9th anniversary

D0204552

To Alan + Bethany,

May your marriage grow in love each year and God make your relationship full and satisfying.

Love.
Mom + Dad.

CREATED
TO BE HIS

Discover how God can make your marriage glorious

Created to be His Help Meet®
Copyright © 2004 by Michael and Debi Pearl
ISBN 1-892112-60-4
First printing: 2005

Visit www.NoGreaterJoy.org for information on other products produced by No Greater Joy Ministries.

Requests for information should be addressed to:
No Greater Joy Ministries Inc. *1000 Pearl Road, Pleasantville, TN 37033 USA*

All scripture quotations are taken from the King James Holy Bible.

Reprinting or online posting of our books, booklets, transcriptions of cassettes, videos, DVDs, or CDs is prohibited.

Cover photo and design by Clint Cearley
Interior design by Clint Cearley
Model for cover photo, Shoshanna (Pearl) Easling, youngest of the Pearl children.

Printed in the United States of America

Acknowledgements

There is not a day of my life that I do not wake up and thank God he gave me the wonderful task of being a *help meet* to Michael Pearl. I know God has used that man to instruct me, mold me, and love me into being the woman I am today. This book is as much his product as it is mine. He encouraged my sloppy beginnings, rewrote my half-hearted second tries, cheered me on when I grew weary and wanted to quit, and then gave me weeks free from my responsibilities as his *help meet* so that I might finish the task.

My son-in-law Gabriel Anast and my daughter Rebekah Joy Anast gave me the idea and much of the information for the section on the three types of men, which made understanding men so much simpler. Beka also provided examples, ideas, and Scripture included in the other parts of this book. I consider her co-author of this book.

The daily letters I have received during the last several years have instructed me and caused me to seek the face of God for answers. By seeing the heartache and/or the truimph of thousands of women, I have been able to identify patterns of success and patterns of destruction. Also, hearing from so many hurting women has given me growing urgency to share what God has taught me. A big "thank you" to all of you whose letters I have used in writing this book.

Introduction

This book has been ten years in the making—four years in its actual writing. It is at my encouragement that my wife wrote it. Many times as she was going verse-by-verse through the Scripture, she would say to me, "I'm not going to include these verses because if I do, the ladies of _____ (some religious group) will not like or promote my book." I would tell her, "If God thought it was important enough to put it in his Word, then you shouldn't exclude it. So she would cringe and add one more controversial subject after another. I am proud of the great job she has done.

I have long wanted other women to have the benefit of her profound wisdom and grace, and I want other men to experience the blessing of being married to a heavenly-gift bride. Debi is my sweetheart and best buddy, my best friend and my only confidante. She is not by nature a passive, "lie down and roll over" woman. In our early marriage, she challenged my authority and occasionally stood against me—sometimes with reasonable provocation—and sometimes because she was just stubborn and self-willed. Admittedly, we didn't start out with a perfect marriage; we grew into it together. Debi has strong opinions that she solidly believes in, but she has learned to be her husband's helper in every way that a man needs a woman's support.

I have never met or read another author who I thought was more qualified by life and experience to write a book to women on how to become the _help meet_ God intended. She exemplifies all that she has written. Every word of this book comes with my blessing and wholehearted agreement.

- Michael Pearl - husband and blessed lover ♥

Contents

Once upon a time there was a silly young girl who grew up to learn what it means to be a *help meet*—God's secret for a heavenly marriage. I start this book with the words *"Once upon a time"* because it really is a wonderful story come true. It should, and could, be your story too. It is God's gift to every woman.

My "wife" story began 34 years ago with the ringing of the phone. I was sitting at the desk where I worked, when my pastor called, asking me to go with him to a gospel meeting that evening. He occasionally called on me to go with him to counsel the girls while he dealt with the men. I was a single, twenty-year-old girl, and my pastor was a single, twenty-five-year-old hunk of a man. Of course, I said I would love to go and help. *He had been my goal* since I was 13 years old. Although I thought that he occasionally cast his eyes at me, I had despaired of ever getting my trophy. With that simple phone call, my despair turned to hope once again.

A few hours later, my old VW Bug buzzed into the church parking lot. I grabbed my Bible and climbed into his oversized, overpowered station wagon, and we were off to a Bible study with a crowd of hippies. This was during the height of the hippie revolution and the Jesus Movement. The birth-control pill was a new and heady thing that drove the hippies into an era of non-responsibility. AIDS was not yet a factor. The theme of the 60s was, "If it feels good, do it." Young people could be seen sleeping in parks or on roadsides, switching partners as the night progressed. Drugs dulled their conscience and destroyed their dignity, but in the midst of all this sin and shame, God poured forth his Spirit, and thousands of those heartsick kids began to seek God. To me, it was a privilege to live in a time when the Spirit of God moved so freely. The Bible tells us in Romans 5:20, **"But where sin abounded, grace did much more abound."**

That evening, our gospel meeting was held in an upstairs apartment where a group of used-up druggies had gathered. The room was crowded with young hippies dressed in worn-out jeans and tie-dyed T-shirts. My pastor began to share the gospel of Jesus Christ, and they listened as if every word were straight from God. It was a simple, quiet, powerful message of forgiveness and hope. Pastor Pearl never gave an invitation, because he did not want anyone to respond to him, only to Christ. But he did tell them that if anyone wanted to pray, they were free to join him. That night, in one accord, everyone fell to their knees and began to pray. The Spirit of God began to move, and I could hear several young men cry out for mercy. In the midst of this movement of God, I felt my pastor reach over and take my hand. Talk about electric shock! I knew there was a strange and wonderful thing happening, because he was ordinarily a real prude! He wouldn't even let the old ladies shake his hand after Sunday morning service. Now he was holding mine during a prayer meeting! I just knew my time had come!

> What I have enjoyed is just too good to bequeath to my daughters only.

He never spoke in the hour's drive home, and I never shut up. Always given to gab, I *really* gab when I'm nervous, and I was really nervous. Since silence was so unusual for him, I thought I knew what was on his mind. Me! Finally we pulled up to the parsonage where he lived and where my VW Bug was parked. I sat in the darkness waiting, but... nothing....Finally, I spoke out. "You remember that boy you baptized Sunday night, the little guy who could barely see over the top of the baptistry? Well, someday I would like to give *you* a little boy just like that!" You would think a man might take a hint, but he was out of the car and running within two seconds. I got out and headed for my car, figuring I might have spoken a little too boldly. I saw him as he came around his house the first time and watched as he disappeared around it again. He made three full laps around the large parsonage before he finally made up his mind. He rushed toward me, picked me up, and threw me into the air. At that point I was beginning to doubt my wisdom and his sanity. Then he said in a loud, confident voice, "Let's get married." And, so we did. Eight days later, on a Sunday night, I made my way to the front of the church building, carefully stepping around the newly-saved ex-hippies sitting on the floor of the crowded aisle, to take the hand of my pastor-husband in holy matrimony. Thus we began our journey.

God's Plan

> You do have a choice in how your life plays out.

This book reveals God's plan for obtaining a heavenly marriage. It is the combined voice of thousands of women who have sent me their stories of heartbreak, or of the glory of a love recaptured. The following pages are filled with simple instructions, examples, and many letters from women, some doing the wrong thing and reaping the bitter fruit, and others doing it God's way and drinking from a fountain of life.

I am not an accomplished, professional writer who has collected and collated material from other writers and speakers. I am a happy, creative wife, homeschool mom, and grandmother who, many years ago by the grace of God, found God's will through his written Word, my husband's instruction, and a mother's example. I followed the plan and have enjoyed the blessed fruits of love for many years. I write to you because what I have enjoyed is just too good to bequeath only to my daughters and the few women I reach one at a time.

God commands older women to teach the younger women the wonders of wifehood. I can think of no better way to obey this command than to write to you of God's beautiful love plan. Regardless of what kind of person you have been in the past, with instructions from God's Word, you can become a heavenly-gift bride. You can still be your man's dream come true, and in the process your dreams will come true also.

You do have a choice in how your life plays out. Some of you are fighting your present situation and making no more progress than someone fighting quicksand. You fight your husband, and every verbal punch you land leaves a bruise on you as well. It is time to stop struggling in strife, bitterness, frustration, and disappointment. You are about to read

God's plan for a joyful marriage. It has worked for me, for my daughters, for my mother, my grandmother, and my grandmother's mother. It has worked for many other young and older ladies alike. We didn't just happen to marry perfect, or even saved men, but we all learned to be *help meets* to our men, resulting in heavenly marriages.

You are going to learn God's design for a woman, the place of fulfillment as a properly-fitted helper. We will discuss what God's Word says of a *help meet*; what she does, what she shouldn't do, and the rewards she can expect. Each day is a decision, each hour a challenge, and each response starts you toward either the quicksands of divorce or the solid ground of being blessed **"heirs together of the grace of life."**

As I described above, my marriage began rather spontaneously, but it didn't begin perfectly. In our early years, I experienced a considerable amount of defeat. On one occasion, I even threw rocks at my husband. Eventually, I grew out of that, but from time to time I threw barbed words—and with much greater accuracy, pain, and effectiveness. Through God's grace, I finally discovered his way to a heavenly marriage. I didn't step into it; it worked its way into me, graciously from God. It has been worth every sacrifice many times over. It is my urgent desire to share this glorious knowledge with all young women. If you will turn to God, asking him to open your eyes to his instruction for wives, he will open his Word to you, just as he did for me those many years ago. So, as my mother taught me—so, I teach you. *—Debi*

PART I
The Help Meet

In the beginning. . .
"And the LORD God said, It is not good that the man should be alone;
I will make him an <u>help meet</u> for him... And the LORD God caused a
deep sleep to fall upon Adam… and he took one of his ribs…And
the rib, which the LORD God had taken from man, made he a woman,
and brought her unto the man" (Genesis 2:18, 21-22).

What does being a *help meet* mean? What does God teach
concerning my role as a *help meet*?

Chapter 1

God's Gift

*A wise woman doesn't take anything
for granted. She is thankful to be loved and seeks
to make herself more lovely.*

He Loves Me

Dear Mike and Debi,

*I want to thank you both for explaining what I was doing to
my husband. I was definitely a Jezebel type, but I have changed! I
felt broken inside when I read your article. I asked God to help me
learn what His views were of marriage and how He wanted me to
respond to my husband. At first, I only made little changes in what
I did for him, but at least my attitude was different. The truth has
set me free.*

*I want to let you know that the changes in me have astonished
me—and my husband! And, the changes in him have left me
dumbfounded. He is more caring, eager to please, spends more
time with the girls and myself, and the level of intimacy is
wonderful! I had spent years scratching my head and wondering*

why he would not take a position of leadership in the home. I did not realize that I controlled many situations because I feared my husband would not handle them correctly. We had both grown bitter, and love-making was not love; it was necessary sex—when it was unavoidable. When we first married, I started this little nonsense thing where, if we had a blow-up, I would say the "flower petals chant" under my breath, ". . .He loves me not." And if we were having a fun time, I would say, "He loves me." After several years, I realized that I had stopped saying, "He loves me," and almost daily I was saying, "He loves me not."

> If God created a special woman, perfectly suited to be your husband's helper, would you be that woman?

Guilt washes over me when I think of the wasted years and how blind I was to my own faults. It has been hard to confess. I am so thankful to now know my place as my husband's helper and friend. Yesterday my husband slipped in and grabbed me from behind. I felt his whispered breath in my ear and realized he was saying over and over again, "He loves me, He loves me, He loves me." Tears poured down my face in thanksgiving, and while safe in his arms, I took up the chant, "He loves me, he loves me, he loves me." No one knows how precious those words are until you almost lose them. Thank God he helped me see the truth before I had totally lost my one true love. Learning to be the help meet God created me to be,

Liz

So He isn't Mr. Right!

As you have probably already discovered, you don't just marry "the right man" and live happily ever after. Every man I know is a bona fide sinner. And, considering that you, too, are a selfish, fallen creature, it will take real effort to make a heavenly marriage. A good marriage, just like anything worthwhile, takes doing the right things every day…every hour…every moment.

God's Gift to Man

God gave Adam the most precious gift a man will ever receive—a woman. I know it to be so because my husband tells me quite often. According to him, I am indispensable. He says I am his best buddy, his preferred helper. **"And the LORD God said, *It is* not good that the man should be alone; I will make him an <u>help meet</u> for him"** (Gen. 2:18). And then God **"brought her unto the man"** (Gen. 2:22). Later, he tells us, **"Whoso findeth a wife findeth a <u>good thing,</u> and obtaineth favour of the LORD"** (Proverbs 18: 22). Do you see? God says it is not good for a man to be alone, and the answer to his need is a wife—called **"a good thing."** Furthermore, a man obtains God's **favor** by getting a wife.

If you are a wife, you were *created* to fill a need, and in that capacity you are a **"good thing,"** a helper suited to the needs of a man. This is how God created you and it is your purpose for existing. You are, by nature, equipped in every way to be your man's helper. You are inferior to none as long as you function within your created nature, for no man can do your job, and no man is complete without his wife. You were created to make him complete, not to seek personal fulfillment parallel to him. A woman trying to function like a man is as ridiculous as a man trying to be like a woman. A unisex society is a senseless society—a society dangerously out of order.

> When you are a help meet to your husband, you are a helper to Christ.

The Gift Received

Adam must have been excited when he woke from his divinely induced sleep, with a missing rib, and first laid eyes on God's birthday gift to him. My husband, who is a learned student of the Word, assures me that Eve was indeed a birthday present, as seen by the fact that they were both wearing their birthday suits.

If God created a special woman, perfectly suited to be your husband's helper, would you be that woman? Just imagine your dull husband waking up one morning, opening one lazy eye, and there sitting on his bed is a large, beautifully wrapped box. Mr. Dull is shocked, surprised, and quite curious, so he stretches out his arm and pulls gently on the vibrant red ribbon. Voilà! That is your cue, so you push back the lid, and out you pop with an inviting smile and a welcoming body. His gift-bride straight from the hand of God! My, oh my! How undull Mr. Dull would be!

That's exactly what happened to Adam, everything but the box, that is. I am sure Adam was anything but dull when he awoke from deep sleep to find beautiful, naked Eve sitting there looking him over.

Does your husband share Adam's feelings of delight when he looks upon you? Do you wake each morning ready to make your husband happy and blessed, to serve him to the best of your ability—to be his helper? Are you engaged in active goodwill toward your man? That is God's perfect will for you.

When you are a help meet to your husband, you are a helper to Christ, for God commissioned man for a purpose and gave him a woman to assist in fulfilling that divine calling. When you honor your husband, you honor God. When you obey your husband, you obey God. The degree to which you reverence your husband is the degree to which you reverence your Creator. As we serve our husbands, we serve God. But in the same way, when you dishonor your husband, you dishonor God.

It is now time for my reader to pull out one of those twisted exceptions to make God's will appear untenable.

"How can I be my husband's helper when he cheats on his taxes?"

"How can I honor my husband when he wants me to view pornography with him?" We will come to exceptions eventually, but don't miss the point by hurriedly jumping to the twisted and perverse. Women who do not want to do the will of God in regard to their husbands remind me of atheists always ready with a few reasons *not* to believe, but never considering the many reasons *to* believe. <u>It is your nature to be your husband's helper.</u> Don't fight it.

God Hasn't Changed His Mind

"For the man is not of the woman; but the woman of the man. Neither was the man created for the woman; but the woman for the man" (I Cor. 11:8-9). Four thousand years after creation, Paul, Timothy, and Peter wrote to us, telling us God's original plan was still the same as it was in the beginning when Adam and Eve were first learning how to be husband and wife. Now, two thousand years since Paul's teaching, amazing as it seems, God still has not changed his mind. Regardless of who you are or what your talents may be, God's will is that *you be a suitable helper to your husband.* Paul says, **"But she that is married careth for the things of the world, <u>how she may please her husband</u>"** (I Cor. 7:34).

I know that as you read this it almost sounds like blasphemy, because it is so weird to think that your husband deserves you as his **help meet**. But who said anything about what he deserves? You can only realize your womanhood when you are functioning according to your created nature. To covet his role of leadership is to covet something that will not make God, you, or him happy. It is not a question of whether or not you can do a better job than he; it is a matter of doing what you were "designed" to do. If you successfully do the job of leading the family, you will not find satisfaction in it. **It is far better that the job be done *poorly* by your husband than to be done well by you.** Your excellence as a help meet to him may very well be God's plan for improving his leadership role in the family. Your female nature cannot be retrofitted to the male role without permanent damage to the original design.

Your Divine Calling

The role of being a *perfectly fit helper* does not make one inferior to the leader. In our office there is an entire staff of workers. Every person in the office spells better than I do; most know the computer better, and they certainly know finances better. Yet, when I walk into the office, I can tell any one of them what to do and how I want it done, and they all are *glad* to do my bidding—including the men. My *place* of authority does not mean I am better, it only means that they are there to help me do my job—better!

> A woman trying to function like a man is as ridiculous as a man trying to be like a woman. A unisex society is a senseless society—a society dangerously out of order.

Men are created to be helpers of God. Jesus willingly became a helper to the Father. The Holy Spirit became a helper to the Son. Society is structured so that men and women must submit to authorities like government, employers, police, the Internal Revenue Service, child protection agencies, the courts, etc. There is no loss of dignity in subordination when it serves a higher purpose. God made you to be a **help meet** to your husband so you can bolster him, making him more productive and efficient at whatever he chooses to do. You are not on the board of directors with an equal vote. You have no authority to set the agenda. But if he can trust you, he will make you his closest advisor, his confidante, his press secretary, his head of state, his vice-president, his ambassador, his public relations expert, maybe even his speech writer—all at his discretion.

A perfect **help meet** is one who does not require a list of chores, as would a child. Her readiness to please motivates her to look around and see the things she knows her husband would like to see done. She would not use lame excuses to avoid these jobs.

A man would know he had a fine woman if she were this kind of **helper.** Such a blessed husband would receive honor from other men as they admire and praise his handy wife. **"A virtuous woman is a crown to her husband"** (Proverbs 12:4). It is our job to learn how we can help our husbands in every way possible. The very fact that you are reading this book indicates that your heart's desire is to honor God by becoming a real help meet to your man.

The word **help meet** appears in the KJB just two times—Gen. 2:18 and 20. However, it is the translation of one Hebrew word—*ayzer*—which is found 21 times in the Hebrew Bible. Other than being translated *"help meet"* two times, it is translated just plain *"help"* 19 times. The Hebrew word studies tell us that it means *to succor* or *one who helps.* My proofreader kept trying to get me to join the two words with a hyphen (help-meet), which is commonly done. But throughout this book I have written it just as it appears in the Word of God—two words (help meet), which is to say Eve was created to be a helper (noun) who was meet (adjective), suited to Adam's needs. The New Testament use of the word *meet* throws some light on this word: Acts 26:20, Romans 1:27, I Cor. 15:9, 16:4, Phil. 1:7, Col. 1:12, II Thes. 1:3, II Tim. 2:21, Heb. 6:7, II Pet. 1:13. I encourage you to look up these verses. You will be enlightened as to your position before God as a helper "meet" for your man. As I read these verses, the words *proper, fit, perfect, good,* and *well-equipped* came to mind. I want to be that kind of help to my husband.

I want to be what God created me to be ♥

Time to Consider

God's perfect will for my life is that I be a help meet to my husband.

I do have a choice in how good my marriage will be. **"For the man is not of the woman; but the woman of the man. Neither was the man created for the woman; but the woman for the man"** (I Corinthians 11:8-9).

➢ *Make a new habit*

Think of ways you can be a helper to your husband. Start today.

➢ *Getting Serious with God*

Locate in Scripture (King James Bible) the following words or traits as they relate to a woman of God. Write the verses in your diary, and ask God to work each of these attributes into your character.

> *1. Virtue*
> *2. Graciousness*
> *3. Wisdom*
> *4. Prudence*
> *5. Goodness*

➢ *A Good* **Help Meet** *has a Passion to be of Service*

The words *help meet* bring up images in my mind of a woman who serves others. A good help meet will have a passion to be of service. Her first calling is to be of service to her husband, then her children, and when time affords, her passion of service will spill over to serving others.

Chapter 2

A Merry Heart

The Joy of the Lord is my Strength

The Bible tells us that the **Joy** of the Lord is our strength. For this marriage-making journey you're on, you will need all the strength afforded by the joy of the Lord.

God says in Proverbs 17:22, **"A merry heart doeth good like a medicine."** A merry heart is the foundation of health and happiness. And the day you have a merry heart will be the first day of rebuilding your marriage into the heavenly gift it was meant to be.

I have listened to the longest-faced women trying to assure me that they do indeed have the joy of the Lord, and I sat there wondering where in the world they were hiding it. The last part of the verse above says, **"but a broken spirit drieth the bones."** How are your bones doing? I mean <u>your</u> bones. The Bible is far more literal than you may think. A broken spirit and dry bones result from not having a merry heart. A merry heart is very good medicine. It is a love potion.

When he first fell in love with you, you were a sweet little thing, full of laughter and fun. From the very bottom of your soul you were thrilled with him. Every day you woke up planning some activity that involved you both. Is he still married to the

> When he first fell in love with you, you were a sweet little thing, full of laughter and fun.

same sweet little thing, or have you become a long-faced, sickly complainer? Love is like a flower: you can't expect it to grow without sunshine. Has your lover seen your sunshine lately? Is he still your lover? What would he say?

Proverbs 15:13 says, **"A <u>merry</u> heart maketh a cheerful countenance..."** Everyone is drawn to a smile. Who and what you are is reflected in your face. Does your husband see you as a **happy** thankful woman? Does he smile when he looks at you, amused at the **cheerful little grin** on your face and the totally delightful things you think and say—even the dumb things? Learn to charm him with your mischievous "only for him" grin.

One Ugly Hillbilly!

A few years back, there was an overweight hillbilly woman who worked in the local store in our hometown. Every time we went into the hardware store, several men would be standing around the counter talking to her, and they were always laughing. We usually had to wade through the cheerful crowd and interrupt the gaiety to get served. Her swarm of admirers reminded me of bees around the honey, buzzing with high interest. The strange thing was that this woman was ugly, I mean, *hillbilly ugly*, which is worse than regular ugly. One day as we were leaving the store, I laughingly brought to my husband's attention all those men standing around talking to the sales clerk. His reply really surprised me, "Oh, you mean that cute little lady?" Live and learn! And apparently I really had something important to learn. In his mind that lady was cute! The truth is, she was not little, she was not cute, and she was not young. But she did **smile, laugh, and giggle**, and she was always ready for a good clean joke. I loved being in the store talking to her as much as the men did. She was delightful. A few weeks later, we saw her in the grocery store. She was mad at her very obese daughter for grabbing a handful of candy. Gone were the smiles, giggles, and radiance that had so captivated everyone at the hardware store. In their place was a bitter, ugly snarl. My husband remarked when we left the grocery store, "Haven't we seen that woman somewhere before? She looks familiar, but I just can't place her." When I told him who she was, he was stunned. "No, it's not possible; it just can't be her. The woman in the hardware store does not look like that." I could see the truth dawn on him, and he was so disappointed. The funny thing was that the woman looked just like she always did. She was the same size, same scraggly

Men are highly attracted to <u>smiles.</u> That includes your husband.

hairstyle, the same clothes style, the same everything she was when we saw her in the hardware store. All she lacked was her **glorious smile**. It was her most valuable asset. Her face was always so **radiant,** her **smile** so infectious, her **laughter** so sweet, and her eyes so **earnest** that people simply saw her as cute. I don't know if she had a husband, but I am sure she could have had a dozen different men in that small town—as long as they never saw her in the grocery store, mad at her daughter.

Everyone is drawn to a smile and wants to be a friend to someone overflowing with goodwill. Men are highly attracted to smiles. That includes your husband. Do you want your husband to stay home more? A **merry** heart and a mischievous **giggle** are good drawing cards. **"A merry heart doeth good like a medicine: but a broken spirit drieth the bones"** (Prov. 17:22). You may not be an ugly hillbilly, but there are other kinds of ugly. Women spend billions of dollars every year to make themselves more attractive, but the most effective beauty aid is free—**a joyful smile**.

The Desperate Wife

Here is a letter from a desperate wife who needs to learn how to win.

Dear Mrs. Pearl,

I am going nuts. My husband has been in an emotional affair with his secretary. He says it is over now, but I do not trust him. He gave her a small box of chocolates for Valentine's. He has never remembered me on Valentine's Day. He often goes out to eat with her and the other men of the office. She has twice confided to my husband about problems in her marriage. I know I am supposed to honor, forgive, and not be bitter, etc. This is the hardest thing I have ever gone through, including the death of my mom just 3 months ago. I think he is foolish to place himself in her company when he does not have to, after he has already proven he can't handle it. We are at an impasse. How do we find stuff to talk about? I am nervous as a cat, can't sleep, etc. Desperate, but holding on and eagerly waiting to hear from you,

Beth

Love fogiveth all things

Dear Beth,

Your husband is, without doubt, wrong. It would be wonderful if he were wise and godly, but he isn't. God has provided for your husband's complete sanctification and deliverance from temptation through you, his wife. Your man, like many men before him, is a fool to wink at sin, to play with temptation. But you already know this. That is why you react in jealousy and anger, "**...for love is strong as death; jealousy is cruel as the grave: the coals thereof are coals of fire, which hath a most vehement flame**" (Song of Solomon 8:6).

You now stand where millions of wives have stood. Your reactions are the norm, and as the norm continues, and as you stand on your rights and withhold yourself until he proves his loyalty to you alone, you will come to the normal end — divorce.

You must face the facts — life is not fair. Marriage is not fair. And most of all, the woman at work is not playing fair. And, your husband is not playing by *your* rules. Obviously, he doesn't feel the shame that you do. He is motivated by baser instincts and drives.

Yes, he is wrong, but your response, though justified, will certainly lead to the destruction of your marriage. You can rear up in rage and indignation; you can stand on your rights and stand on truth, but it won't save your marriage. When you have lost your husband and are alone, and the children are at a daycare or public school, and you are trying to pay rent on the dumpy duplex and keep food on the table, you can always know that you stood on principle, you called him to repentance, and you didn't allow him to humiliate you and play the hypocrite. You called his hand. There he will be, living in sin with that other woman, and you, the righteous one, will still be standing for your rights — but sleeping alone. If you get another husband, he will be like your old one, cast off by some other woman. It is a merry-go-round where the scenery gets uglier every time you go around.

I am not suggesting that this is your fault, that you are the cause of your husband's sin. I am just warning you that **if you really, honestly want to win your husband back to yourself, you must change your game plan.** Face it: you have a competitor. She is your rival, the enemy of your heart's desire. Your negative responses are *not* going to make your carnal husband suddenly be the mature man who does what he ought. My husband says, "No man has ever crawled out from under his wife's criticism to be a better man—no matter how justified her condemnation."

Your husband will never be pressured into loving you, even if you are his wife. He will never willingly leave a smiling secretary to come home to a frowning wife. **You cannot be pitiful enough to force him to love you.** You can tell him how he hurts the children, how he destroys his testimony, how he forsakes God and the church, and he will respond by taking his secretary to dinner so he can see a smile that has no strings attached. It is cruel. But that is the way of carnal men. It is the way of humanity. He is not functioning on the plane of moral duty. **He is a lonely man seeking identity in a *woman's approval and admiration*.**

You know that if he were a godly man, he would not consider his needs; like Daniel, he would do what was right, regardless. You also know he needs to repent and love God. But what you don't know is that men do not repent for the sake of an angry, critical wife. You can hold out for repentance and most likely lose your husband, or, you can "court" your husband and win back his favor. Recognize that you are at war for the preservation of God's most noble institution on earth—the family, *your family!* Make yourself more attractive than the secretary. You can win if you are willing to lose your pride.

> Never demand that a man love you and cherish you because he ought to. Earn every smile and shared moment.

If you want to keep your man and the father of your children, you are going to have to forget your rights as a wife and forget his Christian obligation to his vows. You must act as if you and the secretary are engaged in open competition for this man. **Your husband is going to love what is lovely to him.** You must be more lovely than she. You must beat her at her own game. A man is attracted to vulnerability in a woman—the blush, the need, the dependence. When she is physically aware of him, impressed by him, emotionally aroused by his presence, he is excited by her. If a woman lets a man know he brings her comfort, and that she feels safe with him, he will respond. I think the secretary knows this and uses it to her advantage. She has appealed to his wisdom in helping her when she is hurt and down. She looks at him adoringly, and you can be sure that on more than one occasion she has said, "Oh, why can't my husband be like you?" I suspect if your husband were not lapping at her feet, some other man in the office would quickly take his place, and she would be using the same line on him. You would like to wring her neck—and I would like to help you—but don't forget that rundown duplex. Get down on your husband's emotional level, and make yourself more attractive than that office wench, and do it now, today!

It is a mistake for a wife to take her position for granted, to assume that love and contentment exist because "we are husband and wife." In a perfect world, being married to a perfect man, your vows would be sacred. Never demand that a man love you and cherish you because he ought to. **Earn every smile and shared moment. Cultivate his love for you.** Pray that you can remind him of the loveliness and beauty that first attracted him to you.

It is in your best interest to learn to use feminine wiles. A woman holds her man with the fragile threads of adoration, thankfulness, delight, and just plain fun. He needs to hear gladness and appreciation in your voice when you speak to him, even when you are talking of everyday things. He needs this as much as, or perhaps more than, sexual release.

> God stands with you when you stand by your man.

So knock the chip off your shoulder, and fight for what is yours. When I read letters like yours, and I have read many, I often think about that old song performed by Loretta Lynn, "You Ain't Woman Enough to Take My Man." When she wrote that song, her husband was being tempted away by some cheap slut. Rather than recoil in disgust and self-pity, Loretta fought back like a woman should. The words to her song go something like, "Women like you are a dime a dozen; you can buy them anywhere. For you to get him, I've got to move over, and I'm gonna stand right here." Loretta won back her man and kept him.

Just remember, you are fighting a woman who is in the dime-a-dozen class. They are everywhere, ready to steal away the heart of the man who feels uncared for and unappreciated. **The tool of your warfare is your loving, kind, delightful, radiant, adoring self.**

When you are faced with a situation that calls for jealousy, it is appropriate to get mad and threaten to wring his neck. There is a **godly jealousy** (II Cor. 11: 2). One of God's names is **Jealous** (Ex. 34:14). You can threaten to go down to the office and tell the wench to bug off. Do it if you like; just don't humiliate your man. A man will appreciate and be attracted to a woman who cares enough to fight for her man. But your anger must stop before the sun goes down and the covers are pulled back.

It is God's will that your marriage last ♥

Write love notes he will find when he gets to the office. Don't ride him with suspicion. Don't play detective and follow him around. But do call his work with a giggle in your voice, and give him fair warning that you expect "some loving" when he gets home, then giggle and ask him if he is blushing. Once or twice a month, show up at work during lunchtime for a brief unexpected visit. Make sure you are looking radiant and delightfully in love. Your very sweetness and thankfulness toward your man will make that cheap office hussy feel she is beneath your class. And your "innocence" and confidence will cause all the men in the office to be angry at "the woman" for her underhanded advances. It will fortify your husband's spirit.

Be creative and aggressive in your private, intimate times. Keep him drained at home so he won't have any sexual need at work. If you feed him well, emotionally and sexually, her cooking won't tempt him. **God is on your side. Fight and win.**

-Debi

Cherished

Many women think their husbands are not worth the effort. They feel they are forced to humble themselves in order to love him when *he* is the guilty party. Do not be deceived. When a woman is willing to forgive and win back her husband's affection, she is winning more than just his affection. Once a man comes to his senses and sees how close he came to losing all that he holds dear, he will be profoundly thankful to the good woman who loved him through his foolishness. She will win his respect as well as his love, because he will know that she is the kind of woman who will **stand by her man**. Few women ever know what it means to be cherished by their husbands, but if you love him through this kind of trouble, you will be cherished. Being cherished is much, much more than being loved. It will be worth all your effort.

God stands with you when you stand by your man, but you will stand alone if you insist on standing by your rights. Always remember that the day you stop smiling is the day you stop trying to make your marriage heavenly, and it is the first day leading to your divorce proceedings.

> **Stand by your man.**

TIME TO CONSIDER

God's perfect will is that I learn to be the best *help meet* possible.

My husband is highly attracted to my smile. I want my husband to love me.

> **"A merry heart maketh a cheerful countenance:**
> **but by sorrow of the heart the spirit is broken"** (Proverbs 15:13).

Being pitiful, hurt, discouraged, and even sickly is one side of a "bad marriage" coin. Men, in general (your husband in particular), are repulsed by women who project this image. A man's spirit tells him his woman is rejecting him and manipulating him when she regularly manifests a broken spirit, and he will react with anger. The other side of the bad coin includes having a bitter, angry, and resentful spirit.

Toss that old, destructive coin out the door before it buys you a divorce. God's will is for a wife to have a merry heart, a cheerful countenance and a glow that will refresh the most stressed and tired husband on the planet. Bubbling cheer goes a long way to maintain or even restore a marriage. Make a decision right now to break the "poor me" habit. Today, put it down as sin and rebellion, and then tomorrow, wake up with joy in your heart and home.

Establish a new habit.

What can I do today that will make him smile?

➤ *Getting Serious with God*

Do a study on the word *JOY*. You will find that the word *joy* is found 167 times in God's Word. The word *joy* is often coupled with shouting, music, the playing of instruments, dancing, gladness, and praise. Write down and memorize your favorite verses on joy. God's Word is effectual. As you read, memorize verses on joy, and ponder the word *joy* in God's Word, real joy will be worked into your heart.

➡

Every morning, let the first thing your husband sees on your face be a gentle smile, even if your eyes are still closed. Any time your eyes meet or your hands touch, let it be a reminder to smile and offer a word of gladness. When you eat, always show thanksgiving by means of a smile and a joyful spirit.

During the day, sing and play and dance as you work around the house. Your children will be delighted as you dance around the house with the broom or mop, and this lighthearted mood (visible joy is the only joy children understand) will be an encouragement to your children. The lightness in your soul will help put you in a good frame of mind for your husband when he comes home. If you have reason to be hurt or discouraged and yet you sing with thanksgiving, this is a true sacrifice of worship to God.

"And let them sacrifice the sacrifices of thanksgiving, and declare his works with rejoicing" (Psalm 107:22).

Think of other ways and times during the day that you can establish a habit of praise and thanksgiving by showing joy. Write them down, think of yourself doing them, and then practice this new and wonderful habit *all day long*.

"Make a <u>joyful</u> noise unto the LORD, all ye lands. <u>Serve the LORD with gladness</u>: come before his presence with <u>singing</u>. Know ye that the LORD he is God: it is he that hath made us, and not we ourselves; we are his people, and the sheep of his pasture. Enter into his gates with <u>thanksgiving</u>, and into his courts with <u>praise</u>: be <u>thankful</u> unto him, and <u>bless</u> his name. For the LORD is good; his mercy is everlasting; and his truth endureth to all generations" (Psalm 100).

Chapter 3

A Thankful Spirit

A wise woman sets a joyful mood in her home. Through laughter, music, and happy times, she creates a positive attitude in her children. She knows that a lighthearted home relieves her husband of stress.

A Merry Heart vs. a Poor-Me Attitude

"All the days of the afflicted are evil: but he that is of a merry heart hath a continual feast" (Prov. 15:15).

You might be one of the women who often complains about her family's lowly financial state and how she must "do without" because her husband "cannot support the family decently." **This downcast, unthankful attitude is a dishonor to God** and an attack upon your husband's ego. If you have ever been guilty of this attitude, now is the time to say, "Never again."

I know women who remain perpetually discontented because they must live with stained carpet and damaged furniture. Some women feel their family is in desperate straits if they cannot afford to serve fresh broccoli and salad. Tension rules their home. Their sad, withdrawn faces reflect their suffering. They cultivate expressions of grief, reflecting, they suppose, the heart of God sorrowing on their behalf.

Some women learn to accept the poor state of their physical surroundings. They don't want to be carnally-minded. They live only for the eternal. So they save their disapproving expressions for those times when they think it necessary to remind their husbands of how sad they are that he sits in front of the TV, plays video games, or engages in any number of carnal activities. They keep the pressure on—just like the Holy Spirit would do. At least, that's their justification for doing his job so "faithfully."

Some women get it in their minds that if the family would just move to the country, they would be happy and their children would not be getting into sinful habits. Or, if they lived closer to the church, or away from bad neighbors, or spent more time in family devotions, or any number of ifs, ands, or buts, then life would be better. This is a sure recipe for disaster. Discontentment is not a product of circumstances; it is the state of the soul. Remember, **"All the days of the afflicted are evil: but he that is of a merry heart hath a continual feast"** (Proverbs 15:15). Paul said, **"... for I have learned, in whatsoever state I am, therewith to be content"** (Philippians 4:11). The author of Hebrews says, **"...and be content with such things as ye have"** (Hebrews 13:5). In I Timothy we read, **"But godliness with contentment is great gain. For we brought nothing into this world, and it is certain we can carry nothing out. And having food and raiment let us be therewith content"** (I Tim. 6:6-8).

> Discontentment is not a product of circumstances; it is the state of the soul.

Contentment

Recently, I walked into a home that did not have running water, nor did it have an indoor bathroom. It had none of the things we consider necessities today, no washing machine or dryer and no kitchen cabinets, though they did have carpet—a remnant that covered about half the room, with its cut and frayed edges showing. Yet, this sweet new bride was smiling from ear to ear, telling me how thankful she was to have her own place. She told me over and over again how her husband made this shelf, and that place to store stuff, and how he is going to build a cabinet right here later. *Thankful people have a view of life that begins somewhere deep in their souls*, and outside circumstances just can't mar their joy. To them, life is a wonderful, continuous dream come true. All of life is blessed, and they see themselves as being in a continual feast.

•• ♥ Joy begins with thankfulness. ♥ ••

Granted, this new bride is just starting married life, and she is filled with the optimism and energy of youth. But we can take a lesson from her. Joy begins with thankfulness. Quite often our attitudes hang in the balance; by making a conscious choice, we can tip our souls into dark moods of complaining, or into thankfulness and praise. It is amazing how much your mouth controls your soul. You can smile with your mouth and say, "Thank you, God; thank you, husband; thank you, children," and your spirit is directed into gratitude with joy following. Thankfulness is *how* you think; joy is the *abundance* it produces.

Practice Makes Perfect

Practice makes perfect. Practice having a merry and thankful heart. I have known people who, though they did not have a natural knack for music, started piano lessons and practiced every day. After two or three years, their fingers moved across the keys easily and their music sounded sweeter and more fluid every time I heard them. If you ask them, "How do you know to hit all those notes?" They answer, "Practice. I've practiced so much, I don't think about it. It just happens." Life is like that. Most people have practiced hitting the notes of bitterness, sourness, hurt feelings, and frustration so long that their soul finds the discordant notes easily, almost without thought. But, you don't have to keep on practicing discord; you can practice joy and thanksgiving just as easily, and certainly with more pleasure. Every day, every right response makes the fingers of your soul find the notes of joy and thanksgiving easier and easier, until it is so natural that people will say to you, "I am not like you; I just don't have a bubbly personality. I'm not a happy person. How can *I* have joy?" And you will be able to tell them, "Practice makes perfect." Learn to enjoy life. **Be thankful. Smile.** When you catch yourself becoming irritated or disturbed at circumstances, stop and laugh at the little things that steal your peace. **Count your blessings** and learn to be appreciative. My daughter once wrote a song around the words, "Thanksgiving is good; thanks-living is better." Colossians 3:15 advises, **"And let the peace of God rule in your hearts, to the which also ye are called in one body; and be ye thankful."**

> You can practice joy and thanksgiving. Every day, every right response makes the fingers of your soul find the notes of joy and thanksgiving easier and easier.

The Queen of His Heart

Dear Debi,

One day my husband came in while I was reading your literature about joy, and he asked me to do something for him. I cheerfully did what he asked with a smile on my face, and, boy, was he surprised. That was the beginning of our new life.

*The sweeter I am to him, the more he likes me, and the more I like myself. I know most of my depression was because I hated myself over how I treated my man and how he reacted to me. How dumb we can be. We make life so complicated with our demands to be treated fairly. You know, the attitude of, "You do this, and if you do it right, then I'll do that, and if you don't, then you can just suck it up, because I will not do your part." Boy, I am glad to be finished with that stupidity. Now **I seek to always delight my husband**, no matter what. I do not know why I expected him to "like" me when I was so "unlikeable and mean." I want my face to reflect joy and thanksgiving to him.*

Anyway, he has been treating me like a princess. His face lights up when he sees me. He holds my hand, puts his arm around me, smiles at me all the time, tries to help any chance he gets, and wants to just sit and talk. I am the Queen of his heart and the fire in his bed, at last!

Marie

Time to Consider

"**But the fruit of the Spirit is love, joy, peace, longsuffering, gentleness, goodness, faith, Meekness, temperance: against such there is no law**" (Galatians 5:22-23).

Joy is a fruit of the Spirit. If you are a child of God, joy will be a visible reality in your life.

1. Where does joy start?
2. Have I been discontent about my lot in life? Am I, on occasion, a "poor-me" person?
3. Do I verbally show thanksgiving every day?
4. Do I daily remember to thank God for my husband?
5. Would my friends describe me as joyful, thankful, and content?
6. How can I add practicing joy and thanksgiving to my life?
7. Am I willing to lay down my grievance toward my husband for the hope of a heavenly marriage?

"**Brethren, I count not myself to have apprehended: but this one thing I do, forgetting those things which are behind, and reaching forth unto those things which are before, I press toward the mark for the prize of the high calling of God in Christ Jesus**" (Philippians 3:13).

➤ *Getting Serious with God*

The book of Philippians is full of instruction to help us learn to become a woman of God. Phil. 4:6 tells us to "**be careful for nothing**," which is to say, don't worry and fret about everything being just perfect, but be content with what you have. Paul tells us in chapter one that every time he thinks of his friends, he prays for them. Philippians has only four short chapters. Instead of reading a romance novel today, read the book of Philippians and ask God to work his Word into you.

Chapter 4

Thanksgiving Produces Joy

Live with thanksgiving,
forgiveness, and joy, and enjoy all your
moments as if they were your last.

My Jolly Playmate

You have control over whether or not you and your husband will be "**heirs together of the grace of life**" (I Pet. 3:7), or partners together in the tension and stress of life. **You have much more control than you know.**

As a general rule, my husband *just doesn't* take the trash out. I could be annoyed, or I could learn to enjoy taking the trash out. I'm smart; I have learned to really enjoy taking trash out. One day recently, my husband saw me struggling out the door with a huge sack of trash in one hand and several empty boxes in the other. Since he was headed in that direction, he volunteered to carry the heavy sack. He walked about ten feet ahead of me, holding the sack out from his body with one hand. I knew he was just showing me how strong he was. I was amused, as usual, with his display of manhood. After nearly thirty-five years of having me appreciate his muscles, you would think he would tire of showing off, but he knows that I have never tired of watching him perform. When he got near the large trash trailer, he was really getting into his macho thing. With great fanfare, he flung (I would say *tossed*, but it was like a sideways catapult) the large trash bag as if it were a cement block instead of a thin plastic bag too loaded down for its own strength. Of course, the string broke, allowing the bag to hit the side of the trailer, bursting open and dumping trash all over the ground. I could tell he was a little embarrassed as I rushed over to clean up his mess, but he continued on his merry way. I remember a time when all this would have irritated me to the point of bitterness. I would have made sure that he felt my irritation, and our relationship would have been strained, all for a bag of trash. Such a stupid waste of our lives.

But now, as I watched him humbly slink off, I had to grin. I think I have finally come to understand the male psyche, at least this male's. I know that the dumped trash bag was hard on the old boy. It is funny that men think women are so difficult to understand, but can you imagine a woman flinging a heavy garbage sack to prove how strong she is and then, having spilled it, leaving it for someone else to clean up? Having come to this lofty understanding of the male ego, I knew Big Papa would look for any chance to take out the trash from now on, and always do it right. His chance came about two weeks later when I was heading out the back door with another heavy sack. I graciously showed my thanks as he offered to take the bag out. Just as he stepped out the door, I raced for the laundry room window. Quickly raising the window about three inches, I waited for him to come around to the trash trailer, which is directly in front of the laundry room window. This time he carefully and gently pitched the heavy sack, and I was ready. Just as the sack left his hand, I let out a bloodcurdling scream. You would think he would get used to my tricks after all these years, but I got him again. I wish you could have seen his reaction. His T-shirt shook as if a strong wind had hit it, as every inch of his body quivered with shock. Of course, my own body was in spasms of wild laughter. It took him a moment or two to realize that the sack had landed safely and that the scream was in no way related to the trash bag he had just thrown. I had so rattled his nerves with my wild war whoop that it seemed to take him a second to realize that *I had done it again.* Oh, it was a grand moment — until he turned to meet me eye to laughing eyes, and I knew I would have to pay for my rowdy entertainment. His addled brain came quickly back to the present, and he took off running back to the house at a speed the likes of which I thought he had long since become incapable. I knew there was no sense in trying to hide, because he would find me sooner or later, so I decided

Speak your thankfulness out loud ♥

to use my "innocent lady" pose. I sweetly stepped in front of the sink and began to wash dishes, suppressing my laughter with great difficulty. He sounded like a big Mack truck coming through the door, but I just kept my back turned and continued to wash the dishes. My demure stance did not stop him. He grabbed me by the arm and started pulling me into the bedroom. Since he outweighs me by a hundred pounds, it was no contest, although he had to drag me all the way. I could only imagine what the office staff (right next door) might think if they happened to drop in at that moment. I was ready with another scream just in case our very reserved business manager appeared. It would have been really funny to see the manager's horrified face. I can just imagine him thinking with horror, "And THEY teach marriage relationships."

> ♥ ———— ♥
> Because I have known such love and closeness with a man, it makes my understanding of and appreciation for God much deeper.
> ♥ ———— ♥

Mike thought he was going to scare me with his show of force, but he was dragging me to my favorite winning spot: the bedroom. While he shut and locked the door, I quickly arranged myself in a very inviting, seductive pose. It gets him every time. It sure is handy being a woman. So he started smooching on me, while I continued giggling for a little longer. He smooches better than he throws a garbage sack. Well, that's enough of this story! But can you see how much better a merry heart is than an ugly pile of hurt feelings?

Make Love Fun

Mike is my **playmate**. He needs someone to play with every day. I am his **help meet**. That is, I am his **helper**, suited to his needs. I meet his need for conversation, companionship, and a playmate. Anytime we take a walk, we end up racing each other. When we walk up hills, I grab his belt and he pulls, just for fun. The other day we were walking up a steep incline, both of us puffing hard. He looked back to where I was and asked, "Do you need a pull?" "No, I can make it," I said. Wheezing, he presented his posterior to me and said, "Then, push!" We laughed to the top of the hill. It didn't make the hill any easier to climb, but *laughter always makes life easier to climb.*

Most mornings, we greet the day with what we call "wallowing," which is a rolling around, alternately snuggling, tickling, and hugging wrestling match that, on occasion, ends in a real wrestling match or a king-of-the-bed game where I try dumping him off. If he gets tickled enough, he loses his strength, and I can sometimes get the best of him.

I am his **playmate**. He thinks I am perfectly wonderful, not because I am a beautiful woman. Those days passed more years ago than I care to remember. Our delight in each other did not happen because he is the perfect man, or because he "loves me like Christ loves the church," or because he is "sensitive to all my needs." It didn't happen because he takes the trash out, or cleans up after himself, or has always made a good living, providing me with all the things most women take for granted. It didn't happen because he is a strong spiritual leader and always does the right thing. It happened and continues to happen because of the choices I make every day. I never have a chip on my shoulder, no matter how offended I have a right to be—and I do have reasons to be offended regularly. Every day, I remember to view myself as the woman God gave this man. This mind-set helps me be just that: *a gift, a playmate, his helper*.

> I want you to know something wonderful about Jesus; with Him it doesn't matter where you have been or who you have been with, because His love and forgiveness can reach down and make you His bride.

Early in our marriage, we each made a commitment (independently) to please and forgive the other no matter how hurtful the actions or words that were spoken. Somewhere over the years, having goodwill and a merry heart toward each other has become as natural as breathing. We have learned that all of life is fun and needs to be shared with our best *friend, playmate, and lover.* This, then, is the rule of life for wives: Live with thanksgiving, forgiveness, and joy, and enjoy all your moments as if they were your last. Someday, soon enough, they will be.

The marvel of my story is that it has been playing out for close to thirty-five years. No one would ever guess that the two old folks sitting at the corner table in the restaurant, getting their senior citizens' discounts, would still be having so much fun. Yet, we continue to enjoy each other, playing, laughing, loving, and sharing. We have been heirs together of the grace of life, not partners in stress and bitterness. Our relationship has been a living testimony of Christ and the Church. My husband has been my *head*, and I have been the *body*. He likes to remind me I am THE body. At my age, this is not only funny to me, but should give you a chuckle too. This is exactly what

God meant marriage to be between a man and his wife. It is the great mystery spoken of in Scripture. Webster's dictionary tells us that a mystery is something that is fitted to inspire a sense of awe; an enigma. For two earthly beings, here in this cursed world, to have a joyful relationship throughout their marriage is truly awe-inspiring.

Because I have known such love and closeness with a man, subsequently my understanding of God and my appreciation for him are much deeper. A relationship based on law, rules, willful humility, and formality is death. I have learned to approach God just as I approach my husband with love, joy, and delight.

From This Day Forth

Now, I know what some of you are thinking. You think it is too late for you. You are struggling on your second or third marriage to an unbelieving porn addict, or you are suffering through emotional scars from your godless youth. I want you to know something wonderful about Jesus. With him, it doesn't matter where you have been or who you have been with, because his love and forgiveness can reach down and make you whole. He is willing to love you and make you His bride, just as you are. And he asks you to be a bride to your husband, just as he is. When a weak sister fulfills her divine purpose of being a true help meet, it brings great glory and joy to God.

Do you remember the great story in Luke 7:38, where the former promiscuous woman intruded upon a private dinner at a Pharisee's house? She hurried to where Jesus was seated and fell down behind him, weeping at his dusty feet. Her intention was to anoint his feet with costly ointment, but her tears of repentance and gratitude fell upon his feet. I think she was shocked to see that she had defiled him with her tears and, finding nothing at hand with which to wipe them away and rectify her intrusion, she unbound her long hair and used it to wipe away her unworthy tears. The Pharisees were sure that if Jesus knew who and what she was he would not have accepted her devotion. But they didn't really know Jesus. Jesus turned to the lady and said to all those present, **"Wherefore I say unto thee, Her sins, which are many, are forgiven; for she loved much: but to whom little is forgiven, the same loveth little. And he said unto her, Thy sins are forgiven…Thy faith hath saved thee; go in peace"** (Luke 7:47-48, 50).

> When a weak sister fulfills her divine purpose of being a true help meet, it brings great glory and joy to God.

Forgiven ~ Forgiven ~ Forgiven ~ Free

Gratefulness

Dear Debi,

 I wanted to send my testimony because you have greatly encouraged me. I send it with my husband's approval.

 As a young child, I was messed with by family members and non-family members alike. I don't ever remember feeling pure. At age 4, my parents divorced, and my mother had custody of us. I think my mom just gave up when they divorced. She didn't take care of us. We were left to ourselves for the most part. We were dirty and unkempt. Because these things took root in my person, I never really knew what it was to be loved. God certainly couldn't love me, because I was so dirty, inside and out. I didn't just think that in my head; it was the way I lived.

 After I was married, I experienced deep personal pain in my marriage relationship—my husband's adultery. It was awful. I reacted terribly toward him. I defied him, used it to get my own way, and tortured him with it. You name it; I did it. The only thing I didn't do was leave him. We went through much hurt, anger, and bitterness. I had great difficulty trusting anything or anyone, even God.

 I asked God if he would please show me one way that he loved me. I felt bad for even asking, in light of the fact that he had sent his only begotten Son to die for me. But I did ask, and God answered me. That night I went out of the living room to pray, and God opened up a small part of what felt like heaven to me. He reminded me that he loved me when I was that dirty, ill-mannered, messed-with child.

 Here is how he did it. There was a lady in our neighborhood who was a Christian. When I was 5 years old, I was wandering by her house one day with a dirty cookie in my hand, and I offered it to her. She accepted it and took me on her lap and told me all about Jesus, Creation, and how Jesus would come for us one day. **It was God's lap I sat on that day; it just took me years and years to know it.** Because God loved a dirty little girl, all the while I was going through public school, I never believed in evolution. I had a basic knowledge of Jesus Christ, sin, hell, and heaven. God had laid a foundation in my life, when I was a rejected, lonely child, that would one day lead to my salvation through faith in Jesus Christ and his finished work on Calvary. That lady also took me to church with her for the next 5 years. She was a true vessel for God's love.

There came a time during all our marriage troubles that I knew I was stagnating. I got on my knees and began to pray, **asking God to make me grateful.** That Sunday at our church, the ladies from the Roloff Homes were there. [Roloff Homes take in troubled, drug-addicted or street ladies who come for help.] God began to remind me where he had brought me from and what he had saved me out of. About the time God was doing this, our pastor asked the ladies of our church, who would, to come and stand with the Roloff ladies because, really, but for the grace of God, we could have been standing where those ladies were. I went and stood with them, and we all began to sing, "At The Cross." I began to weep, thinking about the miry pit that God had rescued me out of. The Roloff ladies put their hands on me to comfort me—me, who should have been comforting them! I silently thanked God for making me grateful, and thanked him for doing it so gently.

Being grateful and thankful is the key to spiritual victory.

It was at this point that the battle turned. There came a time when God dealt with me about my bitterness towards him. I had carried bitterness towards him for not protecting me while a child, when I thought he should have. He showed me that he hadn't shielded Jesus either. It was a battle to lay it down and trust that

> Being grateful and thankful is the key to spiritual victory.

God would do the necessary things with it. I learned a good lesson about bitterness. It drives everyone away. I was now willing to let God have it. The next few weeks, I noticed that I had freedom to go to God with everything.

Who would believe that now I <u>want</u> to be married to my husband; that I like being around him and spending time with him. I enjoy talking to him and enjoy the fact that he balances me out so well. Who would believe I am looking forward to having more children with him, Lord willing. **Some people would say I am weak and foolish or extremely co-dependent. What people think is nothing compared to what God thinks.** I know that God has brought me out on the other side. I don't know what the future will bring, but as the women of old, I am trusting in God. He is up close and personal now. I am learning to rest in him. I love him. He has not done anything in my life as I thought he would, but he has done exceedingly above all I could think or ask.

Sara

*The message to you is simple. From this day forth,
starting right now—today—be the woman who honors, obeys,
and loves Jesus, by honoring your husband.*

Thanksgiving Produces Joy

Open your mouth and begin to thank God for his grace towards you. Thank him for every good thing that he has brought into your life. Thank him, thank him and thank him again. Joy is the result of a thankful heart. A thankful heart is the result of a person who decides to give thanks. So say, "Thank you, God, for…"

TIME TO CONSIDER

Traits of a Good Help Meet
- She is joyful.
- She makes love fun.
- She is thankful and content.

"And let them sacrifice the sacrifices of thanksgiving, and declare his works with rejoicing" (Psalm 107:22). **"But I will sacrifice unto thee with the voice of thanksgiving; I will pay that that I have vowed. Salvation is of the LORD."** (Jonah 2:9).

➤ *Getting Serious with God*
Joy is often lacking in a woman's life because she is not thankful.

The word *thanksgiving* is found in God's Word 30 times. Thanksgiving is often coupled with joy, praise, gladness, melody, and sacrifice. God values thanksgiving and sees it as an act of sacrifice toward him. Read these verses on thanksgiving and ask God to teach you to be thankful. Make a written list of ways that you can start showing thankfulness; then start living your list and show a thankful life. Thankfulness starts by saying *thank you*, and continues by making a mental note to appreciate all those people God has placed around you. If it is not already in your heart, then it needs to be by an effort of sacrifice that you show thankfulness. Start walking on the water of thankfulness. God will give you the wherewithal as you are willing to walk in thankfulness and joy.

"For the LORD shall comfort Zion: he will comfort all her waste places; and he will make her wilderness like Eden, and her desert like the garden of the LORD; <u>joy and gladness</u> shall be found therein, <u>thanksgiving</u>, and the voice of <u>melody</u>" (Isaiah 51:3).

Chapter 5

The Gift of Wisdom

*Do you have enough fear of God
not to question his Word?*

The Eternal Vision

> Dear Debi,
>
> How can I have a merry heart when my husband treats me harshly? Do I just pretend he is a good man instead of a lazy, TV-watching, selfish jerk? Do I just let him walk on me? How can I have a merry heart when all I feel is pain?
>
> Linda

Dear Linda,

You have two choices. You can doubt God and say, "I know God does not expect me to honor this mean man." Or, you can say, "God, I know your Word teaches me to be a woman who is there to help meet all my husband's desires and dreams. Make me that woman." God made you to fulfill this eternal vision. Until you embrace that divine plan for your life, your life will never make sense. You will always be struggling. When you can finally let go and believe God, life will become so simple that you won't have to wonder what you should do. You will know. This eternal vision will change your mind, thus changing your actions, and, most importantly, it will change your reactions. Ask God for wisdom to become the very best help meet.

-Debi

It doesn't take a good man, or even a saved man, for a woman to have a heavenly marriage, but it does take a woman willing to honor God by being the kind of wife God intended. It takes one woman willing to be a help meet—a suitable helper. If you look at your husband and can't find any reason to want to help him—and I know some of you are married to men like that—then look to Christ and know that it is He who made you to be a help meet. You serve Christ by serving your husband, whether your husband deserves it or not.

For many ladies reading this, it will take a miracle for you to have a merry heart, to be joyful and full of thanks. Think of it: God performing a miracle in you! The challenge is bigger than you. You will need an eternal vision. You will need to take God at his word and become a help meet for his sake, knowing you are fulfilling your mission here on earth. You are being God's helper on earth.

Women who have difficulties in their marriages usually follow their feelings and just react. But you must stop trusting your hurt responses or the advice you receive from the world, for today's media communicates a worldview that is skewed at best. You are not thinking from God's perspective, but the good news is that God is prepared to give you divine wisdom, just for the asking. **"If any of you lack wisdom, let him ask of God, that giveth to all men** [and women] **liberally, and upbraideth not; and it shall be given him"** (James 1:5). It is a gift, but it is not given unless you ask for it. Just think of all the wisdom Christian women could have if they would only ask!

A woman's calling is not easy. To allow someone else to control your life is much harder than taking control of it yourself. It can be a challenge, even for veteran wives. Don't despair. With wisdom from on high, you can be the woman God uses, if not to change that old man into a wonderful fellow, then at least to ease your own burden and become a heavenly bride fit for the Son of God himself. God very clearly spelled out to us exactly what he expects of us as wives. His plan is eternal. It involves more than just our relationship with our husbands. God designed marriage to be an earthly pattern of the divine marriage of Christ and the Church. In God's design, we play a leading role. Therefore, God left no margin for error of misunderstanding. His Word speaks abundantly and clearly of our role.

Is your marriage a good picture of Christ and the Church?

What Does the Bible Say?

Now, before we go any further, we must first consider a pertinent matter. You must come to terms with the fact that the biblical well from which I would have you drink this living water has already been put off limits in your mind by timid Bible teachers who have themselves never tasted the gift of a heavenly marriage.

There are many books written by men, "scholars," that undermine the beauty of a woman's help meet position. They do so by casting doubt on the Bible itself. They talk in elaborate and "learned" terms about "the original languages" and the "cultural settings" in which the words of Scripture were written. Of course, there are many other scholars who believe the Bible just as it is written. Can we, ordinary housewives and mothers, jump into the arena and compete with these "scholars," deciding which verses in the Bible should be believed and which ones should be dismissed for various reasons? That is not for me.

But I do have a solution. There is one verse that they have not yet contested: **"The <u>aged women</u>…may teach the young women to be sober, to love their husbands, to love their children, To be discreet, chaste, keepers at home, good, obedient to their own husbands, that the word of God be not blasphemed"** (Titus 2:3-5). It reads basically the same in all my English translations. And my husband says it reads the same in his four Greek Bibles as it does in the King James. According to the Word of God revealed to the apostle Paul (a man!), aged women are to teach the younger women to be obedient to their own husbands. It is clearly God's plan.

The following letter is typical of many I have received about this topic. Someone is trying to get this woman to believe his opinion about the words of God. He would block her way to the well of water that produces heavenly marriages.

Dear Mrs. Pearl,

I am asking you to investigate something for me, and I trust that you will use many resources, and that you will do as the Bereans in Acts 17:11 did. I was raised Catholic, and they always served wine during mass. As an adult, I joined the Christian Church and I was perplexed that they used grape juice. Finally, someone explained to me that the Scripture says wine, but it means a drink made from grapes. This made me realize that a topic that has burdened my heart for many years should be addressed in the same manner. I have been deeply blessed by women speaking on the platform. I don't understand how God could move so profoundly through women who are not in accordance with his will.

There is a book out by H_____ who analyzes the Scriptures that have kept women bound for centuries, and he rightly divides them, illuminating God's plan for women to be the same as for men. He shows that in the original languages there is just one word for women (nothing for wife) and one for man, which would help explain why the women obeying and not teaching their husband passages are wrongly translated and received. The Full Gospel believers have never silenced women and always encouraged women to teach men.

Your ministry has meant a lot to our family. I know your teachings saved my marriage and helped us with our children, but I know that you could be blind to this beautiful truth and wish you would study to show yourself approved unto God a worthy servant.

Kristin

Dear Kristin,

If you were trying to convince me of the truth of your argument by telling me the "full gospel" crowd encourages women to take positions of leadership, you sure used the wrong argument. Check out their divorce rate, and you will understand my amazement in your choice of arguments. Statistics reveal that, on the average, modern Christians have a higher divorce rate than does the general population.

You will notice the huge amount of Scripture we will present that deals with God's will for a woman. I have not had to redefine, retranslate, restate, or deny the words as they are recorded. I believe God has given and preserved his words so that the average woman can know what he means without having to go to a man who claims to be smarter than the words of God. If God's words are so misleading and difficult to translate that the fifteen English translations I have and the four Greek versions my husband has (all in agreement on these verses) are not able to speak the truth about women, then He is not the God I have worshiped these many years. Why would God allow his words to be consistently misleading, teaching the exact opposite of his will? How is it that for over 1,900 years, all translations in Greek, Syriac, Coptic, German, French, Spanish, English, and two hundred other languages have

Chapter 5 – The Gift of Wisdom

gotten it wrong? Would you have me believe that only in these last few decades, as the world shifted to a "women's liberation" philosophy, that suddenly a few preachers who "studied Greek" in college for three years should discover that the world is right after all? Do you believe the Bible has been taught in error ever since it was written, and that all the Christians during the first nineteen centuries were living in error? We are not talking about two or three verses in one or two books. They would have us believe that 500 verses, found in twenty-five different books of the Bible, from Genesis to Revelation, have been consistently mistranslated or misunderstood by all sects, Catholic, Protestant, Jewish, and Baptist alike.

You will have to go to a "pop" TV evangelist or conference speaker, who depends on monetary gifts from women, to get the modern view that you say is taught by men like H_____. There is a reason why those people attempt to appeal to the modern woman. Nine out of ten gifts to these ministries, and nine out of ten purchases of books and tapes, are by women. **Women who can't be close to their husbands have a propensity to develop a self-absorbing, spiritual intimacy with spiritual leaders—be they men or women.**

> I have not had to redefine, retranslate, restate, or deny the words as they are recorded.

My husband started studying Greek forty years ago. (He daily uses three different Greek Bibles in order to correct the teachers who attempt to correct the Bible with the Greek.) When my husband, who is a Bible scholar and, for many years, also a student of Greek, <u>wants to know what God says</u>, he always opens his KJV Bible first.

You are asking me to adopt a philosophy that is contrary to the Bible, has destroyed countless homes, has put thousands of women on Prozac, and has driven men to pornography, in exchange for something that has worked perfectly for the past thirty-five years in my marriage. I am a supremely happy and content woman, in submission to my husband, but I am not altogether gullible. I suggest you believe God, and let the snake deceive some other dumb lady (just like he deceived Eve in the garden). -Debi

Now let us see what <u>*God*</u> says, just as he said it.

God's Blueprint for Marriage

"Wives, submit yourselves unto your own husbands, as unto the Lord. For <u>the husband is the head of the wife</u>, even as Christ is the head of the church: and he is the saviour of the body. Therefore as the church is subject unto Christ, so let the wives be to their own husbands in <u>every thing</u>" (Ephesians 5:22-24).

"Wives, submit yourselves unto your own husbands, as it is fit in the Lord" (Colossians 3:18).

"But I would have you know, that the head of every man is Christ; and <u>the head of the woman is the man;</u> and the head of Christ is God." (I Corinthians 11:3).

1. God commands wives to *submit* to their OWN husbands.
2. God informs men that they are the head of the wife.
3. God tells the wives to be *subject* to their husbands in everything, every decision, every move, every plan, and all everyday affairs.

There will be times in your marriage when it will take faith and wisdom to believe that God is good, kind, and just in his command for you to submit to your husband in everything. Note that what God commands a woman to do does not hinge on the man loving his wife as Christ loved the Church. If it did, there is not one single husband who ever lived and breathed who would be worthy of his wife's submission or reverence. Each of them, the man and the woman, has been given their own directive from God with a model or pattern to attain to. What God said stands, regardless of the man's goodness or the apparent lack thereof. You were given your blueprints with words like *honor, submit,* and *reverence.* This is God's will and way, his directive and pattern for you to model. It is up to us to believe and obey God.

Just knowing God's will from his written Word will help you become that kind of person. There is peace and joy in knowing that you are right where you were created to be. The more you seek to obey God by being a good help meet to your man, so much the more you will come to know God; and the more you know him, the more you will care about the things he values.

You Think I'm Some Kind of Spiritual Giant?

It has taken wisdom for me to understand a man, his ego, his tender heart, and his strong needs. It was nothing short of *divine wisdom* that enabled me to understand the destructiveness of taking personal offense when my husband did things that seemed unfair, selfish, or harsh. It has been the *gift of wisdom* that has helped me to understand that God is delighted in me when I want to delight and please my man.

A gift is something you receive that has not been earned or merited. God wants to give you the gift of wisdom. It is this precious gift of wisdom that has enabled me to see beyond the piles of dumped trash bags.

Do you think I am some kind of super-spiritual giant? I am just like you, flesh and blood. I can pitch a hissy fit just as well as the next woman. I can get stone-cold and freeze my man down to cracked ice. Thankfully, God has offered us women wisdom that allows me daily to choose what my future will be. **I thank God that *wisdom is not earned; it is a gift*.**

Your life will be full of dumped-trash-bag situations. Your husband will be selfish. He will be unkind. He will not respect your rights. He will be foolish. He may be cruel, and that son of Adam may actually walk in sin. **But he cannot victimize you unless you react outside of the wisdom of God.** You can decide to be in a constant state of anger and bitterness, or you can ask God for the wisdom to live each day in a state of honoring your man for God's sake.

You need the precious gift of wisdom to be able to hold your tongue and be thankful when your flesh would strike back in anger. **You need wisdom to see how feeling sorry for yourself is far from the heart of God.** You need this gift of wisdom as a constant reminder of the limitations of your female understanding. The gift of wisdom will remind you that God's rules are not there to put you in bondage, but to help you make a man want to cherish, protect, and love you. Most of all, the gift of wisdom will enable you to serve and honor your husband because you are serving and honoring God. You will find fulfillment in your nature as a woman. **"If any of you lack wisdom, let him ask of God, that giveth to all men** [and women] **liberally..."** *(James 1:5).* God gives us wisdom liberally, like a "gift," but first we must ask for it.

TIME TO CONSIDER

Today, as you read this, you have two choices open to you. You can excuse yourself from responsibility by mentally assigning various excuses to your situation, or you can choose to believe God and become a 100% help meet regardless of anything that would stand in your way. Which will it be?

➤ **Answer these questions from the text of this chapter:**

1. What is the key to understanding our roles as wives?
2. Where are peace and joy found?
3. If your husband does not love you, does that negate your responsibility or prevent you from fulfilling your role?
4. What is the gift that God gives that will help you in your pursuit of becoming a help meet?
5. List three words that are part of the blueprint for help meets.
6. What can you do that will cause you to know God more and cause you to care about the things he cares about?
7. Are you committed to a heavenly marriage?

To commit your way unto the Lord is to say, "**Not my will, but thine, be done**."

"**Trust in the LORD, and do good; so shalt thou dwell in the land, and verily thou shalt be fed. Delight thyself also in the LORD; and he shall give thee the desires of thine heart. Commit thy way unto the LORD; trust also in him; and he shall bring it to pass. And he shall bring forth thy righteousness as the light, and thy judgment as the noonday. Rest in the LORD, and wait patiently for him: fret not thyself because of him who prospereth in his way, because of the man who bringeth wicked devices to pass. Cease from anger, and forsake wrath: fret not thyself in any wise to do evil**" (Psalm 37:3-8).

Chapter 6

The Beginning of Wisdom

*We live under a law of sowing and
reaping that is as certain and unrelenting
as disease and death.*

Fear

Wisdom is conceived in a strange place. It is **fathered by fear**. Many
Christians—even many ministers—are unwilling to speak of fear. It doesn't sell well
with a public that is lustful for pleasure. The commentators try to convince us that
biblical fear is just *respect* for God, not real fear. Their God is like a paper cut-out with
only two dimensions. If our actions were without consequence, or if consequences
were never painful or permanent, then fear would be foolish. **But our actions and
reactions *do indeed* reap painful results in this present life as well as in
eternity. We live under a law of sowing and reaping that is as certain and
unrelenting as disease and death.** One might forestall the day of reaping, but
it always comes with the surety of an eternal lawgiver. If women never slump onto
a couch and weep for their loss and loneliness, if children never curse their parents,
if no one ever experiences shame and regret, then fear is foolish, and anyone who
would promote it would be an enemy of humanity. But if our choices can bring us to
miserable ends, then fear is the healthiest deterrent we can have. It is the beginning of

wisdom. Life without fear is a fool's paradise. *What physical pain is to the preservation of the human body, fear is to the preservation of the soul*. A Christian life without fear is a religious life without a living God.

"The fear of the LORD is the beginning of wisdom" (Psalm 111:10).
"The fear of the LORD is the beginning of wisdom" (Proverbs 9:10).
"The fear of the LORD is the beginning of knowledge" (Proverbs 1:7).

Anything God says three times is worth heeding. Watch out! Much of what you will read in this book was written to put the fear of God into you. I feel that if I can cause young wives to be aware that there are consequences to their actions, they may turn to God now and start sowing to the spirit, rather than to the flesh. By means of letters written to me and from real life examples, I am going to earnestly warn you about where poor choices will take you.

Disappointed Old Failures

When a woman gets old and realizes that there is no man to love and cherish her, it is sad indeed, for she has failed in the very purpose for which she was created—to be a suitable helper to a man.

We receive thousands of letters every year, mostly from bitter, middle-aged, "spirit-filled" women, disappointed with their "unspiritual" husbands, wanting someone to take sides with them against their "abusers." We also hear from younger wives just beginning to cultivate their bitterness. For years, I tried to write a book addressing their many issues raised in the thousands of letters we received. Trying to answer the older women was usually a futile effort. It is much easier to direct someone toward a better path than it is to stop someone that is in a downward spiral. I finally came to understand the wisdom of the command, **"the aged women…teach the young women to be sober, to love their husbands…"** (Titus 2:3-4). I saw that my advice needed to be directed to those young wives who are still trying to find their way. While still young, these women need to be warned, and they need an instruction manual to prevent them from growing into bitter, crazy old women. A woman who

> A woman who really knows God will know that true spirituality is obeying God's recorded Word, not cultivating her "spiritual" sensibilities.

really knows God will know that true spirituality is obeying God's recorded Word, not cultivating her "spiritual" sensibilities.

I have been around long enough to see this process of failure repeated in the lives of many women—too many. I have seen it begin to develop in young brides and eventually bring them to miserable ends. I fear God for those women still in the process, for I know that God is dreadfully faithful to his Word, and when you dishonor his marriage plan, clearly recorded in his Word, he will stand against you while sin eats away your soul and destroys your health. The consequences of sin are always cruel and costly, whether it is the sin of fornication or the sin of neglecting your calling as a help meet. And the collateral damage to children and family members is horrific.

No woman has ever been happy and fulfilled who neglected to obey God in regard to her role as a help meet. As you read the following example, you will recall some woman you know who is in her forties and has a few "emotional issues." Her excuse might be menopause, but you will find that bitterness is the real source. A hormonal change doesn't change a woman's soul; it just tears down her carefully constructed defenses against expressing the carefully guarded content of her heart.

The Crazy Lady

I'll never forget something that happened several years ago. A middle-aged couple with several children moved into our area so they could get counseling. The woman didn't like the counseling they had received in the church where they had met and married. She thought that by moving into our community where there were so many "spiritual men," her husband would "get some help." She wanted my husband to "disciple him," to be "his mentor"—something Mike considers effeminate on the level she expected.

For many years before their marriage, her husband had been a highly successful and prosperous businessman, but after they married, she expressed her disapproval of his participation in the business world. Nor did she like the area where they lived. She thought he should "live by faith," which meant not working, but staying home with the ever-expanding family. He had been "Mr. Steady," a likeable, even lovable, big teddy bear, always friendly and ready with a smile. She was given to "words from the

> He wanted to make her happy, and he was somewhat awed by her other-worldly spiritualism.

Lord." Her spiritual passions and commitments were deep, according to her, and he was convinced so as well. He was intimidated by her because he carried guilt from past sins, which she never let him forget, and he was somewhat awed by her other-worldly spiritualism.

Several years before they moved to our community, because he wanted to make her happy, and because he was awed by her "closeness to the Lord," he relocated and modified his business as "God directed her." But his new ventures never prospered. The lack of success at his age left him shaken, and he lost his courage. He saw himself getting older with a house full of homeschooled children, and he knew the poor business decisions could not be reversed. His frustration and insecurity were, to her, proof of his lack of faith. She tried to "encourage" him to a "walk of faith," a life of miraculous deliverance, and maybe full-time Christian service. He grew more uncertain and desperate. Their marriage bed suffered. They had troubles, and they both knew it and had been receiving marriage counseling. They had also been reading our literature and decided that our community would be their salvation; so, plop, here they were!

> She was totally deceived into thinking that her female intuition, sensitivity, and passions were spirituality.

It didn't take my husband and me long to see the source of their problems. It turned out, as we learned later, that we were in agreement with the counselors from their previous church. **She was not her husband's helper; she was his conscience.** She manipulated him with her "deep" spiritual discernment. She would describe her attitude toward her husband as "encouraging him to a higher walk."

We shared God's Word with her, telling her that her disobedience and lack of reverence to her husband were sin. She was shocked that we would think she was disobedient to her husband. She was very committed to reading and studying God's Word and loved to "share" with other women.

The move to our area took up the last of their financial resources, and they were soon broke to the last dollar. When they did get a little money, she insisted on tithing it, believing God would return it manyfold. We warned her over and over against usurping authority and dishonoring her husband. She just couldn't believe that God would have her, a spiritual woman, stand up for and follow a "carnal" man.

The foremost drive of her life was her own "deep" spirituality. She felt that the "Spirit" was her guide and that what God said about and to women concerning their position in the chain of command was not relevant to her; she was the exception. Furthermore, she had read books and pamphlets and heard sermons that explained away the passages that seem to limit a woman's role in the family and the church. They stated something like, "The original Greek word says.... What that really means is.... You see, Paul was speaking to cultural issues peculiar to that time.... Surely, God wouldn't command a woman to.... In Christ there is no male or female.... Weren't there women prophets?"

She was totally deceived into thinking that her female intuition, sensitivity, and passions were spirituality. She had no idea that she was a woman in total rebellion against God. King Saul of Israel offered sacrifices to God, but he did so in disregard to the clearly revealed will of God. He thought the end justified the means. His motive was to glorify God, but God said his religious service was rebellion equal to witchcraft (I Sam. 15:23). When a woman attempts to live for God contrary to his Word, her "spirituality" is equal to witchcraft, because she is attempting to "divine" the will of God in total disregard of his clear written words. God calls such a woman "Jezebel."

> Having hurt feelings and being angry are just different sides of the same old controlling coin.

It certainly was clear to my husband and me; her sin would be her destruction. It had already reduced her once strong, resourceful husband to a fearful, pitiful man. Over the years, the poisonous bile of her soul had been affecting her mind. One night, immediately after an especially powerful church service, while everyone was fellowshipping, I saw her approach my husband rather overly excited, so I began to make my way to him in case he needed me. Just as I got close, I saw her begin to swing her arms in wide jerky movements and heard her yell out loudly that her husband was in an adulterous affair with Marilyn Monroe (dead then for 50 years or so). She said she had a vision from God, which explained all their troubles. About the time I got to her side, she began to name several of the young mothers with new babies in the church as her husband's sex partners, claiming the babies were his. My husband looked around, horrified at her filthy accusations, which we knew were lies from a deranged mind. Her rantings got louder. In order to drown out her ravings, my husband began to sing as loudly as he could, "What can wash away my sin? Nothing but the blood of Jesus." I followed his lead and began singing with him. The startled congregation turned around and began to automatically sing along. I put my arm around her and forcefully led the now totally crazed woman out the door. **God had visited her with madness. He does "fearful" things like that.** He didn't just allow it to happen, he was there to push her over the edge. The fear of God is the beginning of wisdom. She had no fear of God. She should have. This lady believed she could force her husband to submit because she was "spiritually anointed." She did not reckon on God. A woman who thinks she can walk her own way because she believes herself spiritually gifted has no fear of Almighty God. **"He that soweth iniquity shall reap vanity: and the <u>rod of his anger shall fail</u>"** (Proverbs 22:8). **"Be not deceived; <u>God is not mocked</u>: for whatsoever a man soweth, that shall he also reap"** (Galatians 6:7). God was not mocked. The whole family still reaps what she sowed to this day. A wife without genuine fear of God can drift so far from reality that she needs sedatives to maintain an appearance of sanity.

Practice Makes "Awful" Perfectly Awful

By the time many women are entering their fortieth year, they are teetering on the edge of mental instability. They have spent several years of their life irritated at their husbands, daily feeling hurt and responding with coldness and bitterness. Instead of practicing being thankful and merry, they are practicing bitterness. As practice enables the pianist to find the right keys without effort or thought, so a woman who practices discontentment will, without thought, hit the notes of bitterness when her chain is pulled. Practicing, always practicing, perfecting her bitterness and discontentment.

She has practiced her bitterness until it comes naturally, and she does not even recognize it. She will usually define herself as one who stands against pride and evil. She will "do what is right, even if no one else will."

In the course of time, as her edginess and moodiness grow, she realizes that she can no longer control her nervousness. One day her "nerves" snap and she loses control, screaming like a crazy woman and calling loved ones terrible names. She will say it was "just a bad hormone day," but the family will wonder. The family learns to tolerate her occasional blow-ups, and she keeps practicing. After a trip to the doctor, she is calmer…"more her old self." The doctor changed her medication.

"Mom sleeps more now."

"Shh! Don't wake up Mother; she is having a bad day."

The disturbed woman expects her family to appease her and is offended when they act like life is just fine. God is visiting her soul with a terrible rot called madness. First, she is only mad at her husband. Years pass and she is mad at the family. As time goes on she is mad at the Church. Then she is mad at the mailman and mad at the waitress. **Practicing, always practicing, perfecting her madness. Mad, all the time mad. Madness.**

"The LORD shall smite thee with madness, and blindness, and astonishment of heart" (Deuteronomy 28:28).

"The beginning of the words of his mouth is foolishness: and the end of his talk is mischievous madness" (Ecclesiastes 10:13).

"Because thou servedst not the LORD thy God with **joyfulness**, and with **gladness of heart**, for the abundance of all things; Therefore shalt thou serve thine enemies which the LORD shall send against thee, in hunger, and in thirst, and in nakedness, and in want of all things: and he shall put a yoke of iron upon thy neck, until he have destroyed thee. " (Deuteronomy 28:47-48).

TIME TO CONSIDER

Peace is a fruit of the Spirit. Peace is that tangible presence of a relaxed, confident feeling a person experiences when everything is right (even when things are not right). If you are a child of the living God, those closest to you will be aware that peace can be found in your presence. The fruit of the Spirit is not a party to tension, stress, nervousness, uptightness, or bitterness.

"But the fruit of the Spirit is love, joy, peace, longsuffering, gentleness, goodness, faith, Meekness, temperance: against such there is no law" (Gal. 5:22-23).

Wisdom is a gift, yet we receive it by asking. And it is given to us liberally by God.

Proverbs 9:10 clearly and simply teaches that **"The fear of the LORD is the beginning of wisdom."**

Make a new habit.

➢ When you feel yourself beginning to have a critical spirit, stop, take a deep breath, silently ask for wisdom, then think of something that is on your thankful list. This is remolding a habit, and, in time, *practice makes it perfect.*

Getting Serious with God

➢ Find the definition for the word *odious*. Learn to hate the idea of ever being guilty of such a thing. Any time you are showing irritation and blame toward others, keep in mind that the earth is disquieted due to your being an odious, married woman.

"For three things the earth is disquieted, and for four which it cannot bear: For a servant when he reigneth; and a fool when he is filled with meat; For an <u>odious</u> woman when she is married; and an handmaid that is heir to her mistress" (Proverbs 30:21-23).

Look up in Scripture (KJV) the *fear of God*. How many times does it appear? What do you think God is trying to teach us? How differently would we react to our daily challenges if we truly feared God, if we feared his law of sowing and reaping?

Chapter 7

Wisdom
While There is Yet Hope

A wise woman is always learning.
She is open to change. She is ready to hear.
She pursues knowledge.

Please Listen to Me, Young Mother.

Dear Pearls,

My heart is heavy. I desire with my whole heart to bring our children up in the ways of God (they are ages 2 and 5). My deep concern is this—my husband has been deceived into thinking that various TV programs and commercials are not harmful to him or the children. He lets the fact that they are humorous dismiss the fact that they are crude and subtly being used to chip away at the spirit of our family. I have to work part-time in the evening, and I worry what is being shown on the idol of TV in our home. I have shared my concern with him (and, sorry to say, have nagged some too), but he is just not as convinced as I am about this issue. This has led to my being resentful and angry at him to the point where I feel no respect or love toward him. I am committed to my vows, though. Can you offer any advice or help me in any way? I even feel I must have married the wrong man! He has many positive qualities, but I worry that these influences are causing him to stray.

Thank you for any help you can give.

Susan

Dear Susan,

Just imagine what it would be like if your husband just disappeared one day—no more bad commercials, no questionable TV, no warm beds, just lots of long, lonely nights and days of toil at a job away from the children. The children will not be with their father watching TV; they will be with a baby-sitter who is taking care of them for money. You will wonder if the baby-sitter is having her boyfriend over for a little sex in the bedroom while the kids watch TV alone. The young children will cry when you leave for work, and the older children will be glad to see you go so they can exercise their new found liberties. The car has something wrong with it, but you can't take a day off to get it fixed. Money is in short supply. You discover that the social circle for a divorced woman with kids is rather small. Then the kids get the flu, and the baby-sitter refuses to work because she is not going to take the chance of catching the flu for a few measly dollars. For a year or two, your ex gets the children for the weekend. You have no control over what they do, but you are too tired to care anymore. In time, the child support you thought was required by law stops coming, because your husband has left the state with another woman.

> If you continue to dishonor your husband, the above scenario will likely become your own personal nightmare—soon!

Now, Susan, let's come back to the present. If you continue to dishonor your husband, the above scenario will likely become your own personal nightmare—soon! You describe yourself as resentful and angry. Your soul is being slowly molded into a bitter person. Your letter reveals that you have already considered that your marriage could end over this issue. I have seen it happen hundreds of times. People will ask why he left you, and you will righteously tell them that he got involved with another woman. The truth is, you ran him off because he watched commercials you declared unrighteous. You left his heart. And, he has left you emotionally—all because of your "playing the Holy Spirit." Remember, you told me you didn't feel love or respect for him, and even wondered if he was the right man for you after all. You have telegraphed your thoughts to him and, be assured, he is wondering the same thing about you right now.

Listen to me, young mother. Do not play the fool. You don't know how bad it can get. **The Devil would love to steal your children's souls. He will not do it through your husband's TV; he will do it through your dishonor.** The boys may have a difficult time with their sexual drives as a result of the commercials, but many young men have survived this in spite of the increased temptation. Few survive an unstable marriage where Mother resents Daddy. Your attitude has done nothing to stop the children's exposure to temptation. Just think, if you had lower expectations, you would permit yourself to love and honor your husband, and the children would be better for it. When God gave Eve to Adam, he was giving him a helper, not a conscience. Adam already had a conscience before his wife was created.

I am not suggesting that *you* should have lower standards. In fact, your husband obviously should have higher standards, but your nagging and criticism have the opposite effect of producing righteousness. Ideally, if you could hold your standards, hold your tongue, and hold your man, in time you might be able to put forth an appeal to him that does not offend.

As things are today, you will continue toward divorce, or you will get on the road toward a heavenly marriage by honoring your man. It's a no-brainer.

-Debi

Alone

Dear Pearls,

I would like to tell my story that others might be warned. I am 52 years old and have been alone for 23 years. I never thought this would be my lot in life. It never crossed my mind that my husband would ever leave me.

I made many mistakes in my relationship with my husband. Today, I see and hear young wives, and older wives as well, thoughtlessly making those very same mistakes with their own husbands. They take for granted that he would never leave them and file for divorce. This sense of security seems to give them the feeling that they have the liberty to take their stand, in myriad ways, against the wrongs, failures, and inadequacies of their husbands. I see it as either ignorance or a refusal to obey God's injunction to wives, or a combination of both. This is why I write my story—to open the truths to the wives who are truly ignorant, and to warn the resistant wives.

I cannot answer for my husband's responsibility and duties. That is between him and God. But if I had known then what I do now about God's commands to wives, i.e., what a man needs and what I could do to fill those needs, it would have made a big difference.

The things I did or failed to do were not everyday, constantly overt, in-the-face actions. They were subtle, ebbing and flowing, but there, nonetheless.

• **When** my husband acted selfishly at home, allowed his temper to flare, and sometimes said curse words, and then went to church and acted spiritual, I wish I had prayed positively for him instead of withdrawing a little emotionally from him and letting my cynicism and lack of confidence in him be so manifest. I wish I had openly showed love and acceptance of him for himself, not impatiently waited until he acted right.

• **When** he failed the children, failed to have devotions, failed to be spiritual, failed to lead as he should, I wish I had completely trusted God and maintained unity, honor, reverence, and submission with a glad and trusting heart. I wish I had kept the children honoring him and praying for their dad instead of allowing my martyred attitude to manifest itself so openly.

• **When** he made a statement about someone or something, I wish I had not always put his opinion down, letting him know he was wrong—again.

• **When** he acted like a jerk, I wish I had remained quiet and prayed for him, loved him anyway instead of letting him know what I thought about him and his actions.

• **When** he tried to make up to me for some failure, I wish I had not

Chapter 7 ~ Wisdom–While There is Yet Hope

been so cool, waiting for him to "suffer" a little more and be more intense and sincere about his apology.

- **When** he spent money I thought we didn't have, I wish I had remained quiet and trusted God. I wish I had shown continued confidence in him, regardless of his decisions.

- **When** he wanted me to do something, and I didn't want to do it, I wish I had cheerfully complied instead of making him sorry he asked. Hardheadedness is not a trait to endear any woman to a man.

- **When** he needed a woman to believe in him, admire him, approve of him, accept him, regardless of his failures, I wish now that I had been the one to give him those things.

- **When** I thought that keeping his faults before him—just small things he did and said—and keeping myself a little standoffish in my approval of him, was the only way he would change, I wish someone would have taken me aside and told me how badly mistaken I was to think that it was my place to apply and keep the pressure on.

- **When** he didn't speak up enough in a business deal or with friends, I wish I had kept quiet and not interjected my "help" in the matter.

- **When** we were in the company of his family and our friends, I wish I had not taken on a martyred air when he left to go off and do something on his own.

- **When** he did not know how to show love, and I felt a void emotionally, I wish I had borne all things and hoped all things, and loved him unconditionally, instead of giving up inside and turning to friends and family for my emotional support and needs. I never saw the need to endear myself to him. I took for granted that he would fulfill the husband's moral obligation to love me. I wish I had gone to "God's Beauty School" for the whole woman.

Time passed. The marriage strangled to death from the load of mistakes, sin, and selfishness on the part of both of us. One day, to my shock and surprise, he just left. The children and I were plunged into near poverty. He no longer felt the natural desire to protect and support his family. I received the minimum child support. It was never enough. When the house and the car needed repairs, there was little or no money to have the work done. Things slowly fell apart. People would help, but no one quite knows what to do with broken families.

I dreaded the summertime. As I drove away to work in the mornings, I agonized over my children having to stay in the house behind locked doors for 10 hours a day when I couldn't afford a baby-sitter or find someone trustworthy. They were too old for child-care centers and still too young to be left all day. At the beginning, when my children were sick, there was no one to stay with them unless I took off from work. Then the week-long flu would hit, and my time off work would mean my job. I had no real job training, so I started off in entry-level positions that hardly paid. I became ill with a long-term, debilitating condition, made worse by stress, but had to continue to go to work every day. I had no choice.

But, God was faithful to us, and we never went hungry or cold. Loneliness at home, the feelings of rejection and abandonment, and the financial struggles, however, were there every day, year after year. I know my life could have been so very different if early in my marriage I had known of and obeyed God's plan for the wife.

Some of you don't believe that this could happen to you. In fact, you may well be thinking that it would be a relief if you could get him out of the house. You think, "Well, I'm healthy and strong. I'm emotionally secure. I can handle it. I am pretty and will find a good man. I have family who will help me. I have a good church to support me, and could get counseling, etc. At least I would have peace in the house and could then live as I wanted to. I wouldn't have all the problems to contend with." These are all things that foolish wives may think. But I know better. My experience, as well as thousands of others, proves this outlook to be a lie.

Carolyn

A New Breed of Women

Look around you. There is a new breed of women today. They serve your table at the local restaurant; they mow grass, work in the hospitals, and direct traffic. There are thousands of these ladies; they are everywhere doing anything they can find to do. They are mostly single moms. They dress cheaply; their hair has a ragged cut, and the dark circles under their young eyes testify to their faded hope. They are a new army of workers. Employers can underpay them because they are desperate for work. You can depend on them because they would not dare take the chance of losing their job. They are always distracted because they are thinking of their unhappy children or the baby-sitter's new, weird boyfriend who comes over when she is at work.

> Satan didn't even give me a chance to get properly bedded before he introduced himself to me, just as he did to Eve, and I, like my big sister Eve, fell for his line.

Sometimes they team up with another single mom to share resources, childcare responsibilities, and troubles. Lately, I have been reading how many of these single women are turning to each other for comfort—sometimes for intimacy. Do you think anything might ever drive you to that? A *new breed* of women. They are independent, in charge, and stressed. They grow old early, trying futilely to care for unruly children whom no man wants to stepfather. They grow bitter as they watch eligible men look over their heads at girls much younger than themselves, who have no strings attached. And they grow fearful when they realize that the men who have shown interest in them are hiding perverted intents toward their cute little youngsters. Their kids are angry and often get into trouble.

But all this was not your fault. No, it was *your husband* who committed adultery, *your husband* who was angry or got into porn, but he seems to have a life of ease now with plenty of money compared to your miserable condition. He takes the kids every other weekend and spoils them, making them hate you all the more. He seems to be so vital, so alive and full of smiles. He has money to entertain them, and they know you as a grumpy penny-pincher. They think his young girlfriend is really cool. When you discover a lump in your breast, your teens don't care or understand the gravity of the situation. You struggle alone with your fear and take yourself to the doctor, knowing that even though this might not end in death, it is the end of hope.

It all started when you were mad about a TV commercial, or when he watched the car races on Sunday afternoon. It all got worse when he wanted you to do something exotic sexually. **Divorce is never planned, but is almost always preceded by certain <u>avoidable</u> reactive behavior and events. Don't let it happen to you.**

You Poor, Dumb Man

I remember the night Michael and I married. My new husband decided we needed to go shopping and cook a meal before we went to bed. I had no idea how much money he made, or how much he had for our honeymoon. Money had never been an issue in my life. Yet, here we were in the grocery store at 10 P.M. on Sunday night, having been married for less than an hour, when I first felt the critical spirit rise within me. He was picking out ground beef and was about to pay a very high price. I tried to reason with him. "Don't you think that is priced too high, and wouldn't it be better to buy a cheaper priced meat?" He was twenty-five years old and had never had a woman question him about how he was spending his money, and I will never forget the bewildered look on his face. It was as if he were trying to remember who I was and why he had put himself into a position to be criticized. I must have sounded as though **I was patronizing him, speaking to him as if he were a stupid kid, because that is how I felt about what he was doing.** I was suddenly shocked at my attitude. What right did I have to treat him like a stupid jerk? How did I know how much money he had? I wasn't even his wife yet, in the biblical sense, yet here I was thinking, "You stupid nincompoop. I wouldn't spend MY money like that!"

Satan didn't even give me a chance to get properly bedded before he introduced himself to me, just as he did to Eve, and I, like my big sister Eve, fell for his line. I was amazed at my critical spirit. There, standing at that meat counter, I made up my mind I would not allow this to be the story of my life. **I would learn to be a woman of God,** regardless of what my husband bought or how dumb he seemed to be in the way he spent money.

What Did You Practice Today?

Were you mad at your husband this week over something he did, like being late, speaking to you rudely, or yelling at the kids? Did you seethe with bitterness and intentionally avoid looking into his eyes so as to express your disdain? You know what I am talking about. You remember the ugliness of your own heart and soul. Yes, your husband deserved it. Yes, it is your right. But is there any satisfaction in

♥ Practice forgiving, Practice loving, Practice being thankful ♥

your punishing responses? Does he now bend to your anger and do better in hopes of escaping your condemnation? **He practices his *faults*, and you practice your *bitterness*. You are both practicing divorce.** Your children watch and are practicing being poor future mothers and fathers.

Have you forgotten why you were created? Please come to Jesus just as you are and say to him, "From this day forth I want to be the help meet you created me to be." Tell him. He is waiting to forgive and love you. God's way works.

I know I have been hard on you, but no harder than reality. For a moment, God has broken through your wall of excuses, and you now know **you** are responsible.

"Therefore to him that knoweth to do good, and doeth it not, to him it is sin" (James 4:17).

"But he that <u>heareth, and doeth not,</u> is like a man that without a foundation built an house upon the earth; against which the stream did beat vehemently, and immediately it fell; and the ruin of that house was great" (Luke 6:49).

"For God hath not given us the spirit of fear; but of power, and of love, and of a sound mind" (II Timothy 1:7).

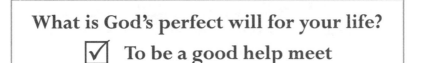

What is God's perfect will for your life?
☑ To be a good help meet

TIME TO CONSIDER

God had a plan for women from the beginning. You are not an exception to his plan.

Sin causes women to self-destruct. Because this self-destruction is a slow, almost indiscernible process, women do not see the destruction coming until it is too late and their husbands are gone. This slow, eroding process often blinds a woman from seeing her part, thus she will repeat her mistakes over and over until she is too old or broken to attract another man to be a part of her life.

"Doth a fountain send forth at the same place sweet water and bitter?" (James 3:11).

➤ *Make a new habit*

Think of the thing your husband does that irritates you the most. Now say to yourself, "I do not see the whole picture. I do not know what God is doing in my life or my husband's life. My critical attitude is a far graver sin than his bad habits. I am guilty of blaspheming the written Word of God when I do not love and obey my husband. Therefore, I am laying down my campaign against him concerning this issue. And, as far as I am concerned, it is God's business to direct my husband and convict him. I am trusting God."

➤ *Getting Serious with God*

Go back through the previous story called, **Alone**. Every time you read the word *"When,"* stop and ask yourself, "*When* my husband acts as her husband acted, do I react as she did?" Write your own new response to each *"When."* Ask God to give you the wisdom and courage to follow through on your new commitment.

Chapter 8

Wisdom to Understand Your Man

Co-authored by Rebekah (Pearl) Anast

A wise woman learns to adapt
to her husband.

Three Kinds of Men

Men are not all the same. I have become aware that there are basically three types of men. The different types are just as marked in one-year-olds as they are in adult men. It seems that God made each male to express one side of his triad nature. No single man completely expresses the well-rounded image of God. If a man were all three types at the same time, he would be the perfect man, but I have never met, heard of, or read in a book of history or fiction of a man who is the proper balance of all three. Certainly Jesus was the perfect balance. Most men are a little of all three, but tend to be dominant in one. And all the training and experiences of life will never successfully make a man into a different type of man. There is nothing clumsier and more pathetic than a man trying to act differently from who he is. As we review the types, you will probably readily identify your husband and be able to see where you have been a curse or a blessing to him.

By the time a young woman gets married, she has developed a composite image of what her husband ought to be like. The men she has known and the characters in books and movies provide each woman with a concept of the perfect man. Poor guys!

> If you fight his inadequacies, both of you will fail. If you love him and support him __with__ his inadequacies and __without__ taking charge, both of you will succeed and grow.

Our preconceived ideas make it tough on them. They are never perfect—far from it. God gave each one a nature that in part is like himself, but never complete. When you add in the factor that all men are fallen creatures, it makes a girl wonder why she would ever want to tie her life to one of these sons of Adam. But God made us ladies to have this unreasonable desire to be needed by a man, and our hormones are working strenuously to bring us together.

When a girl suddenly finds herself permanently wed to a man who is not like she thinks he ought to be, rather than adapt to him, she usually spends the rest of their marriage—which may not be very long—trying to change him into what she thinks her man ought to be. Most young girls are married only a short time when they make the awful discovery that they may have gotten a lemon. Rather than bemoan your "fate," ask God for wisdom.

Wisdom is knowing what you "bought" when you married that man, and learning to adapt to him *as he is*, not as you want him to be.

Men are not alike. Your husband most likely will not be like your father or brother or the man in your favorite romance novel. Our husbands are created in the image of God, and it takes all kinds of men to even come close to completing that image. No man is a perfect balance; if he were, he would be too divine to need you. **God gives imperfect women to imperfect men so they can be heirs together of the grace of life and *become something more together than either one of them would ever be alone.* If you fight your husband's inadequacies or seek to be dominant where he is not, both of you will fail. If you love him and support him __with__ his inadequacies and __without__ taking charge, both of you will succeed and grow.

Mr. Command Man

God is **dominant**—a sovereign and all-powerful God. He is also **visionary**—omniscient and desirous of carrying out his plans. And, God is **steady**—the same yesterday, and today, and forever, our faithful High Priest. Most men epitomize one of these three aspects of God.

A few men are born with more than their share of dominance and, on the surface, a deficit in gentleness. They often end up in positions that command other men. We will call them *Command Men*. They are born leaders. They are often chosen by other men to be military commanders, politicians, preachers and heads of corporations. Winston Churchill, George Patton, and Ronald Reagan are examples of dominant men. Since our world needs only a few leaders, God seems to limit the number of these *Command Men*. Throughout history, men created in God the Father's image have all surrounded themselves with good men to help get big jobs completed. *Command Men* usually do more than is required of them.

They are known for expecting their wives to wait on them hand and foot. A *Command Man* does not want his wife involved in any project that prevents her from serving him. If you are blessed to be married to a strong, forceful, bossy man, as I am, then it is very important for you to learn how to make an appeal without challenging his authority. We will discuss how to make an appeal later in this book.

> It is very important for you to learn how to make an appeal without challenging his authority.

Command Men have less tolerance, so they will often walk off and leave their clamoring wife before she has a chance to realize that she is even close to losing her marriage. By the time she realizes that there is a serious problem, she is already a divorced mother seeking help in how to raise her children alone. A woman can fight until she is blue in the face, yet the *Command Man* will not yield. He is not as intimate or vulnerable as are other men in sharing his personal feelings or vocation with his wife. **He seems to be sufficient unto himself.** It is awful being shut out. A woman married to a *Command Man* has to **earn her place in his heart** by proving that she will stand by her man, faithful, loyal, and obedient. When she has won his confidence, he will treasure her to the extreme.

She is on call every minute of her day. Her man wants to know where she is, what she is doing, and why she is doing it. He corrects her without thought. For better or for worse, it is his nature to control.

A woman married to a *Command Man* wears a heavier yoke than most women, but it can be a very rewarding yoke. In a way, her walk as his help meet is easier because there is never any possibility of her being in control. There are no gray areas; she always knows exactly what is required of her, therefore she has a calm sense of safety and rest.

The *Command Man* feels it his duty and responsibility to lead people, and so he does, whether they think they want him to lead or not. Amazingly, this is what the public is most comfortable with. Very few people have enough confidence to strike out on their own; plus, the feeling of being blamed for mistakes holds them back. The *Command Man* is willing to take the chance, and for that purpose God created these king-like men. Their road is not easy, for James said, **"My brethren, be not many masters, knowing that we shall receive the greater condemnation"** (James 3:1).

On 9-11, when the World Trade Center was destroyed, another plane flying over Pennsylvania was being highjacked by other terrorists. Mr. Todd Beamer was on that plane. It was his voice we all heard saying the now famous line, "Let's roll." He must have been a strong *Mr. Command Man*. He, and others like him, took control of a desperate situation and saved many other lives while sacrificing their own. It could have been a terrible mistake, but Mr. Beamer evaluated the situation, made a decision, and then acted upon it. He knew the lives of all those people were in his hands. It was a heavy responsibility, yet he was "willing to do what a man's gotta do." You will remember how strong and queenly his young widow seemed when we watched her on TV after the attacks. **A good *Mr. Command* sees the bigger picture and strives to help the greatest number**, even if it costs him his life and the lives of those he loves. If he is an honest man, he will take financial loss in order to help lead those who need him, but in the end he will usually come out on top. If he is not an honest man, he will be selfish and use the resources of others to further his own interests.

> A King wants a Queen, which is why a man in command wants a faithful wife to share his fame and glory.

A King wants a Queen, which is why a man in command wants a faithful wife to share his fame and glory. Without a woman's admiration, his victories are muted. **If a wife learns early to enjoy the benefits of taking the second seat, and if she does not take offense to his headstrong aggressiveness, she will be the one**

sitting at his right side being adored, because this kind of man will totally adore his woman and exalt her. She will be his closest, and sometimes his only, confidante. Over the years, the *Command Man* can become more yielding and gentle. His wife will discover secret portals to his heart.

If you are married to a king, honor and reverence is something you must give him on a daily basis if you want him to be a benevolent, honest, strong, and fulfilled man of God. He has the potential to become an amazing leader. Never shame him, and do not belittle him or ignore his accomplishments.

If the wife of a *Command Man* resists his control, he will readily move forward without her. If he is not a principled Christian, he will allow the marriage to come to divorce. Like King Ahasuerus of Persia, if she defies him, he will replace her and not look back. If his Christian convictions prevent him from divorcing, he will remain stubbornly in command, and she will be known as a miserable old wretch.

His vision is like a man looking from a mountaintop; he sees the distant goal.

If a *Command Man* has not developed working skills, and thus accomplishes little, he will have the tendency to tell stories about himself and brag until people are sick of him. If he has left his wife and lost his children, thus having no legitimate "kingdom" of his own, he will be obnoxiously garrulous.

A *Command Man* who has gone bad is likely to be abusive. It is important to remember that much of how a *Command Man* reacts depends on his wife's reverence toward him. **When a *Command Man* (lost or saved) is treated with honor and reverence, a good help meet will find that her man will be wonderfully protective and supportive.** In most marriages, the strife is not because the man is cruel or evil; it is because he expects obedience, honor, and reverence, and is not getting it. Thus, he reacts badly. When a wife plays her part as a help meet, the *Command Man* will respond differently. Of course, there are a few men who are so cruel and violent that even when the wife *is* a proper help meet, he will still physically abuse her or the children. In such cases, it would be the duty of the wife to alert the authorities so that they might become the arm of the Lord to do justice.

- *Mr. Command* will not take the trash out, as a general rule, and he will not clean up the mess at the trash area. He may organize and command someone else to do it. Any woman trying to force *Mr. Command* into becoming a nice trash man will likely end up alone, trashed by her man.

- *Mr. Command* will want to talk about his plans, ideas, and finished projects. He will be very objective, very unemotional, and **he will not enjoy small talk. His vision is like a man looking from a high mountain; he sees the distant goal.** He will expect his wife to help him remember individuals' needs.
- *Mr. Command Man* will be most uncomfortable and at a loss when dealing with the sick, helpless, and dying. Where there is no hope, there will be no need for a *Command Man*.
- A born leader is a man who can, when necessary, adapt principles or rules to circumstances for the greater good of the greatest number of people.

Mr. Visionary

God is a *Visionary* as seen in his person, the Holy Spirit. He made some men in the image of that part of his nature. Prophets, be they true or false, are usually of this type. Some of you are married to men who are shakers, changers, and dreamers. These men get the entire family upset about peripheral issues, such as: do we believe in Christmas? Should we use state marriage licenses? Should a Christian opt out of the Social Security system? The issues may be serious and worthy of one's commitment, but, in varying degrees, these men have tunnel vision, tenaciously focusing on single issues. They will easily pick up and relocate without any idea of what they are going to do for a living at their new location. They are often the church splitters and the ones who demand doctrinal purity and proper dress and conduct. Like a prophet, they call people to task for their inconsistencies. If they are not wise, they can be real fools who push their agendas, forcing others to go their way. One *Visionary* will campaign for the legalization of pot, while another will be an activist to make abortions illegal. Most will just sit around the house and complain, but in their souls they are *Visionaries*.

> Learn how to be flexible, and learn how to always be loyal to your man.

Visionaries are often gifted men or inventors, and I am sure it was men of this caliber who conquered the Wild West, though they would not have been the farmers who settled it. Today, *Visionary* men are street preachers, political activists, organizers and instigators of any front-line social issue. **They love confrontation**, and hate the status quo. "Why leave it the way it is when you can change it?" They are the men who keep the rest of the world from getting stagnant or dull. **The**

Visionary **is consumed with a need to communicate with his words, music, writing, voice, art, or actions.** He is the "**voice crying out in the wilderness**" striving to change the way humanity is behaving or thinking. Good intentions don't always keep *Visionaries* from causing great harm. They can stir up pudding and end up with toxic waste, if they are not wise. An unwise wife can add to the poison with negative words, or she can, with simple words of caution, bring attention to the goodness of the pudding and the wisdom in leaving it alone. **Every** *Mr. Visionary* **needs a good, wise, prudent, stable wife who has a positive outlook on life.**

If you are married to one of these fellows, expect to be rich or poor, rarely middle class. He may invest everything in a chance and lose it all or make a fortune, but he will not do well working 8 to 5 in the same place for thirty years, and then retiring to live the good life. If he works a regular job, he may either not show up half the time or he will work like a maniac 80 hours a week and love every minute. He may purchase an alligator farm in Florida or a ski resort in Colorado, or he may buy an old house trailer for $150 with hopes of fixing it up and selling it for $10,000, only to find out that it is so deteriorated that it can't be moved. He will then have his wife and all the kids help him tear the top off and carry the scraps to the dump, (saving the appliances in the already crowded garage), so he can make a farm trailer out of the axles. Now that he has a farm trailer and no animals, expect him to get a deal on three, old, sick cows, and.... **He may never be rich in money, but he will be rich in experience.**

Come to think of it, maybe my husband is not a 100% *Mr. Command Man*, because he seems quite a bit like this *Mr. Visionary*. I remember, on more than one occasion, helping him tear down someone's old barn in order to drag the junk home to fill up our old barn. Remember, most men are a mixture of types, but usually stronger in one.

The wife of *Mr. Visionary* should be just a little bit reckless and blind in one eye if she is going to enjoy the ride. If this is your man, you need to learn two very important things (beyond how to make an appeal). **Learn how to be flexible, and learn how to always be loyal to your man.** You will be amazed at how much happier you will be and how much fun life can be if you learn to just go with the flow—*his flow*. Life will become an adventure. You will actually begin to feel sorry

> Greatness is a state of soul, not certain accomplishments.

for the gals married to the stick-in-the-mud, *steady type*. And once you get it into your head that your husband does not have to be "right" for you to follow him, you will FINALLY be able to say "bye-bye" to your overwrought parents, even when they are screaming that you are married to a crazy man. People looking on will marvel that you are able to love and appreciate your husband, but you will know better because **you will see his greatness.**

> It will be your face he looks into to see the marvel of what a great thing he has done.

Greatness is a state of soul, not certain accomplishments. Thomas Edison, though not recognized as such, was *great* after his 999th failure to make a light bulb. The Wright brothers were *great* when they neglected their lucrative occupation of fixing bicycles and "wasted time" trying to make one of them fly. If the light bulb had never worked and the plane had never flown, and no one remembered their names today, they would have been the same men, and their lives would have still been just as full and their days just as challenging. Did Edison's wife think him great when he used his last dime on another failed idea? If she didn't, just think what she missed.

The *Visionary* **man needs his woman's support**, and he will appreciate it when it is freely given. Without her, he feels alone. This guy will be a little hard to live with at first. Big, wild fights are the usual beginnings if a nice, normal girl (who had a *Mr. Steady* daddy) marries one of "the weird ones." They will either have a bitter divorce (she divorces him) in the first few years, or she will decide to learn to appreciate him, because he is really rather lovable. I get very few letters from wives married to these high-strung, going-to-reinvent-the-wheel men. I do get lots of letters from their mothers-in-law, asking us to write and straighten out their sons-in-law.

Some of these guys talk with glowing enthusiasm and animation. Usually, they enjoy hashing over ideas, plans and dreams. If you are married to one, he loves to tell you about his newest idea, and he wants your enthusiastic support, not a critique of his idea. He will look at his idea more critically later, but for the moment, the idea itself is invigorating to him. He will have a thousand ideas for every project he attempts, and he will try many that he will never finish, and he will finish some that are worthless, and you "knew it all along." Remind him of that the next time he has an idea, and you will destroy your marriage—but you won't change him. He will share his "dumb ideas" with someone else.

Learn to Enjoy the Trip

Several years back, a newlywed couple decided to take a bicycle road trip for their honeymoon. They had the map all worked out and the bikes and camping gear ready. After riding for a couple days, the young wife noticed that her good husband was going the wrong way. She stopped him and tried to show him on the map that he had veered off the course. She had always been endowed with a natural ability to read maps and knew exactly where they were. He was not so gifted and argued that she was dead wrong and insisted that they were headed the right way. Later that day, when he did discover that he had indeed taken the wrong road, he brushed it off and blamed the signs or gave some plausible reason. Again he took the wrong road, and she argued with him. He kept correcting their course, but they were not getting anywhere by its shortest route. She let him know his error. That part of the honeymoon was not very "honeyed." Nothing would change his mind. He knew he was right, and if not exactly right, then he was as right as could be expected under the circumstances, and criticism was not welcomed.

> He spends his life looking through a telescope or microscope, and he will be stunned that what he sees, others do not seem to notice or care about.

What could she do? The young wife was not pleased with the way they were relating, and she reasoned to herself that this could become the pattern for the rest of their lives. As she brooded on the matter, it occurred to her that it was very important to him to be right and to be in charge, and it really didn't matter which road they took. They were taking this trip to be together, not to get somewhere in particular. God in his mercy and grace gave this sweet young wife a new heart. She decided to follow her husband down any road he chose, without question or second-guessing. So she cheerfully began to enjoy the beautiful day and the glory of being young and in love as she continued to pedal her bike down a road that was taking them to where every marriage ought to go, even though it was not according to the map.

This little lady is married to a 100% *Visionary Man*. She started her marriage right, following him wherever he led, regardless of whether she thought it was the right direction or not. She has been flexible and is enjoying her ride. Someday, when her husband is assured that he can trust her with his heart, he will let her be his navigator— and still take the credit for it. The moral to this story is: the way you think determines how you will feel, and how you feel influences the way you will act.

If you are married to the *Visionary Man*, **learn to enjoy the trip**, for if he ever does make a better light bulb, he will want you to be the one who turns it on for the first time in public. It will be your face he looks into to see the marvel of what a great thing he has done. You are his most important fan. When you know your man really needs you, you can be happy with just about anything.

Overtime, this type of man will become more practical. If you are a young wife married to a man whom your mama thinks is totally crazy—then you may be married to *Mr. Visionary*. Right now, purpose in your heart to be loyal to him, and to **be flexible**; then, let your dreamer dream. Lean back and enjoy the ride; it should prove interesting.

The world needs the *Visionary Man*, for he is the one who seeks out hypocrisy and injustice and slays the dragons. He calls himself and those around him to a higher standard. He knows how to do nearly everything and is readily willing to advise others. In time, he will be quite accomplished in more than one thing.

> The moral to this story is: the way you think determines how you will feel, and how you feel influences the way you will act.

- *Visionary Man* will take the trash out if he remembers it. But, he may also end up inventing a way whereby the trash takes itself out or is turned into an energy source, or he may just waste a lot of time building a cart for you to take it out. He will not mind cleaning up if he notices it needs doing, but he may get so deeply involved that he decides to paint while he is sweeping, and then switch projects before he gets finished painting. And he will likely be irritated when his wife nags him about it.

* *Visionary Man* will talk and talk and talk to his honey if she approves of him. He will be subjective, thinking about feelings, moods, and spiritual insights. **One of his greatest needs will be for his wife to think objectively (proven truth) and use common sense**, which will help keep his feet from flying too far from solid ground. **He spends his life looking through a telescope or microscope**, and he will be stunned that what he sees (or thinks he sees), others do not seem to notice or care about. Every small issue will become mind-consuming, and he will need his wife to casually talk about the big picture and the possible end results of relationships, finances, or health if he continues to totally focus on his present interest. His sweetheart needs to stay in a positive state of mind, yet never jump into his make-believe world, trying to be too much of a

cheerleader on dead-end issues. Let him burn out on things that are not wise. But don't throw water on his fire. Let him find his own balance through bumping into hard realities. The Old Testament prophets of God must surely have been the Visionary types. Remember Elijah, Jeremiah, and Ezekiel and all their trials?

- *Visionary Man* is an initiator and provoker. He is a point man, trailblazer, and a voice to get things done. He will start and keep the party going until the *Command Man* gets there to lead on.

- **Visionary Man's focus is so intense that matters can easily be blown out of proportion**. A wife must guard against negative conversation about people. An idle conversation by her can bring about the end of a life-long friendship. This is true with all men, but especially so with *Mr. Visionary*. Search your heart and discover your motive in what you say about people. What is your intent when you speak? To build him up and give him joy, or to build up yourself and make him think that you alone are perfect? If you mention people and make them look a little bad and yourself a little "taken for granted," your husband may get the idea that friends and family are treating you unfairly, and he may become withdrawn and suspicious. You could unwittingly render your husband unteachable. If

> He is like deep, deep water. The very depth makes the movement almost imperceptible.

you want your husband to grow into a confident, outgoing man of God, then he needs to have a clear conscience toward his friends and family. God says a woman's conversation can win her lost husband. In the same vein, a woman's idle, negative conversation can cripple a strong man and cause him to become an angry, confrontational, divisive man. **"Likewise, ye wives, be in subjection to your own husbands; that, if any obey not the word, they also may without the word <u>be won by the conversation of the wives</u>; While they behold your <u>chaste conversation</u> coupled with fear"** (1 Peter 3:1-2).

- *Mr. Visionary* needs a lady who does not take offense easily. She needs to be tough. He needs his lady to be full of life and joy. A *Visionary Man* is not equipped to be a comforter—for himself or anyone else. His lady will need to learn to tuck in that quivering lip, square those shoulders, and put on that smile.

- *Mr. Visionary* can be a leader, but because he has tunnel vision his leadership will have a more narrow focus.

Mr. Steady

God is as steady as an eternal rock, caring, providing, and faithful, like a priest—*like Jesus Christ*. He created many men in that image. We will call him *Mr. Steady*—"in the middle, not given to extremes." The *Steady Man* does not make snap decisions or spend his last dime on a new idea, and he doesn't try to tell other people what to do. He avoids controversy. He doesn't invent the light bulb like *Mr. Visionary*, but he will be the one to build the factory and manage the assembly line that produces the light bulb and the airplane. He does not jump to the front of the plane to take a razor knife away from a terrorist, unless he is encouraged to do so by *Mr. Command*. He would never lead a revolution against the government or the church. He will quietly ignore hypocrisy in others. He will selflessly fight the wars that *Mr. Visionary* starts and *Mr. Command* leads. He builds the oil tankers, farms the soil, and quietly raises his family. As a general rule, he will be faithful till the day he dies in the same bed he has slept in for the last 40 or 50 years. Older women who are divorced and have learned by their mistakes **know the value of peace and safety, and they will long for a nice steady man of his stature, but such a man is rarely available**—unless his foolish wife has left him. This man is content with the wife of his youth.

> Your husband's gentleness is not a weakness; it is his strength. Your husband's hesitation is not indecision; it is cautious wisdom. Your husband's lack of deep spiritual conversation is not a lack of caring; it is simply the cap on a mountain of intense emotion.

Joys and Tribulations

Being married to a *Steady Man* has its rewards and its trials. On the good side, your husband never puts undue pressure on you to perform miracles. He doesn't expect you to be his servant. You do not spend your days putting out emotional fires, because he doesn't create tension in the family. You rarely feel hurried, pushed, pressured, or forced. The women married to *Visionary Men* look at you in wonder that your husband seems so balanced and stable. The wife of *Command Man* marvels at the free time you seem to have. If your dad happened to be a *Steady Man,* then chances are you will appreciate your husband's down-to-earth, practical life for the wonderful treasure it is.

When you are married to a man who is steady and cautious, and you have a bit of the impatient romantic in you, you may not see his worth and

readily honor him. You may be discontent because he is slow and cautious to take authority or make quick decisions. A bossy woman sees her husband's lack of hasty judgment and calls her *Steady* husband "wishy-washy." His steadiness makes him the last to change, so he seems to be a follower because he is seldom out front forming up the troops. There is no exciting rush in him, just a slow, steady climb with no bells or whistles. You wish he would just make up his mind, and that he would take a stand in the church. He seems to just let people use him. There are times you wish he would boldly tell you what to do so you would not have to carry all the burden of decision-making.

Some women equate their husband's wise caution and lack of open passion as being unspiritual. His lack of spontaneity and open boldness may look like indifference to spiritual things. However, he is like deep, deep water. The very depth makes the movement almost imperceptible, but it is, nevertheless, very strong.

> Let him be the one God made him to be: a still, quiet, thoughtful presence—for you!

He will be confused with your unhappiness and try to serve you more, which may further diminish your respect for his masculinity. **Disappointment and unthankfulness can make you wearier than any amount of duties.** The trials he seems to cause you are really your discontented responses to what you consider to be his shortcomings. If you didn't attempt to change him into something other than what God created him to be, he would not cause you any grief. His very steadiness keeps him on his middle-of-the-road course, and it will drive a controlling woman crazy.

This is why many disgruntled ladies married to Mr. Steadys fall victim to hormonal imbalance, physical illness, or emotional problems.

When a woman is married to a bossy, dominant man, people marvel that she is willing to serve him without complaint, so she comes out looking like a wonderful woman of great patience and sacrifice. A woman married to the impulsive *Visionary Man,* who puts the family through hardships, will stir amazement in everyone. "How can she tolerate his weird ideas with such peace and joy?" She comes out being a real saint, maybe even a martyr. But if you are married to a wonderful, kind, loving, serving man, and you are just a little bit selfish, then you are likely to end up looking like an unthankful shrew. He helps you, adores you, protects you, and is careful to provide for you, and you are still not satisfied. Shame on you!

Know Your Man

Wives are very much flesh and blood, and as young women, we don't come to marriage with all the skills needed to make it start out good, let alone perfect. When you come to know your man for whom God created him to be, you will stop trying to change him into what you *think* he should be. ***The key is to know your man.*** **If he is** *Mr. Steady,* **you need to learn to be thankful and to honor him as the one created for you in the image of God.** God's Word says in Hebrews 13:8, **"Jesus Christ the same yesterday, and to day, and for ever." A man who is created steady brings peace and safety to a woman's soul.** Your husband's gentleness is not a weakness; **it is his strength.** Your husband's hesitation is not indecision; it is cautious wisdom. Your husband's lack of deep spiritual conversation is not a lack of caring; it is simply the cap on a mountain of intense emotions. If he ever speaks of how he does feel, he will most likely become teary.

He wants to please you. **"Counsel in the heart of man is like deep water; but a man** [a wife also] **of understanding will draw it out"** (Proverbs 20:5). You will not need to learn how to make an appeal to him, because your husband is all too willing to hear you.

If this describes your man, you need to learn how to stand still and listen; then let God move your husband in his own good time. Ask God for wisdom and patience. Seek to always have a gentle spirit. Look up "shamefacedness" in the Bible, and learn what it means. Pray for your husband to have wisdom. Stop expecting him to *perform* for you, to pray with the family, to speak out in witnessing, or to take a bold stand at church. **Stop trying to stir him up to anger** toward the children in order to get him to feel as though he understands how badly you are being treated. **Let him be the one God made him to be: a still, quiet, thoughtful presence—***for you! Command* and *Visionary Men* understand and appreciate him, and they, too, lean on this type of man for stability. Learn to seek your husband's advice on what to do, and then give him time to answer, even if it means days or weeks. Show respect by asking him in what areas he would like you to do some decision-making.

Many of these "nice" men prefer their wives to show some initiative. A *Command Man* tells you what to do and how to serve him, and a *Visionary Man* wants you to do what he is doing.

A *Steady Man* likes a woman to walk beside him, yet grow in her own right before God and him.

If you are married to a *Mr. Steady*, you need to get familiar with Proverbs 31 to know how to be an active help meet to your man (see page 222). Your husband will enjoy and share your triumphs in business. He will be proud of your accomplishments. He will want you to use your natural skills, abilities, and drives. Your achievements will be an honor to him, but lazy slothfulness will greatly discourage him. Your wasting of time and spending money foolishly will weigh heavily on him, robbing him of his pride and pleasure in you. **He needs a resourceful, hardworking woman with dignity and honor. It is important to *Mr. Steady* that his wife be self-sufficient in all the mundane tasks of daily living**. You must learn how to pay bills, make appointments, and entertain guests with a competence that brings him satisfaction. Your hobbies should be creative and useful, involving your children so that all of you are busy and productive every day. Your home should be clean

Typically, Steady Men do not become as well known as Command or Visionary Men.

and orderly so that his friends and business contacts will be impressed and at ease. Your skills and achievements are your husband's résumé. If you are wise and competent, then he must be even more so, the onlooker will think. At the end of the day, *Mr. Steady* will enjoy weighing what he has accomplished with what you have accomplished and will rejoice in the value of having a worthy partner in the grace of life.

These men can be some of the most important men in the church, because their steadfastness is sure, and their loyalty is strong. **They make wise, well-thought-out decisions.** They are rarely rash or foolish, although (to their discredit) they will sometimes tolerate foolishness or error without dissent. Their children grow up to highly respect their gentle-speaking dad. If mother has been negative towards Dad, the adult children will strongly resent her to the point of disliking her.

Typically, *Steady Men* do not become as well known as *Command* or *Visionary Men*. They are not odd or stand-out men. They are not loud. They are neither irritating nor particularly magnificent. If they do rise to public notice, it will be because of an enormity of achievement or because they are trusted for their very visible traits of honesty and steadiness. Women and men alike envy and desire a *Command Man*. People are often drawn and compelled by the *Visionary*. But the *Steady Man* is taken for granted. He is seldom a campaigner. He is needed, but not flashy enough to win the spotlight. He will never brag on himself and is typically very poor at "selling" himself and his skills. He waits for another to point out his value and call for his help. It is your job to "sell" him, to speak highly of him until all are convinced and aware that he is the skillful professional they've been looking for.

The vast majority of my letters are from women criticizing their laid-back, quiet, slow, unassuming, undemanding, hardworking husbands for their "carnal" habits. These wives have forgotten to have a life of their own, so they spend their time trying to remake their husbands into dominant types because they admire leadership, authority, and clout. They don't have a clue about the demands that come from being married to a dominant, bossy man.

Most of this book has been written to help young wives learn to honor, obey, and appreciate the *Steady Man* just as he is. If a wife dishonors her steady husband and takes control, he will most likely stay with her; they probably will not divorce. But her dishonor will cause him to lack the confidence to further his business opportunities. He will become satisfied with the mediocre, because it involves no risk. He will know that he pulls the plow alone, that he has no helper. Yet, if that same man had married a thankful, creative woman who delighted in him and thought he was the smartest, wisest, most important fellow around, then he would have risen to the occasion in every area of his life. Many women believe *Mr. Steady* is mediocre and lacks strength and authority, when in actuality, *Mr. Steady* is a manly, steady fellow that lacks a good wife.

- *Mr. Steady* may take the trash out and always keep the area clean, yet his wife will be prone to take his goodness for granted.

- He will be in quiet contemplation much of the time. It will drive his wife crazy, because she will long for him to share his deepest feelings and thoughts with her so she can "feel" loved. He cannot. He might even cry during times of stress or intimacy. He is very, very slow to come to trust and open up to the woman he loves, because he does not understand her. He will enjoy the company of others and be most comfortable spending time in small talk with whoever is around. **Of the three types, he is the one who will be most liked by everyone.**

- *Mr. Steady* is always in demand. People everywhere need him to fix a car, build a house, set up their computer, figure out what's wrong with their phone, heal them of cancer, and the list goes on and on. You begin to wonder if you will ever have him all to yourself. The answer is, no. He belongs to people. When it is time or past time for some special time alone, take a vacation, and *leave the cell phone at home.*

- The *Steady Man* is wonderful with those who are hurt, sick, or dying. **He loves to comfort** and seems to know what a person needs in times of great sorrow. **His still, quiet presence brings peace.** To the *Command Man,* this is nothing short of a miracle. A *Steady Man* thrust into a *Command Man's* position or job will be stressed and, in the end, unsuccessful. He is not meant to lead, but to support.

- He does not focus on the eternal picture, nor is he looking through a microscope, but he does respect both views as important. **His vision is as a man seeing life just as it is.** He can shift his sights to the sky and know there is more up there than he can see, and he wonders about it. Or, he can stare into a muddy pond and appreciate that there is a whole world in there that he knows nothing about. In most of life, he is a bridge between the other two types of men. He is a very necessary expression of God's image.

"Ruination" Wife's Summary

a) The wife of *Mr. Command Man* can ruin her marriage by failing to honor, obey, and reverence her husband's authority and rule.

b) The wife of *Mr. Visionary* can ruin her marriage by failing to follow, believe, and participate as an enthusiast in her husband's dreams and visions.

c) The wife of *Mr. Steady* can ruin her marriage by failing to appreciate, wait on, and be thankful for her husband's pleasant qualities.

Successful Wife's Summary

a) The wife of *Mr. Command Man* can heal her marriage by becoming his adoring Queen, honoring and obeying his every (reasonable and unreasonable) word. She will dress, act, and speak so as to bring him honor everywhere she goes.

b) The wife of *Mr. Visionary* can heal her marriage by laying aside her own dreams and aspirations and embracing her role as help meet to her man, believing in him and being willing to follow him with joyful participation in the path he has chosen.

c) The wife of *Mr. Steady* can heal her marriage by joyfully realizing what a friend, lover, and companion she has been given and living that gratitude verbally and actively. When she stops trying to change him, he will grow. She can, then, willingly take up tasks that will fill her time and give her husband joy and satisfaction when he sees her productiveness.

TIME TO CONSIDER

Who is *your* man?

Make a list of your husband's traits—things that indicate which of the three types he most expresses. It may be a combination, with one more dominant. Now, begin a list of things you can do that will set him free to be the man God made him to be.

"I beseech you therefore, brethren, by the mercies of God, that ye present your bodies a living sacrifice, holy, acceptable unto God, which is your reasonable service. And be not conformed to this world: but <u>be ye transformed by the renewing of your mind</u>, that ye may prove what is that good, and acceptable, and <u>perfect, will of God</u>" (Romans 12:1-2).

Ask God to give you wisdom to see where you need to change to be the perfect help meet for your divinely designed man.

Keep in mind that most men
are a little of all three types,
but tend to be stronger in one.

Ministering Hands

Dear Pearls,

If your husband comes home cold, tired or even bearish, I've got a sure cure. Tell that big old man to lie down on the floor so you can give him a real "sugar-cured" back rub. As I rub warm, sweetly scented oil into my man's stiff, sore muscles, I also rub in love. I whisper endearments, and just a line or two brings a smile. Whispering wraps a normal word in intrigue and gives it a bit of mystery. The moment of secret is sweet. He is reminded how much we need him, appreciate him, and how fine we think he is. Of course, all the children want to bless Daddy, so they rush to help with the back rub. This time of blessing Daddy has never failed to bring on a jolly, relaxed mood.

It works on the little men in your life as well. My little boys have grown up highly appreciating the "moments with Mom." No matter what they are doing, if I tell them I will give them a back rub, they drop on the spot, then say, "Will you put a secret in my ear?" Even the one-year-old plops down with great anticipation at a mere suggestion of a back rub.

All in all, a good back rub is a sure winner. It gives Daddy physical comfort for his big, sore muscles, while it is an outward sign to our children of honor and reverence toward Dad. The ministering of love through my hands seems to prepare the heart-soil and gives the seeds of my words fertile ground in which to grow. On cold, rainy days when the boys are bouncing off the walls, the call of back rubs brings quiet, both to the house and to their little souls. So go bless the men in your family, pour on the oil, and see how much love, joy, and peace it brings.

-Susy

Chapter 9

Finding Your Life
in His

From the beginning, God meant for
us to be a comfort, a blessing, a reward, a friend, an
encouragement, and a right-hand wo-man.

Memories That Matter

I watched a movie one time called "Dad." It told the story of an old couple in their final years. The wife treated her husband as inept, controlling him and always jumping to supply his every need with a patronizing air. She wouldn't even let him pour the milk on his cereal. He seemed to be senile—living in a hazy world. The grown son came home to help the old parents in their last days. The old lady had spent her life controlling and taking care of her Mr. Nice, Steady Husband. But while the old woman was in the hospital with an ailment, the old man, at the encouragement of his middle-aged son, started going places and doing fun things. Suddenly, "Grandfather" seemed years younger. It was like the calendar was turned back fifty years. He was happy now. When Grandma got out of the hospital, she came home to a changed man. With great enthusiasm, he talked of friends and family that actually never existed. He spoke of the dairy farm and their life on it. He spoke of their four children—but they only had two. He spoke with longing of his much loved, gentle, and obedient wife — quite different from the reality he'd experienced over their many years together. His wife was terribly shaken, because she knew there never had been a dairy farm, nor were there more than two children. She knew the woman he remembered so fondly was not her.

A psychologist was called in to try to explain what was happening to the old man's mind. The doctor explained to the family that for fifty years Grandfather had worked faithfully at the same factory, doing the same old job with his hands, but while his hands worked, his mind was dreaming of the life he really wanted. It was a life of sunshine and hard work on a dairy farm with his large family of children helping him. **As Grandfather's mind aged, the pleasant, make-believe world he had lived out in his imagination became more real to him than the caged life he had actually lived.** Because of his wife's controlling hand and his desire to "do his duty" and please her, he had failed to live his dreams. She had weakened him with her control and criticism until he created an imaginary world of hope and fulfillment. This simple story illustrated so well the sad reality of many families.

The CPA

This letter came from a lady whose husband decided to make his dreams come true. It would have taken a book the size of this one to explain to her why she needs to be her husband's dream lady. I know this is what she really wants. She has just temporarily lost her vision.

Dear Pearls,

I have been married for 22 years, and my husband really is a great guy. He knows the Lord, but has not been as consistent with his Bible reading as I'd like to see. I am not saying anything to him about it yet. Our problems really stem from a change he made for our family that started about three years ago.

When we married, he was studying to be a CPA. I helped him through the last year of his schooling and spent 19 years with him going through long hours of tax seasons. I didn't like it much, but I knew that was his career. He wanted to find some job that would let him stay at home and be his own boss. I thought that was a noble cause, and I wanted him to be with our sons as they grew up.

Well, what he has decided to do now, I can hardly handle! He decided to become a dairy farmer. We are city people. I told him all along, I really didn't have a desire to be a dairy farmer. For three years, all he has done is read and research on it. I know he can make it work; it is just not something I want to do. I have had to cope with a lot. He still works in town and rushes home to go work in the barn. I had to wait dinner on him last night until 7 PM, and then he rushes home and goes straight to the barn. I was really hurt. I am tired of working and feeling as though we are getting nowhere. This is tearing the family apart. I know I must be submissive, but I truly do not want to do this. It is not my dream. There was no talk of farming 22 years ago!

Donna

Donna's concept of marriage is all wrong, not at all like God's intention for marriage. God didn't create Adam and Eve at the same time and then tell them to work out some compromise on how they would each achieve their personal goals in a cooperative endeavor. He created Adam, gave him an occupation, appointed him as ruler of the planet, endowed him with a spiritual outlook, gave him commands, and specified his occupational duties. Adam commenced his rule of the planet **before God created Eve to help him in his life's goals.** Adam didn't need to get Eve's consent. **God gave her to Adam to be HIS helper, not his partner. She was designed to serve,** not to be served, **to assist,** not to veto his decisions. Talk about a change of occupation and habitation! Look at Eve. Can you imagine her saying something like this to Adam? *"When God brought me to you in that wonderful garden, and we commenced life together, you never said anything about thorns and thistles, about pain in childbirth, about milking goats and churning butter. I am not a wilderness girl!"*

I wonder if Donna's husband will quit his "dream come true" because she drops frequent reminders that twenty-two years ago he didn't tell her that someday he was

> God made us women to be help meets.

going to be a dairy farmer. Will her unhappy, over-worked expressions break his joy and rob him of his vision? If he does go back to being a full-time CPA, I wonder if he will spend the rest of his life dreaming of a different kind of lady for a wife, a bunch of happy children, and a barn full of milk cows? **Life is now.** Don't make him ruin his life by being forced to count someone else's money. Find your life in his.

God made us women to be **help meets,** and it is in our physical nature to be so. It is our spiritual calling and **God's perfect will for us.** It is the role in which we will succeed in life, and it is where we will find our very greatest fulfillment as a woman and as a saint of God. God said in Genesis, **"I will make him an help meet for him."** Paul said, **"For the man is not of the woman; but the woman of the man. Neither was the man created for the woman; but the woman for the man"** (I Corinthians 11:8-9). **"Unto the woman he said…and thy desire shall be to thy husband, and he shall rule over thee"** (Genesis 3:16).

> God is not looking for happy women to make them into help meets for men. He is looking for women willing to be true help meets, so he can fill them full of joy.

When we fight God's will and our husband's dreams, we are frustrated and disappointed. If our husbands are kind, *Steady Men*, like Donna's husband, they will eventually become discouraged and give up trying to please us. If our husbands are *Command Men*, they may leave us behind and find a dairy-loving woman. If our husbands are *Visionaries*, they will yell and make our life miserable until we run back to mama and end up sleeping in a cold bed and living on food stamps.

Life is full of choices. How you choose to respond will help decide your fate in life. **Life is now.** Learn to really enjoy taking out the trash or milking a cow. You will be amazed at how God will fill you full of himself. You will look back in your "happy" old age and rejoice at your lot in life and wonder how you could have ever been a long-faced sad sack. Someday people will say to you, "Your personality is just a happy type, and that is why you enjoy life. Isn't that right?" You can laugh and know that being in God's will is the only thing that makes you full of joy. God is not looking for happy women to make them into help meets for good men. He is looking for women willing to be true help meets to the men whom they married, so He can *fill* them full of joy.

Life is full of choices ❤   97

His Express Image

We have studied three different types of men and how each one relates to the lady in his life. We have learned that God gives wisdom to those who ask. By now you know that it will take supernatural wisdom for you to come to know, accept, and appreciate your man as God made him. He may be all three different expressions at different times in his life, or he may be some of one and a lot of another. The important thing is for you to understand that he is what God made him, and that you are to be his suitable helper. Knowing what "expression" God has made him to be will help you become a better helper to the man of your life. God says so clearly and emphatically that, **"If any of you lack wisdom, let him ask of God, that giveth to all men** [and women] **liberally, and upbraideth not; and it shall be given him"** (James 1:5). Ask God to help you know and appreciate your man. Pray that God will give you the wisdom and grace to share your man's dreams so it will always be you that he dreams about.

TIME TO CONSIDER

Wisdom is knowing what you "bought" when you married that man <u>and</u> learning to adapt to him as he is, while enjoying the full value of your "purchase."

> **"Unto the woman he said…and thy desire shall be to thy husband, and he shall rule over thee"** (Genesis 3:16).

➤ *Make a new habit.*

Is it God's will for your husband to adapt to you, or is it God's will for you to adapt to him? What habits in your life should you change to adapt to your husband's needs? Start today.

➤ *Getting Serious With God*

The word *WISDOM* appears 223 times in God's Word. As you look up and read each time the word *wisdom* appears, God will do a work in you and give you wisdom as you seek it. The Bible teaches that the sister of **wisdom** is God's commandments, and the kinswoman to **wisdom** is understanding (Prov. 7:4). Add to your diary your favorite **wisdom** verses. Establish one time each day that you will be reminded to ask God for wisdom. For instance, I have resolved for myself that when I stop at a red light, I will remember to pray for my husband. At every meal, we pray for both safety and **wisdom** for ourselves and our children. Write down a certain hour or occasion that will remind you to silently ask God for **wisdom** for yourself and for your husband.

Here are a few of my favorite wisdom verses:

> **"So teach us to number our days, that we may apply our hearts unto wisdom"** (Psalm 90:12).
> **"To receive the instruction of wisdom, justice, and judgment, and equity"** (Proverbs 1:3).
> **"So that thou incline thine ear unto wisdom, and apply thine heart to understanding"** (Proverbs 2:2).
> **"Wisdom is the principal thing; therefore get wisdom: and with all thy getting get understanding"** (Proverbs 4:7).

Chapter 10

Reactions Define You

*A wise woman does not dream of what
"could have been." She does not see herself as "God's
gift to men;" therefore, she is joyful and content
in her present circumstances.*

By the time you married, you already held certain basic convictions. You knew right from wrong. You did what you thought was right, and no one could persuade you differently. But now you find yourself and your convictions challenged by someone who may not share your established standards and worldview. He may be more liberal than you, more permissive, or he may be stricter and more legalistic. The presence of children further complicates the situation. You want desperately to do what is right for them, but you have submitted yourself under the authority of another. Life is not going the way you had planned, and you can't act or react the way you had wanted to. You find yourself pushed to the limits of your patience, and then you react in unsubmissive and selfish anger.

Reactions are not premeditated actions springing from our best motives, carefully thought out, planned, and weighed. They are emotional responses, breaking loose like wild horses when we feel hurt, cheated, used, or misunderstood. They are often retaliatory, sometimes condemning, confrontational, or adversarial, and eventually vengeful and punishing. **Your reactions break you loose from your social**

inhibitions and manifest who you *really* are inside and what you really believe at your core level. We lose our carefully preserved "front" when we are pressed beyond calculated thinking. Then, who we really are is made manifest.

You can control your future reactions considerably by changing the way you think *before* you are pressed into a response. The way you think every day determines the way you feel, and it will determine how you will react in stressful situations.

Researchers have determined that the average person thinks over 40,000 thoughts each day. **The heart is filled with thoughts, and it is out of that reservoir of thoughts that the mouth speaks words of praise or bitterness.** When the pressure is on, and the dam of reservation breaks loose, you cannot control what you say, because you will speak from the abundance of your heart—from the 40,000 thoughts you had *that day,* and all the days before. **"A good man out of the good treasure of his heart bringeth forth that which is good; and an evil man out of the evil treasure of his heart bringeth forth that which is evil: for of the abundance of the heart his mouth speaketh"** (Luke 6:45). If you, as a wife, are going to change the way you have been speaking, it is not a matter of willpower; it is a matter of thought power. **"For as he thinketh in his heart, so *is* he..."** (Prov. 23:7). You must bring **"into captivity every thought to the obedience of Christ"** (II Cor. 10:5). **"For out of the heart proceed evil thoughts..."** (Matt. 15:19). As Paul says, **"Let this mind be in you, which was also in Christ Jesus"** (Phil. 2:5). You will be **"transformed by the renewing of your mind"** (Romans 12:2), not by the strength of your will to hold your tongue. God tells you *how* to think about your role as wife and help meet. If you believe him, you will think differently.

If I were in an airport baggage pick-up area waiting for my red suitcase, and I saw a young man snatch it and run, I would be very upset <u>until</u> I learned that my husband sent him to get it for me. When my thinking changed, my feelings changed.

The lady married to the accountant-turned-dairyman was sitting at home angry because her husband was late. When he finally arrived, he went directly to the barn to take care of his cows. She couldn't hold her tongue. She couldn't help the way she felt, because she had spent the entire day, no, the entire week...month...last three years, thinking how miserable she was for the circumstances her husband had brought upon

> Your reactions define who you really are inside and what you really believe at your core level.

her. She felt it was *her* "red suitcase" that was stolen. "He has no right," she thought over and over again. "This is not what we agreed to when we got married," she repeated to herself many times a day. "He should come in and eat the supper that is already cold from waiting, not go out and milk those cows," she repeated to herself during the last three hours when it was obvious that he was late. She was storing up in her heart an abundance of selfish thoughts. Her actions and reactions became enslaved to her misguided thoughts.

What could she do to change her thoughts? She could learn something she does not know, not just from this book's advice, but from God's book, the Bible. She was not created to choose her husband's vocation, nor to choose his or her lifestyle. She was created by God to be her husband's helper. In her case, that meant becoming a country girl—a dairyman's helper. She doesn't have to like cows, but she was created to help the man who does like cows.

> You are what you think, and God tells you how to think.

Think how different it would be if, when he were three hours late, she thought about how blessed she was to have a good man coming home to her at seven in the evening with a paycheck, and to have love, security, a father for her children, a warm bed all night, and the promise of a bright future with more cows, better milking equipment and, hopefully, a rise in milk prices. How thrilling life would be! How exciting and new every day would be—an adventure out in the country, not stagnating like the rest of the old fogies in town. Many a woman is sitting alone at seven in the evening, afraid that her ex-husband might try to break in again, and she's wondering where she and the kids are going to move to next month when they are evicted from their duplex. She, and many others, would love to be in this lady's kitchen, waiting peacefully for her grass-roots husband to come in late for supper, only to go out and tend to his cows. When he did finally come through the door, his dinner would be warm and the smiles and hugs would be warmer, with promises of an even warmer bed.

You are what you think, and God tells you how to think: **Think the truth.** This is not the power of positive thinking; **this is the power of the truth as God defines it.** You are created to be your husband's helper, not his conscience, not his vocation director, and certainly not his critic.

When you develop an adversarial relationship with your husband, you do so on the premise that you are right and he is wrong. You are also assuming that you have the duty to resist, confront, and challenge him. In thinking he is wrong and you are right, you declare yourself wiser than he, more spiritual, more discerning, more sacrificial, etc. All this adds up to the obvious conclusion that you have assumed the role of leadership, teacher, and judge. This is sinful and odious, and it displeases God greatly. **No woman will ever have peace and joy until her mind is filled with goodwill toward her husband**, and she is committed to becoming a good help meet for him. Is much of your life a reaction to real or perceived wrongs? Are you truly as wise as you think? Take the wisdom test below.

Wisdom Test

1. Do you have enough fear of God to not question his Word?
2. Do you sometimes feel God is punishing you by telling you to obey your husband?
3. Would you give God excuses like, "My husband is mean," or, "I am a strong personality, and he is weak"?
4. How would you respond if God gave you directions on how to talk, when not to talk, or how to dress and even wear your hair?
5. Are you comfortable with dismissing the Bible's role for women by saying we live in a different culture?
6. When God says to reverence (meaning, stand in awe of) your husband, do you think that is demanding too much?
7. Will you say, "If God says it, or even suggests it, then that is what I will do"?

If you can say, **"Not my will, but thine be done,"** then you can know that your prayer is based on the fear of God. It is the beginning of wisdom. Ask God to give you the beginning of wisdom by asking him to teach you to fear him.

TIME TO CONSIDER

- We have learned that our created nature is to be a help meet to our husbands.
- We have learned that a help meet is someone who helps her husband in any and all of his life's projects.
- We have learned that the joy of the Lord is our strength and that a merry heart is a real asset in becoming a godly help meet. A smile keeps our man looking our way. Our desire is to become a jolly "playmate" to our husband and to be an heir with him of the grace of life.
- All of us have decided that we do not want to grow old and become crazy old, religious fanatics who think that they are obeying God while disregarding his written Word. We have learned that the fear of God is the beginning of wisdom, and we shudder to think we might have ended up being like some of the old reprobates we know who dishonor their husbands.
- We have learned that wisdom is a gift that God promises to anyone who asks. Through wisdom, we have discovered that each of our husbands are made in the image of God, either as a *Command Man,* a *Visionary Man*, a *Steady Man*, or some mixture of the three, with one dominant.
- We know that it is our job as a help meet to always be looking for ways to better meet our husband's needs and desires.

➤ *Traits of a Good Help Meet*
- She asks God for wisdom.
- She learns to understand and appreciate her man for who he is.
- She learns to be flexible.

➤ *Getting Serious with God*
Now that you have thought more about your role as a help meet, it is time to go back and add to the list of things you could be doing that will free your husband to be the man God created him to be.

Chapter 11

The Nature of Man and Woman

*Man was created to subdue; woman
was created to assist*

God Made Them That Way

God created man with a nature that is aggressive, and then commanded him to exercise dominion over the earth (Gen. 1:28). He created the male sex with an extra dose of testosterone, which provokes him to want to work hard, conquer everything in his path, and subdue all things. That is why the male sex is at the forefront of military conquests, exploration, architecture, science, inventions, etc. No woman would ever go out and tame a wild horse and make a rope out of its mane and tail, and then go out and find a bear and lasso it just to prove that she could—laughing the whole time.

If women were the inventors, they would make minivans. Men make four-wheel drive vehicles and then modify them so they will stand higher and drive faster. They will even put a winch on the front so they can traverse places meant only for alligators or mountain goats. Men fly to the moon, climb treacherous mountains, fight wild animals, challenge each other at any sport, and laugh with loud hilarious delight the whole time. They like to play or watch games where they knock each other down, just to prove who is the strongest and toughest. Everything they do must end with a testosterone-driven climax. And they think we ladies are hard to understand! A woman can do about anything a man can do, but it is always the men who invent it and then eventually invite the ladies along just to make it more interesting. Testosterone again! A few ladies will always step out and play the men's games, trying to prove a gender point. The men don't need a point to prove; they just need to vent. Men are different. We must face it.

> God created the male sex with an extra dose of testosterone, which provokes him to want to work hard, conquer everything in his path, and subdue all things.

Thankfully, men and women were not created alike. Men were created with traits that I do not want as part of me! But, when I married, it was, of course, to one of those strange male creatures with those traits. When we ladies discover traits in a man like sensitivity, spirituality, and understanding, we are thrilled, because they contrast so starkly with the many coarser and visible traits that so strongly drive his nature. After all, having a nature to subdue all things, he likes best a woman who will give him a token struggle and then surrender to his wit, charm, and strength. He must thoroughly conquer. It is a battle I always enjoy losing. I like to be conquered and consumed by my man. That is my created nature.

The Woman Was Deceived

When Adam was created and placed in the garden, Lucifer, the fallen cherub, was jealous of Adam's position as master of the renewed planet. Lucifer, having become the Devil, had previously made himself the enemy of God and his program. He did not want God to be successful at replenishing the earth. From the very beginning, it was in the Devil's dark heart to lure Adam into disobeying his Creator. Satan would make Adam into the same rebel that he himself had been for such a long time. But Satan did not approach Adam. He waited and watched.

When God finished with Adam, he gave him the job of naming all the animals. He commanded the first man not to eat of the tree of the knowledge of good and evil, and he told him to subdue the earth and have dominion over the animal kingdom. His

Satan waited

principal job was to dress and keep the garden (Gen. 2:15). So, even before Eve was created, Adam was a full-grown man, firmly rooted in his relationship with God and fully engaged in his life's work.

Adam was alone for a period of time as he attended to his vocation and obeyed the command of his Creator. In going about the task of fulfilling his duties, he became aware of a need that he could not define, even though he observed it daily in the male and female behavior of the animals. He was lonely. He had no one with whom to share his achievements and conquests. God, in watching Adam, said, **"It is not good that the man should be alone; I will make him an help meet for him"** (Gen. 2:18). In time, God put Adam to sleep and took a rib from his side to make of it a woman to be his helper and to meet his needs.

> God knew that in order for man to survive, and even prosper, he would need a natural armor that would drive him to keep pushing against the odds, while enjoying the challenge.

Satan could have tempted this lonely man at any time, for he had no knowledge of good and evil. But Satan waited—waited for the creation of the weaker vessel. **"For Adam was first formed, then Eve. And Adam was not deceived, but the woman being deceived was in the transgression"** (I Timothy 2:13-14). Satan knew that the man could not be deceived, but the woman could. So, when she drew near to the tree, he convinced her that life would be better if she sought the higher state of being, "like the gods"—gaining spiritual insight into the nature of good and evil. Eve was deceived in three ways:

1. She followed her flesh in desiring the tree for its food properties.
2. She succumbed to its beauty, desiring it for its pleasant appearance. She did not follow logic; she followed her "sensibilities."
3. She wanted "deeper" spiritual insights than those provided by God.

The source of Eve's failure was her unwillingness to believe God and her husband.

> **She was meant to be Adam's helper, but she helped herself to spiritual knowledge and acted independently, becoming his downfall instead of his help meet.**

Why did Satan avoid Adam and approach Eve with his offer of greater spirituality? Lucifer is a male being (Isaiah 14:12-20). He understands the natural resistance of the male. He knows males say "no" just to prove they are in command. But Lucifer could see that this soft, sweet female was vulnerable. God had made her by nature to be responsive, and she was trusting and naïve. Being willing to rationalize, she could be deceived—having the best of intentions.

In my mind, I picture the man being created heavily armored. His armor is helpful both spiritually and physically. God loaded him down with resistances, giving him a nature that is doubting, skeptical, forceful, and pushy. God knew that in order for man to survive, and even prosper, he would need a natural armor that would drive him to keep pushing against the odds, while enjoying the challenge. God knew that Satan was a liar and the master of deceit, so he created man to question first and believe later. Man's objectivity and lack of intuitiveness make him appear less spiritual than the sensitive, believing female. As a general rule, man is ruled more by his mind than the female, who is governed more by her sensibilities.

Picture God as deliberately creating the woman without this armor, because he intended for her to stand behind her husband's armor. He was to be her covering, her shield, and her protector. Satan was able to deceive her when she left Adam's side and confronted the Devil's logic alone. She didn't have the armor to ward off his fiery darts of deceit.

> Vulnerability is a woman's greatest natural asset and the point of her greatest weakness.

God designed the woman to be sensitive and vulnerable for the sake of the little ones whom she must nurture. The soul of a mother had to be vulnerable, the outer shell thin. She must be quick to feel, to hurt, to love, to have compassion, to take in the broken, and to believe the best. Vulnerability is a woman's greatest natural asset and the point of her greatest weakness. A woman *can* become tough and hard, skeptical, and cautious in relationships, just like a man. She can become guarded and cynical, but in so doing, she is no longer feminine, no longer attractive to a man, and she will even begin to not like herself. Unprotected by the covering of her husband, she will grow miserable fighting her own battles and trying to survive on an equal footing with men. Just look at the faces and mannerisms of outspoken feminists and lesbians. In their attempt to shed their vulnerability and express their independence, feminists begin to exhibit traits and behaviors completely outside of their created feminine nature. They lose their beauty and charm, and become very poor excuses of men.

The soul of a mother had to be vulnerable

Beautiful, Deceived Dreamers

Women, in general, give the appearance of being more spiritual than men. They like to dabble in soulish thoughts. There are many ways of expressing spirituality, but most of them have nothing to do with the Spirit of Jesus Christ. We ladies are more inclined to trust in our feelings and intuition than are men, which makes us more subject to deception, just like sister Eve. Feelings and intuition are ever-changing. **The Word of God is objective and dogmatic—unchanging. It is to religion what hard facts are to science.**

You rarely hear a man say, "God told me to do this," or, "God led me to go down there." The few men I have known who talked that way did not demonstrate that they were any more led by the Spirit than other Christian men. I know that when God does speak to my husband and leads him in a supernatural way, he will not speak of it in public. He doesn't feel the need to promote himself in that manner, and furthermore, he believes that if he has truly heard from heaven, God doesn't need <u>his</u> publicity. God will vindicate himself. But many Christian women habitually attribute nearly every event to divine guidance. Experience proves that women are prone to claim God as their authority, when God had nothing at all to do with their "leading." It is really quite appalling to see this shameful behavior still in action today, especially when

> That a man is less sensitive than a woman does not make him inferior to her, nor does her being more subject to deception than her husband make her inferior to him—just different.

God so graciously gave us the example of Miriam, Moses' sister. Her desire to be on an equal footing with Moses has left her name in infamy, for our admonition (I Cor. 10:6,10) and **"for our learning, that we through patience and comfort of the scriptures might have hope"** (Rom. 15:4). God seems to be gracious to us "dimwits"—and that is what we are when we lightly use God's name (a form of blasphemy) to give authority to our intuitive decisions. **The bottom line is that women "enjoy" their own self-effusing spirituality.** It is a feminine trait that few men share or understand. Men *can,* however, become totally absorbed in their own personal ambitions and, in the process, neglect their "spiritual" side altogether. Women often see this "carnality" in men and assume that women, being more "spiritually" minded, are closer to God—a completely false assumption.

Nearly all spiritualists, past and present, are women. Women are the palm readers, crystal ball gazers, fortune-tellers, and tarot card readers. Witches' covens are headed by women. Most mediums (those contacting the dead) are women, as was the witch of Endor whom King Saul consulted concerning long-dead Samuel. When Jesus spoke a parable about the kingdom becoming corrupted with false doctrine, **he illustrated it with a woman bringing in the corruption** (Matt. 13:33). In the book of Revelation, it is a woman, typically called Jezebel, who deceives the church. We are told that she did it through her *teaching*. John wrote to the church of Thyatira and warned them against allowing that woman Jezebel to teach (Rev. 2:20). Women are either directly or indirectly responsible for most of the past and present cults in Christianity.

> The "last days" profile of Christian women is that of the religious prophetess, Jezebel.

The Bible makes a point of revealing the inherent nature of women when it gives a reason why women should not teach men: **"And <u>Adam was not deceived</u>, but the woman being deceived was in the transgression"** (I Tim. 2:14).

That a man is less sensitive than a woman does not make him inferior to her, nor does her being more subject to deception than her husband make her inferior to him—just different natures. It is in recognizing that difference that wives should fear God and distrust their natural tendencies. Things that are not the same have different capacities and different offices.

Adam Knew

God had instructed Adam, and Adam had instructed Eve. Adam clearly understood that Satan's promise of spiritual enlightenment was a diabolical lie against God. The natural armor God had given Adam granted him enough understanding to doubt the Devil and resist his lies. But Adam's armor had one small weak spot. **He was not ruled by his feelings except where it concerned his woman. Adam's soul was exposed and vulnerable to the woman he loved.** He wanted her happy, even if it meant disobeying God or going against his natural understanding of truth. He was willing to set aside reason for his woman. Eve's influence over Adam changed the course of history. We need to be aware of the power we have to seduce our husbands into following us into disregarding the clear, objective words of God. **Adam**, the first man, **Samson**, the strongest man, **Solomon**, the wisest man, and even **David**, the man listed as being after God's own heart, were all brought down by the women they loved. When a man loves a woman and wants to make her happy, he will often acquiesce in spiritual matters because of the affection he holds for her in his heart. Your husband may set aside reason and good judgment if you pressure him and let him feel your displeasure and unhappiness. In a man's heart, the place a woman holds will lead him into great strength or great weakness, depending on the woman and the man. It is there that men rise to great glory with their women, or they are dragged into shame and disgrace by them, or worse yet, are left unused by God.

Remember the crazy lady who drove her family to financial ruin because she felt led of God to move and change her husband's business? Her husband KNEW it would not work, but he could not stand against her constant pleading and her spiritual intensity. **He wanted desperately to be the man of God she wanted him to be, but in doing so, he gave up the glory of the man that God expected him to be.** Then she badgered him into giving what little they had left as a tithe, in hopes that it would move God to bless their lack of effort with unearned wealth. What foolish rebellion—all in the name of spirituality! In the end, they lost everything, and she lost her mind. Men are still allowing women to take the spiritual lead, and women are confidently leading just as Eve did. They believe they are doing what is good for the family. It is not an act of carnal lust. It is a religious act driven by rebellion. Women are simply deceived. This is why God has so carefully taught us ladies to observe and maintain our roles as help meets. It is why we must implicitly trust God's judgment as to our duties, regardless of how we "feel."

God gave us a careful and stern warning as to what women would become in the last days. The prophetic picture of this woman is now in full array. It is the spiritual Jezebel, who is the exact opposite of a help meet, that is the death knell of the most noble institution on the earth—the family. As you read the next section about the prophetess Jezebel, learn to hate all that she is so you will not fall victim to her wicked practices of deceit.

> Women often see this "carnality" in men and assume that women, being more "spiritually"-minded, are closer to God—a completely false assumption.

The following is an abbreviated account of an article first published in its entirety in our **No Greater Joy** *magazine, March-April 2002. To read the complete version, go to www.nogreaterjoy.org.*

The Jezebel Profile

When the name *Jezebel* is mentioned, most of us see the painted face of a seductively-dressed woman gazing into the eyes of a man who lacks good sense. The Bible portrays Jezebel in a different light. Revelation 2:20 says that Jezebel "**calleth herself a prophetess,**" and men received her as a teacher, showing that she was part of structured Christianity, "ministering" to the saints. Jesus warned the Church against the teaching woman, Jezebel. Any woman who defies the scripture's prohibition against women teachers in the Church is following in the grave tradition of Jezebel.

> We need to be aware of the power we have to seduce our husbands into following us into disregarding the clear, objective words of God.

I went back to I Kings to see what the Bible had to say about the historical Jezebel. **The first thing** I noticed was that she was *more spiritual and religiously devoted* than her husband. She used her insights to guide him. He was a weak man, so she took the lead to motivate him. The Bible says in I Cor 11:3, **"But I would have you know, that the head of every man is Christ; and the head of the woman is the man; and the head of Christ is God."** Regardless of our circumstances, when we women take the spiritual lead, we step out from under our designated rightful head.

The second thing I observed was that Ahab was emotionally volatile—unstable. Is your husband prone to retreat? Is he bitter, angry, or depressed? When a woman takes the lead in marriage, her assuming of the masculine role makes a weak man weaker, to the point of "sending him to bed"—as did Jezebel to Ahab.

The third and most significant thing I noticed was that she used his emotional stress to endear herself to him—a strange way of lording over her husband. If you read the story, you will see how Jezebel manipulated and accused an innocent man, then had him murdered so that Ahab could obtain his vineyard. Ahab, in depression, kept his "face to the wall" and let her do her dark deeds. Today, if a woman is willing to play her husband's role in directing the family, her husband will lose his natural drive to bear responsibility. He will turn his face to the wall.

The fourth thing that jumped out at me was how Ahab was easily manipulated by his wife to suit her purposes. She stirred his passive spirit, provoking him to react in anger. Jezebel used him to set up images and to kill God's true prophets. Often a man becomes involved in the local church, not because God has called him, but because he is trying to please his wife by at least LOOKING spiritual. When a husband steps into a spiritual role at his wife's beckoning or emotional pressure, he is susceptible to her "guidance" in that role. Jezebel took steps to help promote her spiritual leaders. In the process, she provoked her husband to destroy those in spiritual authority whom she did not like. Have you influenced your husband to think evil of those in authority because you did not like something about them?

> Dominance and control are always masculine characteristics.

Jezebel knew that she was not the rightful head, so she invoked her husband's name to give her word authority. Have you ever said, "Oh, my husband will not let me do that," when you knew he would not care? It is a way to maintain control and to stop those who would question you. When a woman steps outside her divinely ordained nature and assumes the dominant role, she will soon become emotionally and physically exhausted, <u>and dangerous</u>.

Ruth

In contrast, God reveals the ideal woman in positive stories about women who honored him. The story of Ruth is about a young girl who had known tragedy, extreme poverty, and hard menial work. Yet, she maintained a thankful and submissive attitude. Read the book of Ruth and see a **beautiful example of bold femininity** that caused Boaz to love and admire her. Take note of her humility and the deference she paid to all in authority. Note her willingness to work and her willing obedience to the Scriptural teaching of her aged mother-in-law, Naomi. And lastly, see the wonderful blessing God showered on her in placing her into the lineage of his only begotten Son.

Esther

Esther is the story of a Jewish girl who lost her family and was taken by force to become the wife of an older, divorced, heathen man. **She could have asked herself the silly question, "Did I marry the right man?"** Or even a sillier question, "Since he was divorced, is he really even my husband?" If she had, there NEVER would have been a book in the Bible describing her courage, honor, and fortitude.

She was put (by her husband's decree) in danger of losing her own life and the lives of all her people, the Jews. Yet, she rose above her circumstances and her natural fear to honor her husband, even as she made an appeal to save her own life, along with the lives of her people.

God has laid down only a few simple rules for women to follow, because they are consistent with our feminine nature and the nature of men. It was Esther's submission to these principles that won the King's love and his appreciation for her as his queen. These two women, Ruth and Esther, showed themselves womanly and lovable in the midst of extreme circumstances. God honored them with his favor and favor from the men in their lives.

The Virtuous Woman

Proverbs 31 defines the virtuous woman. She is NOT a mousy, voiceless prude. **She is confident, hardworking, creative, and resourceful.** Her first virtue is that the heart of her husband is safe with her. That is, he can trust her with his thoughts and feelings, never fearing that she might use the private knowledge she has of him to hurt him in any way. A man will maintain a distance from his wife, never really opening up to her, if he senses she might give this knowledge out inadvertently or use it against him when they are out of sorts. A man whose heart is not safe with his wife

A virtuous woman is hardworking.

will never tell her what he intends to do or how he feels, because on previous occasions she has assumed the role of overseer by taking it upon herself to be his conscience and the manager of his time. She reminds him of what he said he was going to do in a manner that says, "I am holding you to it. What is wrong with you? Are you a sloth or something?" He finds it more peaceful to keep his own counsel. Wives, never use your special knowledge of your husband as leverage to get your way.

If this passage in Proverbs had been written from our modern perspective, it would have extolled her for having a "quiet time" and being a "prayer warrior," teacher, or counselor. In all the Scriptural profiles of righteous women, including Proverbs 31, no such concepts are ever mentioned. In our culture, we have lost a clear understanding of what constitutes a virtuous woman. We have accepted the modern idea of the "spiritual" woman circulating in the realm of religious power, and have forgotten that God does not see them in this same "glorious" light. What we think is spiritual, God labels "Jezebel."

"For my thoughts are not your thoughts, neither are your ways my ways, saith the LORD" (Isaiah 55:8).

A woman working beside her man is a spiritual force for them both. A woman providing good sex and fun company is offering her husband a spiritual benefit. A woman preparing healthy meals and cutting the grass so he can go fishing on Saturday is a spiritual woman, because she is placing him above herself. There is no greater love than to put another, first.

Dominance and control are always masculine characteristics. It is important for a woman to understand that she must be feminine (devoid of dominance and control) in order for her man to view her as his exact counterpart, and thus willingly respond to her protectively, with love and gentleness.

A woman who criticizes her husband for watching too much TV, playing too much golf, or indulging in any frivolous activity is expressing dishonor. When the relationship is properly balanced, a wife can make an appeal at the right time and in the right manner, and it need not be a challenge to his authority. We will speak of how to make an appeal in due course. But know of a certainty that when a woman continually tries to assert her own will against her husband's, throwing it up to him that he is wrong, she is usurping authority over him, lording over him, and dishonoring him. A woman who continues in this behavior blasphemes the Word of God and can expect God's sure "reward."

I say again: when a woman steps outside her nature and assumes the dominant role, she will soon become emotionally and physically exhausted.

A man cannot cherish a strong woman who expresses her displeasure of him. You say that *he* should model Christ's love regardless of how *she* acts. Is that what you want? Is it what Christ wants? **Do you want your husband to be forced to seek supernatural power just to find a way to love you?** Do you want to be another of his trials—his greatest example of overcoming adversity? The home front should not be a spiritual battlefield; it should be the place where a man relaxes and can be vulnerable with the woman he cherishes. Men will always want to reclaim those times when love was fun and free, with no demands, like the times when she would smile at him with that sweet, girlish, "I think you are wonderful" expression. She was so feminine then, so much the woman. He wanted to hold her just because she was a bundle of delightful joy. He would do anything for her.

> A virtuous woman is resourceful.

TIME TO CONSIDER

God placed man in the position of HEAD of the family, not because he is wiser or more capable, but because it is part of God's eternal design.

When people think of your family, do they see your husband as the principal player, or do they think of you as the main character? Would they refer to your family as "Cathy's family" or as "John's family?" Have you usurped the position of headship?

The very first command God ever gave to a woman was, **"Thy desire shall be to thy husband and he shall rule over thee"** (Gen. 3:16). Is your desire toward your husband? Do you live to please him? Or, do you expect him to live up to your convictions and whims? Do you spend your days in angry frustration over his unwillingness to change to your specifications? If so, you have become a Jezebel.

Biblical Profile Contrast

Jezebel Profile

1. Prophetess
2. Teacher
3. One who pities
4. Religious
5. Controller

Virtuous Woman Profile

1. Help meet
2. Silent
3. Encourager
4. Prudent worker
5. Submissive

Chapter 12

By Divine Appointment

The only position where you will find real fulfillment as a woman is as a help meet to your husband.

"**B**ut I would have you know, that the head of every man is Christ; and <u>the head of the woman is the man;</u> and the head of Christ is God**" (I Cor. 11:3).

"<u>**For the husband is the head of the wife**</u>, **even as Christ is the head of the church: and he is the saviour of the body**" (Eph. 5:23).

Your husband, dud that he may "appear" to be, is appointed by God to be your immediate Superior Officer in the chain of command. Your position under him is where God put you for your own spiritual, emotional, and physical safety. It is the only position where you will find real fulfillment as a woman. Don't worry about the quality of his leadership, for he is under the oversight of Jesus Christ. He must answer to God for how he leads his "troops." You must answer to God for how you obey the one he placed over you. It takes faith in God to trust him when all you seem to see is one carnal man leading you—to "God only knows where."

In all of this submit-to-your-superior talk, remember this: **God is focusing our attention on the heavenly pattern.** The emphasis is not on women submitting to men, but rather on women showing, here on earth, the heavenly pattern of the Son submitting to the Father.

"He is not saved!" you say. God's Word remains the final authority. Your husband is your knight in God's protective armor. Even if his armor appears a bit rusty and dull, it is still the armor of God, your safe covering in everything.

God tells us that we are to be **help meets:** We are to submit, obey, and even reverence our husbands. He also tells us WHY we are assigned the role of helper.

1. We came forth *from* man's ribs and were created *for* him. We are a part of him.
   "For a man indeed ought not to cover his head, forasmuch as he is the image and glory of God: but the <u>woman is the glory of the man</u>. For the man is not of the woman; but the woman of the man. Neither was the man created for the woman; but <u>the woman for the man</u>" (I Cor. 11:7-9).

2. Our position in relation to our husband is a picture of the Great Mystery, which is Christ and the Church. We, as the body of Christ, are *for* Him, our living Head. It can be no other way!
   "But I would have you know, that the head of every man is Christ; and the head of the woman is the man; and the head of Christ is God" (I Cor. 11:3).
   "This is a great mystery: but I speak concerning Christ and the church… and the wife <u>see that she reverence her husband</u>" (Eph. 5:32-33).

God tells us WHY our husband is to be the one who rules the home. God explains why it is never his will for the wife to rule.

1. The fall into sin was due to a woman's inherent vulnerability.
   "For Adam was first formed, then Eve. And Adam was not deceived, but the woman being deceived was in the transgression" (I Timothy 2:13-14).
   "For a man indeed…is the image and glory of God: but <u>the woman is the glory of the man</u>" (I Cor. 11: 7).

2. Curses were placed on the guilty in the fall.
   "Unto the woman he said, I will greatly multiply thy sorrow and thy conception; in sorrow thou shalt bring forth children; <u>and thy desire shall be to thy husband, and he shall rule over thee</u>" (Genesis 3:16).

It was God's design, **before the fall,** that the woman's desire would be to her husband and that he would rule over her. This relationship was not punishment, but after the fall it would be a source of suffering for the woman. God created the woman to be the helper of the man—a sinless man. Now that she has led him into sin, she is still his helper, her desires are still focused on him and his goals, and he will still rule over her as before—**but now he is sinful, selfish, and carnal.**

Chapter 12 ~ By Divine Appointment

Limitations God Put Into Place

God expresses a clear and sure mandate when he tells us: **"But I suffer not** [do not allow] **a woman to teach, nor to usurp authority <u>over the man,</u>** [that includes your pastor] **but to be in silence"** (I Timothy 2:12).

I call your attention back to the argument in the letter we read in chapter 5.

"I have been deeply blessed by women speaking on the platform. I don't understand how God could move so profoundly through women who are not in accordance with his will."

The assumption of this woman's argument was that the only reason God would command women not to preach is because they are not very good at it. She has been blessed by women ministers; therefore, in her thinking, the words of the Bible cannot be the words of God, or possibly the Bible does not apply to us today, or maybe it is not translated correctly. What she does not realize is that it is on the very grounds that women *can be* effective public ministers that God commands them not to do so. It is not a question of being qualified; it is a matter of being authorized. God has established an order for the home, a chain of command that is consistent with the very nature of men and women. It is an order from the throne of Heaven that is healthiest and best for the rearing of children and for the good of marital relationships. For the woman to become the channel of spiritual blessings is to put her into a position not suited to the nature of her created being. If she is effective *as a replacement* for her husband's ineffective leadership, that makes it all the more wrong! For then she is, as the Bible says, usurping authority over the man—usurping glory…usurping honor…usurping control…usurping leadership. That is, she is doing what a man should be doing, and thus is getting the recognition a man should get. It is an inversion of God's design for males and females.

"Let your women keep silence in the churches: [Paul gives this as a New Testament mandate] **for it is not permitted unto them to speak; but they are commanded to be under obedience, as <u>also</u> saith the law"** (I Cor. 14:34).

Paul anticipates those who would say that his commands concerning women are unique to a specific culture and not universally applicable. He points out that there is nothing new or unique about this command, for the law of the Jews had made such a distinction for hundreds of years.

"Shame is the mind's uneasy reflection on having done an indecent thing." What is more indecent than for a woman to quit her rank?

God took precious space in his Holy Word to try to help us understand this extremely important point, about which we have been so sadly misled. Modern Christianity has steered women into a perversion of their nature, allowing, and even encouraging, them to be in spiritual authority over men. The fruit of this false doctrine is evident in the unhappy women and dissatisfied men of the last couple of generations. It is a shameful matter of statistics that the fundamentalist Christian home is not as enduring as the general population's.

"And if they will learn any thing, let them ask their husbands at home: <u>for it is a shame</u> for women to speak in the church" (I Cor. 14:35).

Shame—Shame—Shame—Yes, it is a shame. *Matthew Henry's Bible Commentary* says, "Shame is the mind's uneasy reflection on having done an indecent thing." What is more indecent than for a woman to quit her rank?

What About Deborah?

The Bible means just what it says, even though this, and other passages like it, dealing with a woman's position in the chain of authority, have been explained away by today's educated *Scribes, Pharisees, and hypocrites.*

Many times I have read or heard the rebuttal, "What about Deborah who was a judge in Israel?" If you actually read the story, you would know that the text makes much of the fact that the men were shamed by allowing a woman to take the place of prominence. There is no question that Deborah performed the job well, that she saved Israel, that God used her; that is just the point. When the men allowed a woman to take their role and perform the job successfully, it resulted in shame to the nation of Israel. Deborah knew this to be the case and warned the men as such. To build a doctrine on this story, while ignoring the majority of the doctrinal passages on the leadership of women, is as foolish as Deborah leading the armies of Israel instead of a man.

The argument that is often given for ignoring God's Word concerning our role as women is that "we can do just as good a job as the men, maybe even better." God's rule that women not take the lead is not a statement about our being inferior or not as capable as men; **it is a statement by God** about it not being within our sphere of authority and nature to take leadership over men, to teach them, or to gain a place

God's chain of command

of prominence among them. Yes, we are capable of teaching, and teaching well. I am teaching you, but this book is not written to men. It is written by an "aged" woman teaching younger women to obey God and their husbands—just what God commanded me to do (Titus 2:3-4).

What About Priscilla and Aquila?

The naysayers also draw our attention to the ministry of Priscilla and Aquila, as if the inclusion of the woman with her husband somehow negates the hundred or so doctrinal verses that teach about a woman's role as a helper to her husband. On the contrary, although they are mentioned five times in the Bible, Priscilla is never mentioned alone. She is always with her husband, as I am with mine. When my husband goes to speak at a seminar on family and child-training issues, they usually advertise us as "Michael and Debi Pearl." He takes the stage and does the teaching, while I sit in the audience and support him. He sometimes calls on me to publicly answer questions about child training or homeschooling, but I never publicly teach doctrine to anyone, men or women. I counsel women and make sure my husband gets plenty of rest, has something good to eat, and is able to remember where he is and what he is to do next. He often asks me my opinion on issues, and I help him formulate ideas as we discuss points of concern for the seminar. **My role is a support role**, as I am sure was the case with Priscilla.

Marriage Made in Heaven

So, is a woman a second-class citizen of the kingdom? Is she to be a subdued, brow-beaten servant to the male species? Certainly not! What the Bible teaches will not put women back into the Stone Age, nor will it turn us into a bunch of Muslim-like women who stay covered in black, sweaty bourkhas. If you knew me (and by the time you finish reading this book, you will know me), you would know that I am the farthest thing from a mousy, brow-beaten wife. But I know what God teaches about women, and I know that for you to be happy—really happy—as I have been happy, you *must* follow and abide in God's role for women.

God has spoken frankly as to why he made us as he did and what our role is to be.

Key

Yet, so-called Bible teachers today tear apart what God has said and make the average young wife reading these Scriptures feel as though what God has said to her is an insult. I, too, am a woman. I have spent my life counseling women. After almost 35 years as a wife, counseling ladies, reading thousands upon thousands of letters, and chalking up my own life experiences, I have concluded that what the Bible says on this subject is rock-solid truth, and it works! I have also seen the sad results of the teachings that reject the plain sense of Scripture.

My conclusions can be said to be scientifically correct. **That is, the "evidence" that leads to my conclusion is reproducible: Anyone can test it and get the same results. The Creator knows best, and *His* way does work. His Word is meant to be taken at face value.** And, when any woman does as I have done, the blessings are incredible! I have received thousands of letters from women who have entered into God's miraculous, blessed plan by simply believing and obeying his Word concerning our place as women. I have seen lesbians set free and become wives fit for the kingdom. I have seen broken whores, drug addicts, and church-taught, rebellious ladies all become women who honor their men and become good help meets. I have seen marriages born in hell and then remade in heaven. Do you KNOW even one couple who says they have a heavenly marriage? I know that the angels in heaven stand amazed at how much a man can love a woman, how he can break down weeping at the thought of how precious she is to him. The reason he loves her so is because she IS precious. She has earned his total adoration and love. She is what God asks of a woman, and the end result is a man who cherishes her beyond anything this world can know.

When someone tells you that the Greek doesn't read *submit*, *obey*, or *silence*, just ask that person, "How is your marriage? Would you say it is glorious? Will God use your marriage as an example in Heaven of how he wants Christ and the Church to be?" Those who change the Word of God concerning a woman being a help meet do so because they don't know the wonder of a marriage made in heaven. I do.

If you want what I and thousands of women have, then you must *follow the plan the way God wrote it in the Bible*.

TIME TO CONSIDER

God set up a chain of command, first in Heaven, and then again here on earth. When you do not honor that command, you dishonor God, and apart from repentance, you can expect to reap the sure consequences.

"But I would have you know, that the head of every man is Christ; and <u>the head of the woman is the man;</u> and the head of Christ is God" (I Cor. 11:3). Don't question God's chain of command, and don't attempt to break any of its links.

Make a new habit. Start thinking and acting as though your husband is the head of the company and you are his secretary. Look for ways to help him in his managerial position.

➢ *Traits of a Good Help Meet*
- She fears God.
- She believes God's Word *as it is written*.
- She considers her position as a help meet a privileged command.

➢ *Getting Serious with God*
Make a list for each day of the week.

Monday: Write three new things that you will add to your life that will cause you to become more precious to your husband.

Tuesday: List three things that you can do that will be a help to him.

Wednesday: Write down three things you can do that will be an encouragement to him.

Thursday: Jot down three things about your appearance that you can change, which he is sure to like.

Friday: List three things that you can do to your house that will please him.

Saturday: Write three things you can do (for example, intimate time together) that will make him feel like he is THE MAN.

Sunday: Plan three ways you can respond to him in front of others that will show a heart of respect and honor toward him.

Chapter 13

The Great Mystery

A wise woman understands that her husband's need to be honored is not based on his performance, but on his nature and his God-ordained position. She learns quickly to defer to his ideas or plans with enthusiasm. She looks for ways to reverence him. She knows this is God's will for her life.

"**T**his is a great mystery: but I speak concerning Christ and the church... and the wife see that <u>she reverence her husband</u>"** (Eph. 5:32-33). There are **twelve mysteries** in God's Word, but only the seventh is listed as the **great** mystery. Each mystery is a strange, beautiful truth which is hard for us to understand. The old Webster's dictionary defines mystery as, *"something hidden from human knowledge and fitted to inspire a sense of awe; especially something incomprehensible through being above human intelligence. An enigma; anything artfully made difficult."*

Jesus wants us for a friend. He wants a companion, someone with whom to discuss ideas. He wants a playmate, someone with whom to laugh and enjoy life. He wants a buddy with whom to spend time. He wants a lover, someone to care about and someone to care about him. He wants a help meet, someone to share in his work of creation and management. He wants to be a groom, and he wants the Church to be his bride. This is the great mystery. **He seeks to create in me and my relationship** to my husband a working scale model of his relationship to the Church throughout eternity.

Amazing as it sounds, marriage between a man and a woman is what God chose as the closest example of Christ's relationship to his bride, the Church. You are part of eternity when you submit to your husband. Submission, reverence, and honor are virtues God seeks to establish in his Son's bride. Your marriage to your husband is preparing you for your marriage to Christ. You may say, "But it would be easy being married to Christ." Then you don't know your Bible. What if your husband required you to offer your son upon an altar as a burnt sacrifice? That is what God required of Abraham. What if your husband killed you for lying? That is what God did to Sapphira.

For a woman to usurp authority over a man is an affront to God Almighty, like treason in the camp. It would be like a man taking authority over Christ, or like the Church becoming jealous of Jesus' leadership and taking authority unto itself. It would be doing just what Lucifer did when he said in Isaiah 14:13-14, **"I will ascend into heaven, I will exalt my throne above the stars of God: I will sit also upon the mount of the congregation, in the sides of the north…I will be like the most High."** Lucifer, like Eve, was not satisfied with his station in God's eternal program. He tried to jump rank and ascend higher on the chain of command. God cast him down, as he will do with men and women who attempt to live beyond their created positions.

Knowing that my role as a wife typifies the Church's relationship to Christ has molded my life. As I reverence my husband, I am creating a picture of how we, the Church, should reverence Christ. You have wondered why God would tell us to do such a thing as to reverence our husbands. Now you know.

"This is a <u>great mystery</u>: but I speak concerning Christ and the church…. and the wife see that she reverence her husband" (Eph. 5:32). **Reverence: to revere, to be in awe; fear mingled with respect and esteem.**

1. **Obedience** is doing what you know the other person wants you to do.
2. **Submission** is your heart giving over to the other person's will.
3. **Reverence** is more than just doing what a man expects or demands. It is an act of the woman's will to treat him with a high degree of regard and awe.

Obedience, submission, and reverence are all acts of the will and are not based on feelings. Showing deference toward one's husband is an act of reverence toward the God who placed you in that role.

Queen for the Day

Here is a letter from a woman who has every human reason for leaving her husband; instead, she goes out of her way to show him reverence. She is showing deference to him as being the Number One Daddy. From years and years of counseling, I can tell you that if ever a woman can win a man's heart, this lady will. She is my Queen for the Day.

Dear Debi,

I don't have a question, just a very good report! Thank you for telling the truth, for it has set me free. I believe God is the Author and Finisher of my husband's faith. Shortly after we married, my husband started going to strip clubs and meeting with prostitutes. I know this because when he got too guilty, he would confess. For a while, I really wanted a divorce. I couldn't see how I could stand it much longer, and everyone agreed with me except one couple. The wife talked to me on Sunday morning about God's love, and that same morning my pastor taught on love. God put in me a love for my husband, and I am confident that I am in the perfect will of God to stay with him.

He is a good daddy and provider and stands with me on parenting. He has matured so much. He waits until our son is in bed before watching TV. For all of this I am thankful.

Initially, I would cry and verbalize my disappointments of him. "How can I trust you? How do I know what you are doing?" I did not want my son to see me like that all the time, and I know my husband goes through a lot at work. My rantings and bitter face would not make it easy for him to come home to me. I just wanted to love him. He knows already that I wish he would be home more, and he didn't need to see my daily disappointment.

*Our son is convinced that his daddy has the biggest muscles in the world! We do things to help my husband feel loved. We stapled two huge pieces of poster board together and wrote **#1 Dad** on it and drove to his place of work. We waited until he came out to the*

126   Chapter 13 ~ The Great Mystery

parking lot, then held it high so he and everyone else could see how we felt about him. When we got a new phone and I was putting in the memory numbers, my son said "Daddy's number is number one because he is the #1 Daddy." My son was not trying to be cute; he really thinks that, of all the men he knows, his daddy is #1.

Please keep us in your prayers. I still struggle some days and just want to wring his neck, but I do believe God is able to help me.

Loving him,

Judy

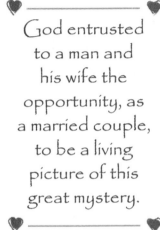

God entrusted to a man and his wife the opportunity, as a married couple, to be a living picture of this great mystery.

I have to confess that as I typed Judy's letter into my book, I wept. Judy has turned her heart to God, for only God could have done such a work of grace in a woman. She is reverencing a man who does not deserve it, and in so doing she is reverencing God.

Do you understand that concept by now? **She is reverencing God by reverencing her husband, not because her husband is a fit representative of Christ, and not because he is a worthy substitute, but because God placed her in subjection to her husband.** And, when it gets humanly ridiculous to obey that lousy man, and when he gives her every reason to not respect him, there is only one controlling factor left—God. This woman is obeying and reverencing God, and no one else. That creep of a husband is the fortunate recipient of honor being given to God. **Her faith sees beyond the sinning man to the God who created us all and "so loved the world, that he gave his only begotten Son. . ."** (John 3:16).

If her faithfulness is never rewarded with a new-birth change in her husband, her commitment will not be wasted, for the grace that God is working in her heart is **making her supremely fitted to be the bride of Christ.** It is an eternal work taking place in her soul. Her obedience to God, and her willingness to go beyond the extra mile, prevents her husband's sin from damaging their son. She has covered a multitude of sins with her love and forgiveness (I Peter 4:8).

"For the unbelieving husband is sanctified by the wife, and the unbelieving wife is sanctified by the husband: else were your children unclean; but now are they holy." (I Corinthians 7:14).

The Power of Reverence

Play It Again, Sue

In our own strength, we women tend to have minds like old LP records that are scratched. We take our husband's faults and replay them in our thoughts over and over again, "he's insensitive…he's insensitive…he's insensitive…he's insensitive…." We get worked up over the smallest offense until our agitation sours into bitterness. He will forget to feed the dog three days in a row. We will look at the empty dog bowl and attribute all kinds of evil motives to him. He will leave us waiting in the car for an extra ten minutes, and we convince ourselves that his lack of consideration is just the tip of the cold iceberg of his heart. Since we are "Christian" ladies, and the kids are watching, we don't rant and rave; we just give him the stone-cold, silent treatment. He must know how much he hurts us, and the best way to retaliate is to hurt him back by depriving him of what he wants most—respect, honor, and love. We know that this will get his attention, and he will eventually have to come humbly asking what is wrong. By then, our miserable countenance should have softened him up for a good case of repentance. Boy, will we make him sorry! But we fully expect that he will try to make up for the birthday he forgot by buying the same kind of candy we told him we hate, and then we hate him all the more for not remembering that we hate that kind of candy. Practice. We are always practicing those thoughts.

> A good marriage is good because one or both of them have learned to overlook the other's faults, to love the other as they are and to not attempt to change them or bring them to repentance.

Remember the 40,000 thoughts a day? Out of the abundance of the heart, the mouth speaketh. How many thousands of negative thoughts are you thinking in the course of three or four hours? It is your *duty* before God to think differently. God tells you how to think. When the emotions will not freely allow us to think what we ought, our will can command our muscles to actions and the thoughts will follow. **"Commit thy works unto the LORD, and <u>thy thoughts</u> shall be established"** (Prov. 16:3).

Remember the passage in II Cor. 10:5? **"Casting down imaginations, and every high thing that exalteth itself against the knowledge of God, and bringing into captivity every thought to the obedience of Christ"**

In the many letters I receive from women who describe the many offenses of their husbands, 90% of the offenses are nothing more than the wife's imaginative response to something that could easily have been overlooked. The difference between a good

Chapter 13 ~ The Great Mystery

marriage and a lousy one is not found in good husbands and good wives versus bad husbands and bad wives, for all marriages are made up of two sinners with lots of faults. *A good marriage is good because one or both of them have learned to overlook the other's faults, to love the other as he or she is and to not attempt to change the other or bring him or her to repentance.* A bad marriage is not one that contains more faults between the two of them; it is a marriage where one or both of them gets worked up over issues that good marriage partners let slide and cover up with love and forgiveness. When a woman gets it in her mind that she must change her husband before she will allow him to relax in the security of her honor and respect, she will never see so much as the bottom side of a good marriage, except when she is kissing hers good-bye.

Eve Has Many Sisters

Where men struggle with fleshly imaginations, we women give ourselves over to emotional imaginations and create a world of hurt for ourselves and those around us. Satan goes after the man directly, offering him pleasure, power, or glory, just as he did with Jesus during his desert temptation experience. But Satan goes after us ladies as he went after Eve, with subtlety. The Tempter asked Eve a question designed to stir her imaginations into supposing that God did not have the best of intentions for her.

"Now the serpent was more subtil than any beast of the field which the LORD God had made. And he said unto the woman, Yea, hath God said, Ye shall not eat of every tree of the garden?" (Genesis 3:1). Satan was leading Eve to question God's motives. He went on to imply that God was keeping something from her, **"For God doth know that in the day ye eat thereof, then your eyes shall be opened, and ye shall be as gods, knowing good and evil"** (Genesis 3:5). Eve was deceived through her runaway imaginations. The root of her sin was doubting God's goodwill toward her. Eve, today, has many sisters. We still doubt the one in authority over us and imagine that he does not intend good for us. Like Eve, we imagine that we can disobey the authority of God's Word and of our husband's word because we "imagine" that we have a higher purpose—to be more spiritual.

We have been tricked into believing that our husbands have committed offenses against us, all the while thinking that we are more spiritual because of the insights we have. We all agree that any man who lives in a lustful daydream is a godless man. And I say to you readers, that any woman who lives on the edge, expecting to be offended and believing ill will on every hand, that woman is living in vain imaginations and is a godless woman. It is time to get yourself under God-ordained authority. Believe God, believe the best of your husband, your neighbors, your church, your family, etc., and get on with the blessings and joy of life and marriage.

Judy, our Queen for the day, has stepped out of being a broken record and has played in her mind those things she is thankful for. God speaks in Philippians 4:8: **"Finally, brethren, whatsoever things are true, whatsoever things are honest, whatsoever things are just, whatsoever things are pure, whatsoever things are lovely, whatsoever things are of good report; if there be any virtue, and if there be any praise, think on these things."**

In the letter above, Judy got over her "Mad Wife" disease before her son became infected with it. The little boy honors his dad because his mother honors him. Someday that little boy will be a man. As he grows up, he will discover that his dad has faults, and he will forgive them as his mother has done. When he is grown and can see the whole picture, he will know that his mom is one of the finest ladies on earth. He will rise up and call her blessed. Someday her husband may grow out of his foolish, lustful stupidity, and if he does, he too will treasure her. She will have earned his love and devotion, because she reverenced him when there was little in him to honor. She loved him because God first loved her.

I would guess that the day Judy held the #1 Daddy sign high in the air, both the angels of heaven and the demons on earth were dumbfounded at the forgiveness and love found in the heart of this "weak" little lady and mother. It was the kind of miracle that proves there is a God on high. I am sure her husband also felt a lump in his throat to see not only her forgiveness, but the honor she bestowed on him. There can be no greater love, and no greater inducement to repentance.

Not one of us honestly thinks Judy's husband *deserved* her reverence, or her love for that matter. He is a first-class worm and deserves to sleep alone in an alley under a cardboard box. But God has called us to a higher plane. It is on this higher plane that we discover the wonder of life, of love, and of forgiveness. And it is the place where we will come to be cherished. Few men are able to continue being angry, lustful, and selfish in the face of such a strong force as being reverenced.

The Promise

In my lifetime, I have known of just two husbands who were able to reverse the course of an angry, resentful wife and make their marriage into something blessed. In all of Scripture, there is no promise to men that they can save their wife and marriage by conducting themselves in a certain prescribed manner. In contrast, the Bible holds a wonderful promise from God to women: they have the power to win their lost husbands both to themselves and to God. The Bible tells us that a woman can win her husband *without the Bible*. In today's churches, many women have failed to win their husbands because they have tried to be evangelists instead of wives.

"Likewise ye wives, be in subjection to your own husbands; that, if any obey not the word, they also may <u>without the word</u> be won by the conversation of the wives" (I Peter 3:1).

A woman wins her husband, just as Judy is doing it, by the manner of her "conversation" or way of living before him. Later, we will discuss how to win **your** lost husband.

> In today's churches, many women have failed to win their husbands because they have tried to be evangelists instead of wives.

Comfort Zones

Men are not the uncaring creatures they sometimes appear to be. They highly treasure their families and like for their homes to be comfort zones. They want respect and a family that gives them security and purpose. Even though home life may get dull, men greatly value their own woman and children.

Men may allow the lust of the flesh to pull them away from that which they value, but they will try to get back to that comfort zone. It is this natural need for his own family that keeps a man caring for and bearing the responsibility for his wife and children. When a woman does not provide for her husband a comfortable nest and a reverent attitude, she has to rely on his goodness to "keep him" faithful. **She is a fool to expect him to be a good husband when she is not being the help meet God has created her to be.** A man coming home to a tense or messy home, lousy meals, and a wife who is critical, might not have the "goodness" to remain faithful if a sweet young woman at work seeks to pull him away with the promise (illusion) of a more fulfilling comfort zone.

It was God who ordained women to be help meets 131

Women take it for granted that a man will be faithful because it is his Christian duty to be faithful (and it is). **It is also a woman's Christian duty to be a help meet: honoring, obeying, serving, and reverencing.** Experience has proven that failure on a woman's part will make it much easier for a man to fail his obligation to the family. A satisfied man will cherish his "comfort zone" enough to resist the "evil woman" and her empty promises.

Counselors agree that in almost all marriage conflicts, both husband and wife share the blame almost equally. A man's guilt is usually easy to see. A woman's guilt is less obvious but just as destructive and just as evil. God ordained a woman to be a help meet. She is to provide a haven of rest and satisfaction, and to be a delight to her husband. When she fails to obey God, there is often "hell to pay" at home. When she obeys God, even if she is married to a "lost" man, she will usually reap heavenly results.

The next story is about a young wife who also discovered how to win her man through ***reverence.***

Earning His Trust

Not all women are as wise as Judy. Years ago I knew a sweet young girl who was really dumb. She had a very tender heart (which she thought was God's love and compassion in her), and she always showed a weakness for guys who "needed" her. Her name was Sunny, and she was as fair and lovely as the Sunshine she was named for. Sunny

always picked up hitchhikers to witness to, even though the older folks told her this practice was not wise. One day she picked up a young man of Arab descent, who looked and talked very romantic. To make a long story short, Sunny married him.

She was soon pregnant with their first child, and in a matter of weeks, the violence began. Over the next seven years, Sunny was regularly subjected to his alcoholic rages and beatings, and she endured his flaunted unfaithfulness. She and the children were alone for days at a time, even weeks, as her husband stayed away with "friends." He returned home to vent his rage and take the few dollars she earned to support their growing family. When Sunny was pregnant with their third baby, Ahmed came home drunk and tried to kill her with a butcher knife. Only the miraculous intervention of Almighty God spared her life.

Every time Ahmed came home raging drunk, Sunny would leave the house with loud, railing accusations and go to her mother's home and cry out her sorrows. She would get on the phone and call all of her friends and tell them what Ahmed was doing to her. But she did not leave him.

One day, I saw her at a church meeting—a huddled, sodden mass of tears and exhaustion. Sunny confessed to plotting her husband's murder. She said she couldn't tolerate life any more as it was, but her children needed her. So she had decided to kill Ahmed instead. Her murder plan was well thought out and could have succeeded if God had not stopped her.

I spent hours in prayer and counseling with Sunny that evening. I asked her to make a decision, either to leave Ahmed once and for all and put the pieces of her life back together, or to stay with him and begin a campaign of winning his heart and saving their life together. I fully expected her to leave him that night, but I discovered something amazing about her: Sunny really wanted God's will in her life. She had grasped an eternal vision about life, and she now believed God could save her man.

> It is amazing how vulnerable a man is when a woman treats him with honor.

I knew of Sunny's weakness to blab everything; she couldn't keep a secret to save her life. I also knew her husband was a very private man, and that her blabbing about his sins kept him in a rage, as it would most lost men. I explained to Sunny that in order to win her husband's heart, she needed to reverence him. This did not mean she had to see some goodness or worth in him that was not really there, but that she needed to show him esteem for the sake of her children and herself. Sunny already did everything else right. She was obedient, faithful, cheerful, a keeper at home, and a help meet. I encouraged her to go one step further and look for an opportunity to reverence her husband. She was not to speak ill of him again. Her conversations with others, as well as with him, would be only praise and appreciation.

Sunny had a learner's heart. She took my advice, and the change in her husband was obvious in just one week. **It is amazing how vulnerable a man is when a woman treats him with honor.** He stopped going off with his drunken friends and got a job so he could help support the family. He came to church occasionally and seemed amazed at the comments people made. "Sunny says you play the saxophone like a genius." "Sunny told us you were a handsome man." "We've been looking forward to meeting you; Sunny has told us...." Ahmed was shocked, and Sunny continued on her mission. A week or so later, she got an encouraging boost in the form of a dream.

She dreamed that a top government official came to the office building where her husband worked on a cleaning crew. The official had a meeting with the manager of the business and told him, "I need to hire a man for a managerial position in my department. The qualifications required are faithfulness, hardworking, honesty, punctuality, and intelligence ... no special education needed. We can always teach him what he doesn't know, but we can't give him work ethics. So do you have anybody who has a good work ethic like that?" The manager answered, "I have one guy who fits that profile, but he is just the clean-up man." In Sunny's dream, the government official said, "I don't care if the guy can't read or write, if he is a faithful, hardworking guy that I can trust and depend on, then I'll hire him and double his wages." In Sunny's dream, her husband was hired by the government official to fill a managerial position.

When Sunny awoke, she excitedly told her husband the dream. She was sure that it was a sign **he was destined for greatness.** Remember what we learned when we studied *Mr. Visionary*, how greatness is a state of soul, not certain accomplishments or the lack of them? Previously, when Sunny called her friends to "tell" them what a creep her husband was, she was reinforcing to him the belief that she thought he was a loser. She publicly shamed him, and he continued to be shameful. Her opinion became his frame of reference. Now Sunny began to publicly exalt him, with miraculous results.

Ahmed thought her dream was silly, but he held his head a little higher when he went to his regular job the next day—on time! Sunny went to her mother's house and got on the phone. She called all of her friends and told them her dream. This time, Ahmed didn't mind her blabbing!

To my knowledge, Ahmed is still on a cleaning crew, and Sunny's dream was just that—a dream. But it expressed her heart toward her husband, and her opinion of him was far more important to him than any job he could ever get. When she dreamed he was a winner and told it around, Ahmed tried to live up to that image. Ahmed found such pleasure and life in his wife's praise that he became interested in her God. In time, he trusted in the Lord Jesus Christ. The last time I saw Ahmed and Sunny, they were growing in the Lord together. As the Scripture says, she won him **"without the word"** (Bible) by her **"conversation"** (I Peter 3:1). God's way works. Who would have ever believed it? Sunny did—but then she didn't have the disadvantage of "culture studies" and modern Greek "scholars."

Chapter 13 ~ The Great Mystery

TIME TO CONSIDER

God admonishes us ladies to see that we reverence our man.

> **"… and the wife see that <u>she reverence her husband</u>"** (Eph. 5:33).

➤ *Make a new habit*

Try to show your husband noticeable esteem at least three times a day. Plan small habits you can establish that will make it easier to remember, until giving him deference comes naturally.

➤ *Traits of a Good Help Meet*

- She acknowledges the "good traits" in her man.
- She speaks of her husband with esteem.
- She defers to him.
- She never responds to him with scorn or ridicule.

➤ *Getting Serious with God*

The word *REVERENCE* appears 13 times in God's Word. Eight occurrences have to do with reverencing men. Look up and consider each of these uses of the word *reverence*. As you read, you will understand from God's Word what God requires of you in reverencing your husband. Make a list of ways you have not shown reverence toward your husband, and then make a list of things you are going to start doing to correct them. Always keep in mind that, when you reverence your husband, you are reverencing God. *It is God's will for you to do this service to your husband.*

Chapter 14

Kings and Kingdoms

*A wise woman always
receives her husband's overtures with delight,
no matter how clumsy he may be.*

God created Adam and commissioned him to take the position of leadership. Since then, every son of Adam has received the same mandate. Man was created to rule. It is his nature. But the only place most men will ever rule is their own little kingdom called *home*. At the least, every man's destiny is to be the leader of his household. To deny him this birthright is contrary to his nature and God's will. When a man is not in command of his little kingdom and is not shown the deference and reverence that goes with that position, his kingdom will not be ruled correctly, and the subjects of that kingdom will not experience the benevolence of a king who truly loves and cherishes them. When you neglect to reverence your husband, you are taking something precious away from yourself, your children, and your husband.

When the President of the United States makes a public appearance in one of the fifty states, even if he is not popular in that state, everyone spends time and energy preparing for him. When he arrives, he is treated with respect. It is not the man or his policies that the people are recognizing, it is the office and all that it stands for. God made your husband the "president" of your family. Your husband is not there to show you deference or to be your helper. It is NOT God's will for your husband to reverence you. It is not God's plan for you to remain seated at the dinner table or in your lounge chair and expect him to serve himself. Our modern society has conditioned us to expect him to serve us. It hurts our feelings if he doesn't do things that we feel he owes us, but that is not the plan God set into place. Our failure to know and believe the written words of God has caused us to accept a cultural lie. Our culture stands diametrically opposed to God at every turn. It is time to realize that feminist beliefs have tainted almost all the public schools and even the best of Christian teachers. God says in Hosea 4:6, **"My people are destroyed for lack of knowledge: because thou hast rejected knowledge, I will also reject thee, that thou shalt be no priest to me: seeing thou hast forgotten the law of thy God, I will also forget thy children."**

> Deference to your man is the height of true femininity. It makes a woman beautiful, gracious, and lovely to all.

Women feel that they will lose some of their self-respect if they surrender to a man who is less than wonderful. Surrendering your autonomy to another is not for wimps. People say of an obedient woman, "Oh, she is just the meek and timid type; she needs to get a life of her own." They know not whereof they speak. This is not abstract, puzzling doctrine; it's practical and pragmatic. The more I show my husband reverence, the more he treasures me and treats me like his queen. God made man so that our deference and respect feed his tendency to show tenderness and to be protective of us.

Reverence is not just how you act; it is how you feel and how you respond with words and with your body language. It is not enough to get up and serve him, your eyes and the quick, carefree swing of your body must indicate your delight to be engaged in serving your man. You cannot fool a man. **He can see your heart as well or better than you can.** Keep an eye on his dinner plate so you can anticipate his needs. Deference is a hot cup of tea while you take his shoes off after a hard day's work. It is a glad face when he returns after being gone for a short time. It is thankfulness for his attention and affection. Deference to your man is the height of true femininity. It makes a woman beautiful, gracious, and lovely to all, but most especially to him.

The next story is an example of the opposite of reverence.

Don't Mess My Hair

A few years ago, I attended a meeting with my husband where a group of leading men were discussing grave matters, trying to come to a conclusion as to what course of action they should take. The men sat in a circle, with their wives sitting beside or right behind them. Sitting across from me was a sober, earnest, young man whom I will call Charles. He was there with his attractive wife. In the midst of an intense part of the conversation, Charles leaned back and draped his arm around his wife's shoulder. She immediately reacted with obvious irritation, shaking his hand off her shoulder, and leaning forward as if to get away from his embrace. Then she carefully fixed her hair where his arm had disturbed it. His mind was jerked off of the serious problem at hand and was focused on her, now — as was the attention of almost everyone in the room. To her, brushing him off was nothing, but to all those in the room (including her husband) it was an act of putting him down like a thoughtless, inept child. Everyone felt his humiliation. After that, Charles had nothing else to contribute. For the duration of the meeting, he sat downcast, properly chastened, with his hands in his lap. I wanted to get up and shake that girl until her teeth rattled. It would have shocked her to know that everyone in the room felt extreme disdain toward her for her self-centered response. She continued to straighten her hair, unaware that she had just shown a complete lack of honor and reverence toward her husband, and unaware that she was wasting her time trying to look pretty, for she had lost all that was lovely and feminine in that one act of disdain.

Carrying that kind of rejection on a regular, daily basis, Charles will never really be able to cherish his wife, and he will never have what it takes to become an effective minister or leader. Yes, she is his wife, and he will undoubtedly continue to love her. But his love will always be more of an attempt to win her. Until she repents, he cannot love her with abandoned joy. A man's ego is a fragile thing. How can a man cherish someone who cares so little for his reputation?

Her act was testimony to the state of her heart. She thought more of her hairdo than her husband's honor. She was rebelling against God in not reverencing her husband. *To reverence* is an active verb. It is something you do. It is not first a feeling; it is a voluntary act. As we reverence and honor our husbands, they are free to mature before God and to minister to others. Charles was not free; he was troubled and bound inside.

Regardless of how a woman may feel about her husband, she can choose to obey and honor him. A husband is told to love his wife. It involves how he feels toward her. You can *will* to do what you ought to do much sooner than you can be motivated by your feelings to act. As we said earlier, when you choose the right way, feelings will soon follow.

"A foolish woman is clamorous: she is simple, and knoweth nothing" (Proverbs 9:13).

"Every wise woman buildeth her house: but the foolish plucketh it down with her hands" (Proverbs 14:1).

Not Fair

It doesn't seem fair that the wife is expected to honor and obey her husband even though he has not earned the right; yet she must also earn the right to be loved. If she has to honor him regardless of how he acts, why shouldn't he love her regardless of how she acts? If my husband were talking to men, he would tell them to love their wives regardless of how they act. But remember, this is me, the aged woman, telling the young girls what they can do to make a heavenly marriage. You cannot command your husband to love you, and you have no right to expect him to love you when you are unlovely. But God has provided a way for a woman to *cause* her husband to love and cherish her. God gave us ladies some keys to the avenues of a man's heart. God made it so that we can actually *manipulate* him into fulfilling his God-ordained duty. His very nature is made to respond to us if we will only treat him with reverence. A man does not have such power to influence his wife. Women are not built with the same response mechanisms. God did not give men the wonderful promise he gave to women, that they can win their wives with proper behavior. But women have a beautiful hope based on the promises of God.

> Accept all of his overtures with thanksgiving and delight.

The Tale of the Purple Flowers PJ Girl

Just last week, while I sat in my van in the parking lot of Wal-Mart, waiting for my daughter, I watched the people as they walked into the store. It was an interesting study in human relations. Of the 25 or so couples who walked into the store together, only three of them were touching each other, and those three ladies were the only ones smiling out of the 25 I observed. On a scale of 1-10, with 10 being the prettiest, all three of these gals were 1s or 2s. One lady looked several (hard) years older than her young, tall, handsome husband. He had a delighted smile on his face as he watched her every move, possessively leading her by the arm. It was clear that she was enjoying telling him her tale. I could see it was a good story, because he threw his head back and laughed freely just as they walked through the door. He was enjoying his woman.

> The very heart of reverence is extreme appreciation and profound thankfulness that this man, just as he is, has chosen to love me, just as I am.

Another couple passed by quietly, deliberately brushing up against each other, saying nothing, but the woman's smile said everything. The third smiling couple took the award of the day. He was a muscled-up, gorgeous hunk, and she was almost past describing. She was wearing flannel PJ bottoms that were cut off just above the knees. The shortened pants had 5-inch purple flowers scattered over the white, almost see-through material. She was short, and at least 50 pounds overweight, with most of the extra weight bouncing in the skin-tight PJ shorts. Her hair was chopped off in an ugly cut and really greasy. Her gorgeous hunk had her in a headlock hug. She was laughing and poking him in the ribs while hollering for him to let her go. You would have thought he was hugging Miss America by the way he was grinning. **He was really enjoying his purple-flowered sweetie**. I caught his eye, and he grinned back at me, not one bit embarrassed. That gal had totally won his heart *and* my respect. He was proud to be her man. Of all those beautiful girls who had walked into Wal-Mart while I waited, it was this girl who was publicly being adored and appreciated. I suspect that she has never removed her husband's hugging arm for any reason, much less to save her hairdo. She has accepted all of his overtures with thanksgiving and delight.

In the coming pages, we will discuss how we need to cook, clean, take care of our children, etc. These are important and necessary, but the buck always stops right here at the action word *reverence*. **A man will allow his woman many, many faults, as long as he knows that she thinks he is great.** If she will just look into his face with adoration, if she is thankful to him for loving her, he will adore her. She can dress awful, be grossly overweight, have terrible hair, not cook so well, be a little lazy and dumb, and not be one bit pretty, but if she will just think and show that he is wonderful, he will love her. It sounds simplistic, but it is the way of a man with a maid.

Chapter 14 - Kings and Kingdoms

Women, on the other hand, want their husbands to perform. They expect them to be spiritual, hardworking, diligent, sensitive, and an attentive parent, or they will take personal offense and begin a campaign to change him into "their" image. I find it amazing that a woman would marry a MAN and then become angry because he continues to act like one.

Elisabeth Elliot, in her book, *Let Me Be a Woman*, wrote to her daughter, "I had been a widow for thirteen years, when the man who was to become your stepfather proposed. It seemed to me the miracle that could never happen. That any man had wanted me the first time was astonishing. I had gone through high school and college with very few dates. But to be wanted again was almost beyond imagination. I told this man that I knew there were women waiting for him who could offer him many things that I couldn't offer—things like beauty and money. But I said, 'There's one thing I can give you that no woman on earth can outdo me in, and that's appreciation.' The perspective of widowhood had taught me that."

As I cast around in my mind and heart for a way to define for my readers what it means to reverence a man, Elisabeth Elliot's letter to her daughter came to my mind.

The very heart of reverence is extreme appreciation and profound thankfulness that this man, just as he is, has chosen to love me, just as I am.

Elisabeth Elliot is a lovely, talented, successful woman, yet she chooses to honor with thankfulness the man who loves her. It is the state of her heart.

My husband tells young men looking for wives that there is really only one absolutely necessary trait that the girl they marry must possess—a grateful heart. He tells them that the girl they choose must be joyful and thankful that you love her. "The more she believes that she is fortunate that you chose her over others, the better the foundation for the true marriage of two souls. If she feels that YOU are lucky to get HER, then you had better run, because that woman is looking for her *own* help meet, and she thinks you are the one to fill the job. She will spend the rest of her life trying to change you."

To reverence a husband is to be delighted and thankful, like the purple flowers PJ girl. It means that you must be the opposite of the "don't-mess-up-my-hair girl" and that you believe in him enough to dream good things about him. You reverence him by teaching your sons and daughters that their daddy is the #1 man, and then help them make a sign and hold it high, so everyone can see how you think and feel about him. In summary, it is to believe that *you* are blessed for being loved by this wonderful man.

TIME TO CONSIDER

Make a list of things you should do that will cause your husband to feel your honor, respect, and reverence. These might be simple things, like meeting him at the door when he comes home from work or reaching out to touch him in the car as you drive down the road. Practice what you have learned, and make a commitment to do these things, come sunshine or storm.

➢ *What Have We Learned?*

- God created us to be help meets. We will find God's perfect will in our lives as we seek to be the help meets he designed us to be.
- A help meet is someone who helps another.
- Joy comes from the abundance of a thankful heart.
- Thankfulness is a result of being content with God's will.
- Control and dominance are masculine traits. A woman's calling is to be submissive and yielding to her husband; to do otherwise is sin.
- In order for us to know God's blessings, we must recognize, appreciate, and honor the chain of command that God has set into place.
- We wives are a picture of the Bride of Christ. It is called the Great Mystery. This high calling should facilitate the molding of our lives into this picture.
- Our obedience in the role of "help meet" is not dependent on our husband's obedience to God.
- God has called us to reverence our husband. A woman who does not submit to and honor her husband in this ministry of reverencing him is a creation of God out of order, out of place, and out of control.

God defined your role when he said, **"the head of the woman is the man."** The man was put in charge before the woman was ever created. God explained his plan clearly when he said, **"I will make him an <u>help meet</u> for him."** God was making it crystal clear that a man is never to be his wife's help meet when he said, **"For a <u>man indeed ought not to cover his head, forasmuch as he is the image and glory of God</u>: but <u>the woman is the glory of the man</u>."**

God even told us *why* a woman was never to be in authority or to think of herself spiritually more able than the man, **"For Adam was first formed, then Eve. <u>And Adam was not deceived, but the woman being deceived was in the transgression</u>."**

When we thoroughly understand our role as help meets, begin to practice joy and thanksgiving in performing that role, and turn our hearts to reverencing our husbands, only then can we expect to experience a heavenly marriage.

PART 2

Titus 2

"The aged women likewise, that they be in behaviour as becometh holiness, not false accusers, not given to much wine, teachers of good things; That they may teach the young women to be sober, to love their husbands, to love their children, To be discreet, chaste, keepers at home, good, obedient to their own husbands, that the word of God be not blasphemed" (Titus 2:3-5).

Over the last several years I have asked hundreds of women, "Can you tell me the eight things God requires of a woman, which if she does not obey she will be guilty of blaspheming God's Word?" Most women respond with a blank look, not having a clue as to the answer.

God told the older women to teach only one message. It is found in Titus 2. The next section of this book covers these eight important things.

Eight Practical Game Rules

When I was a child, the word *blaspheme* struck terror in my heart. My parents were new Christians and did not know much about the Bible, but somewhere along the way, one of our preachers was able to stuff into my little brain the verse on blaspheming the Holy Ghost. As far as I knew at the time, there was only one verse with the dreaded word in it, and it reads like this, **"But he that shall blaspheme against the Holy Ghost hath never forgiveness, but is in danger of eternal damnation"** (Mark 3:29).

Today, now at a much riper age, the word *blaspheme* still causes me to shudder—as it should. To some degree, blasphemy is to put oneself above God, either by what you say or what you do. When the Pharisees heard Jesus speak, and because they wanted a reason to kill him, they accused him of blaspheming, **"making himself equal with God"** (John 5:18).

This is a women's book about wives and mothers, so you must be wondering what blasphemy has to do with the subject. A lot! As I began to write this book in earnest, my mind was constantly filled with Scripture. I woke up one night with the passage of Titus 2:3-5 running through my head. As I lay in my bed, I tried to recall the list of eight things that aged women were told to teach the younger women. It occurred to me right then that God had given me the perfect outline in those eight simple instructions.

"The aged women likewise, that they be in behaviour as becometh holiness, not false accusers, not given to much wine, teachers of good things; That they may teach the young women [1] to be sober, [2] to love their husbands, [3] to love their children, [4] To be discreet, [5] chaste, [6] keepers at home, [7] good, [8] obedient to their own husbands, <u>that the word of God be not blasphemed</u>" (Titus 2:3 5).

The word *blasphemed* jumped out at me, **"…that the word of God be not blasphemed."** Aged women (that's me) are commanded to teach the young women so they will not blaspheme the word of God! Are young mothers in danger of blasphemy? The passage says they are—not of blaspheming the Holy Ghost, which is the unpardonable sin—rather, of **blaspheming the word of God.** Even though it is not the unpardonable sin, it sure is a scary thing for Paul to say about young wives.

The word *blaspheme* in this passage had always seemed to be an overstatement—an emphatic exaggeration. How can a woman be causing the Word of God to be blasphemed if she is not discreet? Does a woman really cause the Word of God to be blasphemed if she doesn't obey her husband? What if he is wrong? What if she dresses a little sexy and is not as chaste as she should be? Should that be judged as blaspheming? What does it mean to be keepers at home? **Why are these eight things so critical to young wives that refusal to do them would be termed *blasphemy?***

As I lay in my bed that night pondering these things, I asked God to give me a glimpse of his mind and heart concerning this passage, so that I might know how to teach the young women to keep his Word from being blasphemed. He did. And, his answer broke my heart. I could never have dreamed the sad horror that would teach me just why the word *blaspheme* is the right word. But first, we will examine the eight characteristics, one by one, that God commands aged women to teach young women.

Chapter *15*

I. To Be Sober

Titus 2:4:"That they may teach the young women to <u>be sober</u>. . . ."

To be sober: To do one's duty, be moderate, self-controlled, thoughtful, and to learn to make wise decisions and judgments. **"And wisdom and knowledge shall be <u>the stability of thy times</u>, and strength of salvation: the fear of the LORD is his treasure"** (Isa. 33:6).

Common Sense

A sober wife is one who faces the fact that she is no longer a freewheeling individual, with time to do as she pleases. She knows that marriage is a joyous, but also a grave responsibility. She cannot be flighty and frivolous. She makes a commitment to be the best wife, mother, and manager of the home that anyone could be. She becomes the acting CEO of a great enterprise of which her husband is the owner.

Her most basic responsibility is to make her husband's home run smoothly. She assumes the role of coordinator of all affairs. If the home doesn't run in an orderly fashion, the marriage will not be joyous and fulfilling, and neither will child training. **When a woman soberly considers the needs, time schedule, and resources of her home, then she will be a more efficient help meet.** This planning will eliminate tension and help set a peaceful mood. It is the simple things in life that can break down a marriage and bring about a bitter divorce. But on the positive side, it is the simple planning of life's activities that can bring health, prosperity, peace, and happiness to a sound marriage and produce gratifying family relationships. Men (and children) appreciate good meals, a clean house, and an atmosphere of peace—a refuge from the stress of life.

Rude, Insensitive Jerk

Dear Debi,

I was totally exhausted yesterday when my husband came home from work. The children were sick. I have a new baby, and she was coming down with a fever. He came in and never inquired how I felt or how my day was. He started off by asking why the place was such a wreck and "when will dinner be ready," because it was the night for choir practice, and he wanted to get there early. He was rude, insensitive, and indifferent to my exhaustion, the kids' sickness, and everything else. He was so selfish, and it hurt so badly. What was I supposed to do? Reward this selfish jerk with loving service?

Jill

Dear Jill, It is your duty, your job, and in your best interest to serve your husband.

-Debi

No one would dispute that Jill's husband is insensitive, but two wrongs do not make a good marriage. One "right" can make a BIG difference in a marriage and change that selfish old guy. Always keep in mind that your job is to do a good job serving him, so **planning ahead is a must**. If Jill had done better at her job, her husband would not have been such a jerk. Your husband expects you to plan ahead. He plans ahead at his place of work, otherwise he would lose his job. If you plan ahead, conflicts like this can be avoided, and your husband will be proud to know he has a better wife than the other guys at work. If you pamper your husband, in time he will become more sensitive to your burden, but you must be a soldier and show yourself strong.

I have had many sick babies, and I know that sometimes it was not easy, but you **can** get the house in order and meals cooked and keep everything running smoothly all the same. As mothers, we will often be stressed over a sick child, but that is no reason to neglect our other duties. A sober wife makes herself the match of every circumstance.

The Assignment

Learn to use the kitchen's "wonder tool"—the crock-pot. Today, as I write this, it is Sunday. This morning at 8 A.M., I put several frozen chicken breasts and some rice into the electric crock-pot. I added some water, celery, bell peppers, and seasonings, and turned it on low heat. When we came into the house at noon, the house was filled with a delicious aroma, and dinner was ready except for a simple salad, which took a scant few minutes. After we had eaten, I added some seasoning and more water to the crock-pot, which now had only a little rice and a few bits of chicken with broth. This simple soup simmered all afternoon and was the basis of our meal that evening. While at church, I asked one of the eleven-year-old girls about feeding their family of twelve, "If your mama asked you to put a chicken in a crock-pot (or three chickens in three crock-pots) with rice and seasonings every Sunday morning, could you do it?" Her twelve-year-old sister laughed and said, "No problem."

> No one would dispute that Jill's husband is insensitive, but two wrongs do not make a good marriage.

Simplify, Simplify, Simplify

Always offer your children only one choice for breakfast. Several options will only confuse the child's spirit. Choices also give room for argument or discontentment. Providing the same simple food every morning (except maybe Saturday) causes a child to look forward to getting cereal on that one special morning. It can actually help your children to become more thankful and will bring about a more peaceful morning. A simple, yet filling meal for the children's daily breakfast is peanut butter toast, which could be served on a paper napkin. Clean up will be easy.

If Dad is not home for lunch, then the plan is to have the same basic wholesome food for lunch each day. You could keep a crock-pot of beans warm for simple burritos everyday, with some vegetables added for variety along the way. This lunch can also be served on a paper plate or napkin.

Just a Meal Idea

✓ Sunday night, put dried pinto beans and water into the crock-pot to soak. Monday morning, turn the pot on low. Monday evening, grill minute steaks and bake sweet potatoes to eat with the beans.

✓ Add water to leftover beans, and let cook on low all night to be used with taco salad as refried beans. An hour before dinner, wash and tear some lettuce, chop up an onion, a bell pepper, and two tomatoes in preparation for a taco salad. Brown two pounds of ground beef, putting half of the cooked meat in a plastic bag in the refrigerator for spaghetti on Wednesday. Season the other half of the meat with taco seasoning and keep warm. Set your table, and lay out sour cream, grated cheese, hot sauce, corn chips, chopped vegetables, beans, and meat.

> *A sober wife is one who considers her options, makes her plans, and follows through in order to avoid the confusion of mismanagement.*

✓ Wednesday at noon, put your reserved, pre-cooked ground beef, chopped and sautéed onions, peppers, and celery in the crock-pot with crushed tomatoes and a can of tomato paste with spaghetti seasonings. An hour before dinner, make a salad and heat water, ready to drop in noodles ten minutes before dinner. Wednesday night, rinse out your crock-pot and put dried black beans into it to soak.

✓ Thursday morning, turn your crock-pot on low with the black beans in it. Two hours before dinner, add smoked sausages to the black beans. Cook enough rice for two meals, and serve the black beans over rice with sour cream, chopped onion and tomatoes, and grated cheese. Add water to the leftover black beans in the crock-pot and a small handful of rice to simmer overnight for you and the children's lunch on Friday. Put the leftover rice in the refrigerator for Friday's dinner of fried rice.

✓ Friday, use leftover crock-pot black beans and rice for children's lunch. Take leftover rice from refrigerator and make fried rice. Chop onions, bits of meat (chicken, ham, bacon, or beef), sauté, mix with rice, then add scrambled eggs and soy sauce to rice. Season with salt and pepper. Make a fresh salad.

✓ Saturday, have a cookout with hamburgers, open cans of baked beans, and cookies for dessert.

✓ Sunday, have your chicken ready for the crock-pot. Early Sunday morning put a chicken, a stalk of celery, and a can of cream of chicken soup in the crock-pot, and season. Just before you leave for church, cut ten flour tortillas into 2-inch-wide slices and drop into the pot with the chicken. Enjoy yummy chicken and dumplings when you come in from church.

It is not a grouchy old husband or bad days that cause the problems of cooking and cleaning for young wives. It is the lack of simple planning.

When I was a child, we always had the same food on certain days. Dinner was ready at 5 P.M.

- We always had peas, potatoes, and minute steaks on Monday,
- Meatloaf with sweet potatoes and coleslaw on Tuesday,
- Wednesday dinner was roast with mashed potatoes and green beans,
- Spaghetti and salad for Thursday evening, and
- Fish, chips, and salad on Fridays (the meal Jesus prepared for his company).

The regular dinners each weeknight made it easier for Mom to plan and buy the week's groceries. My dad would look forward to the meal he knew would be hot and waiting for him when he came home from work. The key is to plan. A grocery list with the week's meals well-defined is a very handy tool.

As wives, our life's work should be to perfect how we may please our husbands.

Sometimes, maintaining a good relationship with your husband simply requires the performing of simple tasks, like having a good meal ready on time and a clean house, even when it is not easy or convenient to do so.

Traits of a Good Help Meet

- ➤ A good *help meet* provides an oasis for her man.
- ➤ She fixes meals that please him; she does not cook to suit herself.
- ➤ She plans and prepares well ahead of time.
- ➤ She exercises self-discipline.

Strawberries and Sweet Love

I have sweet childhood memories of time spent picking strawberries. The thing I remember most vividly is my wrinkled old grandpa down on his knees beside me picking strawberries and talking up one row and down the other about my grandma and how much he loved her. Apparently, he didn't see her bulging country dress, the thin white hair, and her wrinkled old face. The thought of him loving her and of her being a beautiful woman was a novel idea that my young brain found delightful. I remember giggling so much that sometimes it was hard to pick strawberries. His declaration of love was also very comforting. My grandma

Your relationship with your husband is the single most important role you will ever play. If you fail here, then you have failed at your life's work and have missed God's perfect plan.

honored and obeyed my grandfather. It was their foundation of love and honor that made the family (even the extended family) strong. As you read the next story written by my good friend and first cousin (they were her grandparents, too), you will see how we were conditioned to please our husbands. They taught us to resist taking offense, and that we were never to "give him [our husband] a piece of our mind." If Grandma did get offended, no one would know it, because it was well understood that a lady had duties, and she must be sober in the execution of them.

"A wise woman doesn't ever allow herself to be a liability, but strives to always be an asset to the marriage. She looks for ways to make, save, and use money wisely. Her husband knows he is a richer man because she is his wife."

What is a Cold Dinner?

By Freida Lansing, first cousin and childhood friend of Debi

Life is so much different from what it used to be. Several of us ladies were sitting around a dinner table recently, telling about some of our early disastrous cooking experiences. It brought vivid memories of my newlywed days. When I married, I really didn't know how to cook anything. On top of that, my family ate strictly 'country'—peas and cornbread (still my favorite), ham, pork chops, fried chicken, turnip greens, etc., while my husband's family ate a very different type of diet.

I'll never forget that hot afternoon. We lived in an apartment in the back of an old Victorian-style house, which consisted of a living room/kitchen combination and a bathroom. We had no air conditioning, and that far down south could get really miserable in the summer. One sultry summer day, I worked hard to prepare a home-cooked meal for my husband, and had it ready when he came home from a hard day of construction work. When he walked in the door, he was so hot and sweaty, he took one look at that hot meal and said in despair, "This is not a day for a hot meal; this is the kind of day you need a cold meal!" My heart was just crushed. Hot and sweaty myself, I had slaved to serve him the best way I knew how. I had never even heard of a cold meal. What on earth was he talking about? At that point in my life, a tomato stuffed with tuna or chicken salad was totally foreign to me. I must tell you, my story wasn't very funny thirty years earlier, but as I finished telling it to my friends, we were all laughing about how "crushed" I was that day.

I was surprised to see that one of the younger women at the table didn't think it was funny, as she huffily retorted, "Did you throw it at him? I would have!" This stopped me in my "memory" tracks. Was I angry? Did I want to throw the meal in his face? I really don't remember ever having that thought. I do remember being hurt and sad. But my most compelling thought was to figure out how to prepare cold meals. When I married, I became MRS. Lansing. His life, his agenda, and his desires became mine. **I considered my marriage to be my career for the rest of my life, and I intended to be successful at it**. If he didn't like the food that I cooked, rather than refusing to cook anymore, saying that he was just too hard to please, I learned to cook the food **he liked**! I just WANTED, and WAS DETERMINED, to please him. And I found that he really was not that hard to please. Most men are not so hard to please; I heard someone recently say that all a man needs is food, sex, and respect, and he'll be pretty content. That is certainly an oversimplification, but from experience, I know that those things are the basic, rudimentary needs of all husbands. And so, I have worked at it from that perspective for almost 33 years. It is still my GOAL to be pleasing to my husband. I am pleased to tell you that he delights in me. I was determined to earn his delight.

Older and wiser and still very much in love,
Freida

> Carrying a big, ugly chip on the shoulder was considered silly. No self-respecting female would be huffy or get hurt feelings.

"A wise woman doesn't let little things stir
her spirit to agitation. With a quiet and meek
spirit, she seeks to make all things better."

Reflecting on...

1. Was it pleasing to the Lord for Freida to seek to prepare meals to her husband's liking?
2. Would it have been sin to respond with anger or hurt feelings?
3. Would you have sought to please your husband if he had shown such insensitive ingratitude?
4. Do you think her husband was just trying to be cruel?
5. When you first married, did you think of your marriage as a career of pleasing your husband?

"A virtuous woman is a crown to her husband: but she that maketh ashamed is as rottenness in his bones" (Proverbs 12:4).

Make a new habit. Most wives reading this book were trained <u>not</u> to honor their husbands. You were most likely trained by a mother's example to disrespect and resent your dad. You were trained by watching your mom show displeasure at your father's bad habits, and nothing has changed in the way you relate to your husband. It seems natural to be angry rather than to seek change for the better. It is not easy to break a well-established tradition, but it will certainly be worth the effort.

Liberated to Sorrow

Beginning with the women's "liberation" movement in the 1960s, women have been taught and are expected to resent men in authority. All media, magazines, movies, and popular books have promoted eradication of the distinction between male and female. The established churches, as always, are only about one decade behind the world, so Christian books and ministers have followed with their own female liberation theology. Ministers and theologians have devised ways of dismissing the authority of the words of God found in Scripture that speak about the nature and duty of men and women. It has gone so far that the churches are now convinced that the Bible supports this modern view.

When I was a child, no one in our large, extended family could ever remember a divorce on either side of the family, including the many aunts, uncles, cousins, and grandparents. Neither was there a case of wife abuse or child abuse. In the last fifty years, all that has dramatically changed.

Change your lifestyle to reflect his desires ♥

It is hard to believe, but the following assignment was found in a 1950s public high school home economics workbook. When I was in school, this is what the general public was being taught! Can you imagine what an outcry it would cause if someone put this in a public school textbook today?

How to Be a Good Wife Today

(taken word-for-word from a 1950s public high school home economics textbook)

* *Have dinner ready*. Plan ahead, even the night before, to have a delicious meal on time. This is a way of letting him know that you have been thinking about him and are concerned about his needs. Most men are hungry when they come home, and the prospect of a good meal is part of the warm welcome needed.

* *Prepare yourself*. Take 15 minutes to rest so that you'll be refreshed when he arrives. Touch up your makeup, put a ribbon in your hair and be fresh looking. He has just been with a lot of work-weary people. Be a little gay and a little more interesting. His boring day may need a lift.

* *Clear away the clutter*. Make one last trip through the main part of the house just before your husband arrives, gathering up schoolbooks, toys, and papers. Then, run a dust cloth over the tables. Your husband will feel he has reached a haven of rest and order, and it will give you a lift, too.

* *Prepare the children*. Take a few minutes to wash the children's hands and faces (if they are small). Comb their hair, and if necessary, change their clothes. They are little treasures, and he would like to see them playing the part.

* *Minimize all noise*. At the time of his arrival, eliminate all noise of the washer, dryer, dishwasher, or vacuum. Try to encourage the children to be quiet. Be happy to see him. Greet him with a warm smile.

* SOME DON'TS:

* *Don't greet him with problems* or complaints.

* *Don't complain if he is late* for dinner. Count this as minor compared with what he might have gone through that day. Make him comfortable. Have him

lean back in a comfortable chair or suggest he lie down in the bedroom. Have a cool or warm drink ready for him. Arrange his pillow, and offer to take off his shoes. Speak in a low, soft, soothing and pleasant voice. Allow him to relax and unwind.

Listen to him. You may have a dozen things to tell him, but the moment of his arrival is not the time. Let him talk first.

Make the evening his. Never complain if he does not take you out to dinner or to other places of entertainment. Instead, try to understand his world of strain and pressure, his need to be home and relax.

"The goal: try to make your home a place of peace and order, where your husband can renew himself in body and spirit."

D o you see what has happened in the last fifty years? Every high school girl was taught a conservative worldview that was more Biblical in perspective than what the churches teach today.

"A wise woman patterns her life after her husband's. His working, playing, eating, and sleeping habits become hers."

I'm About to Have a Nervous Breakdown

This letter shows how not getting our way often causes us to have a nervous, troubled spirit instead of the quiet (sober) spirit God expects us to have. It was good to hear that this lady finally found peace. The article she refers to can be found on the nogreaterjoy.org website.

> *I heard your article read publicly called "Carnal husbands, Cranky wives, and Cantankerous Kids," while at a seminar in Knoxville. It was the first time I realized my anxiety controlled my husband and was a reflection of my lack of confidence in him. As we left the seminar and were fighting traffic, my husband spoke up that we needed to stop for gas. Miles passed and still the*

traffic was bumper to bumper. Suddenly we were free and in the mountains with no place to buy gas. I was in an extreme state of turmoil. I had worked myself up to a state that I wanted to scream to him to go back into the city and get gas. I could see the gas gauge; it was totally empty. I kept quietly raging to God that "this was the <u>exact</u> reason why I had to take control, since he is the most irresponsible man and does not make wise decisions. I felt that I should tell him what to do." I was so nervous, I was almost sick, but for the first time I kept my mouth shut and looked interestedly at the hills. Ten miles up into the mountains, we finally came to an exit that had a gas station, and my husband turned to me, smiled and said, "What's happened to you? You're not a nervous wreck like you usually are. I'm so glad you've learned to relax. Isn't life a lot more fun when you're not so full of fear? I'm proud of you." I had to stop and think. Even if we had run out of gas, would it have been a tragedy? I could see that I had turned many things into monsters. I had the opposite of a meek and quiet spirit that we are supposed to have. I have learned not to let my fears and irritations over uncertain circumstances control me, and, much worse, my husband. I am learning to lean on my husband.

Sara

Do you think God could have used Mary for the mother of Jesus if she had allowed herself to become an emotional wreck when her environment was not clean or orderly?

"Let this mind be in you, which was also in Christ Jesus" (Philippians 2:5).

Personal Shrines

Many women lack biblical soberness, as seen in the way they treat their houses as shrines to be protected, rather than as spaces in which to enjoy their families. They get emotionally upset if the carpet gets messed up or if the kids accidentally spill milk on the couch. They become emotional wrecks over their physical surroundings. If you have that problem, let me ask you, how would you feel if your husband provided nothing more than an open barn in which to deliver your first baby? That was the case with Mary, the mother of Jesus. Do you think God could have used Mary to be the mother of Jesus if she had allowed herself to become an emotional wreck when her environment was not clean or orderly? Think of the teenage girl, Mary, clinging to the back of a bouncing donkey, contractions pulling at her exhausted body, while her desperate husband searched for a place for her to deliver her child.

Many have speculated as to what virtues Mary had that prompted God to choose her to be the mother of our Lord. I can tell you what she was like. She had eternity in her heart. She was self-possessed, thoughtful, and was always learning to make wise judgments. When a young woman learns to be sober, she will not live for immediate gratification. She will appreciate those things that will last for eternity.

Mountain Ma and Pa

by Rebekah Pearl (age 16), April 1991

O, so much ter do,

So much ter be done.

The work's never through,

An' da work ain't much fun.

No thanks fer yer labor,

No pay fer da job,

Jest, "What's fer supper?"

"How 'bout corn-on-da-cob?"

Ya mop an' ya sweep,

Ya dust an' ya shine.

Then turn around,

An' what do ya find?

His shoes on da floor,

His coat on da chair,

His rear in da couch,

An' his feet in da air!

So ya kick off yer shoes,

An' ya throw down yer broom.

An' ya wink at yer ole man,

So he'll make ya some room!

This is why <u>my</u> Ma and Pa are happily married!

REFLECTING ON
Sober

➤ *Traits of a Good Help Meet*
  - A good help meet establishes a haven of rest.
  - She will adjust to her husband's time schedule and eating habits.
  - She will relax and enjoy her family, instead of worrying and fretting.

➤ *Words God uses to describe a godless woman*

Locate the verses in a concordance, and write them down. Ask God to cause you to HATE any sign of these things in your life. Believe and know that God <u>will</u> set you free.

- Foolish
- Clamorous
- Simple
- Knoweth nothing
- Like a swine (fat pig) with a gold nose-jewel

- Brawling
- Contentious
- Angry
- Odious
- Tattler
- Busybodies

- Without discretion
- Wanders from house to house
- Stubborn
- Loud

➤ *Getting Serious with God*

Think of an occasion in the recent past when you became angry or were hurt because your husband responded in a way that you felt was wrong. Keep in mind that the other side of the coin of being *angry* is being *hurt*. It is one and the same coin, and it buys the same results: a bad marriage and a strained relationship. How different do you think the end of the struggle might have been if you had kept in your mind that your job was to please that man? Write your own story. First, write the one that ended in a big fight, and next, write the story as it should have ended. Remember, he doesn't have to be right or kind for you to react in a godly way. This exercise will help you see the rationale for honoring your husband in a different light.

Chapter 16

2. To Love Their Husbands

Titus 2:4: "That they may teach the young women to be sober, to <u>love their husbands</u>...."

Loving him means putting his needs before your own. I am a minister. If you are a wife, you, too, are a minister. Our ministry is directed toward our husbands and then our children. **We were, and are, created to be help meets. Every day and every night we need to be ready to minister to his needs.**

A Normal Guy

Dear Mr. And Mrs. Pearl,

I am in a dilemma and need you guys to write my wife and tell her what I say is true. My wife thinks I am a sex pervert because I need sex. She feels I am not sensitive to her needs when I want sex and she doesn't, which is most of the time. She will give me sex, but it hurts her feelings that I do not love her enough to consider her first. I tried to explain to her that to a man sex is just like having to eat. When I have missed a meal I unconsciously roam the kitchen, opening cabinet doors, and peer into the refrigerator, just looking and looking. I told her that a few days without sex leaves me in the same condition sexually. No matter how much I love her and respect her feelings and needs, I still have this overwhelming sexual need that drives me until it is satisfied.

There are very few times when everything is just right for her. She is exhausted, or has a backache or not healed right down there or whatever she comes up with. I tried to explain to her that she is setting me up for temptation, and that really set her off. Now I am not only a pervert, I am also unfaithful in my heart, so she is upset every time a good-looking girl walks by.

Please tell her I just down-right need my woman. That's the bottom line; I am normal—all guys need a woman. She said I made it until I was 23 without sex, so why do I have to have it now? I told her when I was single, I did not have to see one undress or lie in the bed and know I could if I wanted to. I just want to come home and be a family man. I want to crawl into bed at night with a woman who is glad I am her man, and I want to make love every few days so I don't have to think about the girls at work. Would you write her and explain all this to her. Maybe if she heard from you she might understand that I have feelings, too—physical feelings as well as emotional feelings.

Micah

> God's ultimate goal for you is to meet your man's needs.

"For this cause shall a man leave his father and mother, and shall be joined unto his wife, and <u>they two shall be one flesh.</u> This is <u>a great mystery</u>: but I speak concerning Christ and the church" (Eph. 5:31-32).

- ➤ God's ultimate goal for you is to meet your man's needs.
- ➤ God's original intention was that a woman would spend her life helping her husband fulfill his dreams and ambitions.
- ➤ From the beginning, God meant for us to be a comfort, a blessing, a reward, a friend, an encouragement, and a right-hand *woman*.

"What can I do to help you, Adam?"

"Pick up the other end of that log, and help me move it over here."

"What should my next project be, Adam?"

"Have my dinner ready every evening, and take good care of my little ones."

"That is a very strong fence you are building, and the gate looks nice. I am so proud of you, Adam. What would you like now?"

"Take your clothes off real slow so I can watch....Yeah, you're a fine help meet."

Frame of Reference

A man's concept of love and marriage is different from a woman's, especially after he has gone without sex for a few days. This book is not a "how-to" for a man. I will skip his part, and deal with the ladies' part. God describes marriage as **"they two shall be one flesh,"** which is, their bodies coming together.

Many men feel that marriage is not quite what they thought it was going to be. Some men spend their youth dreaming about the wild passion they are going to experience with the one woman they love more than life. It is their expression of the oneness they will have with her alone. This is truly God's design for a man in the department of love.

The man remembers the passionate and loving looks his sweetheart had for him before marriage. He had naturally assumed that she would always think of him in that all-consuming, loving way. When they were courting, that is the way she made him feel. **He saw it reflected in her face.** All he wanted was to satisfy that hungry animal he thought she was, and, for a while, she was all he had hoped for; but then it faded away. She wasn't interested anymore. **Her disinterest in him sexually is a reflection of her heart, and he knows it.** There are a multitude of excuses women use to explain why they would "rather not" or why they "cannot respond" sexually. I believe I have heard them all. Her husband knows in his spirit that all her excuses are just that: excuses for not wanting him.

When a woman is not interested in his most consuming passion, he feels that she is not interested in him. When a woman just "allows, cooperates, and tolerates," it leaves a man feeling sick at heart. If, to a man, sex were just copulation, he would make his deposit and be satisfied, but to him it is intimacy, a merging of spirits, a way of saying,

> When a woman is not interested in his most consuming passion, he feels that she is not interested in him.

"I love you…I need you…I like you." A man's most basic needs are warm sexual love, approval, and admiration. For his wife to be willing but indifferent, speaks of neither sex nor love.

A woman is a fool to believe her own excuses or to think she can convince him that what she says is the truth. Her half commitment makes him feel incomplete and unloved. By not obeying God in this area of sex and love, a woman is putting a terrible curse on her husband. When a woman forces a man into that position, it is the equivalent of a man saying to his wife, "You are a stupid, ugly, lousy wife, but I will still be a good husband and kiss you today." A man's wife has more influence on his frame of reference than any other thing or person in life.

Man is driven to succeed. Hormones drive him to be the best at work, to drive aggressively, to build the best building, or write the finest musical piece. But his most pressing drive is to be a successful lover. **Making his wife feel glorious when he touches her is the ultimate test of his manhood—the very measure of the man.** He cannot view life differently; that is the way God made him. He needs a wife, a help meet, a helper who will meet the need God put in him. **If a wife does not meet his intimacy and sexual needs, she is a <u>help-not-meet</u>, a helper** *not suitable* **to the task for which God created her.**

Great Sin

No woman really loves her husband if she does not seek to please him in this most important area. If you are not interested in sex, then at least be interested in him enough to give **him** good sex. If you are not loving your man, you are in danger of blaspheming the word of God—**"to love their husbands."** The Bible says, **"Therefore to him that knoweth to do good, and doeth it not, to him it is sin"** (James 4:17). Hopefully you just didn't realize that your lack of sexual interest in your husband was sin, but now you know.

Your God-Ordained Ministry

Dear Mr. and Mrs. Pearl,

We enjoy your writings and hope you can help us. Our question is what does a Christ-centered, sexually fulfilling, intimate marriage look like? We have an exceptionally wonderful marriage except for our intimacy on the sexual level. My husband feels that

God's ultimate goal: to please your man

a "switch" turned off in me after having the children and that I no longer enjoy relations like I used to. I feel he is correct in his assessment of this. I sometimes feel embarrassed by the whole act and feel that oral sex is wrong, although I used to enjoy it. We have prayed to the Lord for some sort of guidance with this. My husband has turned off his desire for sexual relations, and so we live as best friends who do everything together except make love. Any help or advice you can give us would be greatly appreciated. We both want to get to the bottom of this matter once for all.

Mrs. C

"Nevertheless, <u>to avoid fornication</u>, let every man have his own wife, and let every woman have her own husband. Let the husband <u>render</u> [give] unto the wife <u>due benevolence</u> [sexual gratification you owe her]: and likewise also the wife unto the husband. The wife <u>hath not power</u> of her own body, but the husband: and likewise also the husband hath not power of his own body, but the wife. <u>Defraud ye not</u> one the other, except it be with consent for a time, that ye may give yourselves to fasting and prayer; and come together again, <u>that Satan tempt you not for your incontinency</u>" (I Cor. 7:2-5).

Dear Mrs. C,

You would not be writing unless you are both unhappy with your current relationship. You know it is wrong. When you married you signed over to become a minister to his needs. Your life's work is to minister to your husband. Marriage means becoming one flesh. It does not mean being best friends. In practice, you are not in a marriage relationship with your husband. You and your husband are effectively living in a divorced state, having put each other away. God commands in I Cor. 7:5, **"Defraud ye not one the other, except it be with consent for a time, that ye may give yourselves to fasting and prayer; and come together again, that Satan tempt you not for your incontinency."** God has clearly told us that not having regular sex is giving Satan an opportunity to tempt married couples. Wife, it is your God-ordained ministry to your husband to be his totally enthusiastic sex partner, ready to enjoy him at all times. To do less is a grave error. If you love your husband as God commands, you will always seek to give him pleasure. In so doing, you will fulfill your role as his suitable helper.

> Marriage means becoming one flesh. It does not mean being best friends.

When the angel announced to the 89-year-old Sarah that she and Abraham would copulate and have a child, she responded by laughing and saying, **"After I am waxed old shall I have <u>pleasure</u>, my lord being old also?"** (Gen. 18:12). Pleasure is what Sarah remembered and experienced with her man. She is recorded in Hebrews 11 as one of the pillars of faith.

Sarah's son, Isaac, found comfort for his sorrow after his mother's death through sexual fulfillment with his new wife, Rebekah (Gen. 24:67).

One entire book of the Bible, The Song of Solomon, is dedicated to singing praise to God for the joyful expression of love in the sexual union of a man and his wife. It is so graphic in its description of erotic pleasure that it is embarrassing for some to read or hear it read aloud. My husband wrote a commentary on it called *Holy Sex*.

–Debi

His Arms Are My Arms

Dear Pearls,

I have not felt close to God for a long time. Something was missing. I found myself empty and lonely. I really had no idea what was wrong. I was aimless as a mother, and my discipline of the children was inconsistent and fraught with anger. My household management was wanting. In the past, my husband and I have had a great relationship, but even that was limp. I often cried myself to sleep, not knowing what was wrong.

My husband had been attempting to get intimate with me during "that time of the month," at which time I usually pushed him away. He knew it was "that time" again, but assured me that he wanted to just give me pleasure. Actually, he has attempted to give me pleasurable moments as opposed to "all the way" for years, but I have resisted him. I guess I must think in boxes; it is either all or nothing for me. And so, when I did not think it was "all" a good time, then it was nothing. Last night, after I resisted my husband yet again, my heart cried out to God, and I began to cry and pray. Eventually the sobbing subsided, and I calmed down (my dear husband had sleepily held me and let me cry it out). It was then I felt like God said in that still small voice, "Those arms that hold you so lovingly are MY arms." I felt the warmth and strength of my husband's arms about me. I realized that by pushing my husband away, I have been pushing the Lord away. No

wonder I was lonely! The very one given to be my savior and guide here on earth, I was refusing to receive comfort from.

How eagerly I went to my husband, and how eager I will always remain! Life is an education. Boxes, boundaries, self-imposed rules, they are all the same ink.

Today was like a new day! My children, my house, my chores, I saw everything with different eyes—thankful eyes, a grateful heart, and a soul full of joy and love.

Cheryl

"A wise woman gauges her husband's needs. She seeks to fulfill his desires before even he is aware of them. She never leaves him daydreaming outside the home. She supplies his every desire."

Blaspheming the Written Word of God

Dear Mr. Pearl,

I have a question. Would it be sin to castrate myself? I am a husband and father, and I just cannot satisfy myself with my wife because she does not want sex very often. The Bible says "whosoever looketh on a woman to lust after her hath committed adultery with her already in his heart." Would it not be better in my case to be castrated? I talked with my wife, and she does not care. I am tired of sinning.

Mr. Miller

This is a real letter from a real man named Mr. Miller. We were shocked! What do we tell this man who is willing to lose his manhood to avoid the lust caused by his indifferent wife? The gravity of his wife's sin is staggering. She has NO FEAR of God Almighty. She has blasphemed the Word of God with her selfishness, thinking only of her own needs and not loving her husband. Never, never, never be guilty of such a grave sin. This husband needs to know that God says, **"The wife hath <u>not power</u> of her own body, but the husband…. <u>Defraud ye not</u> one the other…<u>that Satan tempt you not for your incontinency</u>"** (I Corinthians 7:4-5). God grants the marriage partner full access to his spouse's body for sexual gratification. And remember, indifference is unwillingness.

A Matter of Physiology

God made man to need sex. He must be relieved of his built-up sexual desire, even if it means spilling his seed in his sleep. I Corinthians 11:9 states, **"Neither was the man created for the woman; <u>but the woman for the man</u>."** Men are all somewhat different in their sexual needs. If they are sick, tired, stressed, scared, feel rejected, or are even distracted by a big project, their sexual need may be diminished or even put on hold for a week or two. Healthy food makes a positive difference. Vitamins, herbs, and exercise all play a vital part. Men have enhanced sexual drive after excitement or physical exercise. If he is keyed up with success, he may have a stronger than usual need. Even the weather affects a man's drives.

> God created a man with a regular need for a woman, and God commanded a man's wife to see to it that his need is met <u>by her</u>!

A man is negatively affected by a halfhearted response from his wife. The poor guy is never fully relieved and therefore never feels totally satisfied, making him think he is a sexual pervert or something, because he needs sex so often. It is like eating a tiny snack, a little bit here and there, yet never sitting down to eat a big, juicy steak and salad. **A good wife knows that the greater her response, the more pleasurable her man's orgasm can be, and the more complete and long-lasting will be his satisfaction.** When you respond halfheartedly, it says to him, "You only have half of my heart." A halfhearted response from a wife can turn a sweet, teddy-bear of a man into a mean, old dog. It can make a man who is high-strung morph into an emotional jerk at work, home, and even at church.

God created man with a regular need for a woman, and God commanded the man's wife to see to it that his need is met. Do yourself and everyone else a favor, and devote at least 15 minutes every few days to *totally* pleasing your man.

For a wife to defraud her husband of this vital need that God has instilled in him should cause her to tremble in fear of the consequences. And remember, his entire ego is tied up in this sexual experience. **To him it is the ultimate expression of his deepest love for you**, the fullest measure of intimacy with you he can imagine. His entire body, soul, and spirit are caught up into earth's "heavenlies" in this one act of sharing that love with you, the very measure of his person.

Hormones 101

We ladies all have basically the same hormones. Over the last 50-plus years, my hormones have fluctuated some, but I have still been fully a female during all that time. Amazing, isn't it? Through adolescence, marriage, pregnancies, births, periods, menopause, you name it, our hormones were always there, maintaining us as a female. For the most part, all ladies have the same sexual drives.

Do you love your husband the way he needs loving, the way you were created to love him? If you don't score high points here, you are providing an opening for your husband to be tempted by other women. It is a man's duty to walk in truth and have high integrity, but a woman who trusts in a man's ability to endure all things, while providing circumstances that test him to the max, is a fool. **It is *your duty* to fulfill his sexual needs.** His faithful responsibility to you, **and yours to him** are both equally important, and we wives must give an account before God for our faithfulness in this area. **I call it "ministering" to my husband. He says I am a mighty fine minister.**

For a woman, sexual expression starts in her mind and heart. Love is giving up your center, your self-interest. It is choosing another's needs above your own. A woman chooses to be interested or not interested in her husband's needs. So, when a woman's first commitment is to her own needs and feelings, she is necessarily going to view sex as strictly a carnal experience, for then she does indeed have an entirely hedonistic outlook—her self-gratification. But if a woman views sex as a ministry to her husband, then it is a selfless act of benevolence. She need not wait until she is stimulated to desire eroticism; she need only seek to fulfill her husband's needs. I have a tip for you: when you make your husband's needs central, you will get turned on to the experience and enjoy it yourself. That is the way God meant it to be. The principle is universal. Compare our Christian duties. We don't minister to others because we are blessed—we minister to others because we want to bless them. It is completely incidental that the by-product of selflessly blessing others should result in our being blessed also. Eve was created to be Adam's helper. It is not in seeking personal fulfillment that she is fulfilled, rather, it is in doing her duty to bless him, that a blessing is returned upon her.

> When you truly love and reverence your husband, the very thought of him loving the likes of you should thrill your soul and make you long to cause him pleasure.

Hormones respond to stimuli. You remember the story of Ruth. She gave her baby to old Naomi to nurse. It is a fact that an old woman who has not had a baby in twenty or more years can produce milk in her breasts and be able to nurse a baby. It just takes the physical stimulation of the baby attempting to nurse to provoke her glands into producing milk. Even a woman who has never been pregnant can nurse a baby if a baby stimulates her breast by nursing. It might take a few days, or even a few weeks, but if she sticks with the stimulus, it will work.

I will repeat a known medical fact: **Hormones respond to stimuli.** A woman whose heart and mind are focused on pleasing her man has hormones ready to be awakened to answer her husband's desires. Before those hormones kick in and get active, a good woman should respond with great enjoyment toward her husband, simply because she finds joy in _his_ pleasure.

Don't talk to me about menopause; I know all about menopause, and it is a lame excuse. Don't talk to me about how uncomfortable or painful it is for you. Do you think _your_ body is special and has special needs? Do you know who created you, and do you know he is the same God who expects you to freely give sex to your husband? Stop the excuses! Determine to find a way past your "excuses," and provide the pleasure your husband wants only from you. Your Creator knows your heart. **When you truly love and reverence your husband, the very thought of him loving the likes of you should thrill your soul and make you long to give him pleasure. If your heart is right with God, you will focus on his needs and lay aside your own selfish, prudish attitude.** The hormones are there, ready to be unleashed. Go to your husband with the intention of having a good time with him. A sober woman PLANS ahead.

You need to read the book _Holy Sex_ by Michael Pearl. Check it out at www.nogreaterjoy.org.

Awake, My Beloved

Dear Mr. and Mrs. Pearl,

When I picked up your book, Holy Sex, I was afraid to read it. I thought you would tell me that what I was feeling was wrong—but you didn't, and instead you have given me a wonderful gift.

We have been married for twenty-six years, and our love is getting better as we grow older. Sex has always been fulfilling; we each seek to please each other. I have a wonderful partner in bed, and I am blessed!

Enjoying my husband has always been fine with me, but I have experienced a deeper longing and a "hunger" for him. I thought this was wrong. Times when I kissed and touched him from head to toe, for me were feelings of adoration and sometimes worship of him, and I felt it was wrong. I loved him so much, and I desired to pour all of my being into him, but I struggled with whether it was right to do so.

There are times when I am so into him that at the end of our loving, I weep. He has asked me why, and I can't explain, other than, with all that I am, I feel grateful for his love. I feel completely satisfied.

You have helped me accept that our Creator designed us to be spirit, soul, and body, and that "oneness" in flesh can be more than physical; it can have a spiritual and emotional essence that is pure.

It was two this morning when I finished your book. I woke my beloved and shared myself with him without reservation. I wept in his arms afterwards, and all was good. Thank you for your book, Holy Sex.

Brenda

Marriage between a man and woman is a picture of our relationship with Christ. It is a great mystery. The physical union between a man and a woman is so beautiful, so otherworldly, that God uses sexual intercourse to illustrate our relationship with him.

The great mystery includes spiritual closeness, emotional openness, the intensity of feelings, and <u>the act of loving copulation</u>. Marriage in all its completeness is what God chose as an example of Christ and the Church. It wasn't something figured out by Adam and Eve and passed down through the ages to us.

"Marriage is honourable in all, and the bed undefiled" (Hebrews 13:4).

Brenda's great satisfaction did not come because her husband was so spiritual, sensitive, or endowed with some special sexual gift. This couple is experiencing what God intends for all married couples. In husband-and-wife relationships, God always speaks first to the wife, telling her to **submit**, and then to the husband, to **love**. Brenda's relationship with her husband started with her attitude of honor and thanksgiving toward him. You can see where it took her.

"There be three things which are too wonderful for me, yea, four which I know not: The way of an eagle in the air; the way of a serpent upon a rock; the way of a ship in the midst of the sea; <u>and the way of a man with a maid</u>." (Proverbs 30:18-19).

Song of Solomon 3:4
"... I found him whom my soul loveth: I held him, and would not let him go...."

A Great Mystery ♥

A Great Big Thank-You

As I was finishing up this book, I received a large box in the mail. It was full of nice, home-canned apples and pumpkin-bread mix. The office ladies who receive the mail could smell the wonderful aroma through the unopened box! Since I did not recognize the name of the sender, I searched and finally found a letter explaining the wonderful gift. Here is her letter for you to enjoy. We ate apple pie the next day.

Dear Michael and Debi Pearl,

Hello! My husband and I are very thankful to you both. We have just finished watching the videos on marriage (Husbands Love Your Wives, Wives Honor Your Husbands). I found myself apologizing to my husband many times. We watched the wife tape first, and a week later my husband said it was time to watch the husband tape. As he put it in, he jokingly said to me, "I'm a little scared." It was great.

Well, then I read the Holy Sex book and, WOW, thanks a lot! That is when I decided to send you my apple pie in a jar and the pumpkin spice bread, which are two awesome aromas to have baking.

My husband recently commented on how great God is, and he said that a year ago he would have said it was God who was breaking us up (my fault for trying to play his conscience), but NOW it is God bringing us closer together!

I cannot tell you enough how grateful I am. I can see the peace and joy even in our children. I personally think every woman should read the Holy Sex book, and I have already passed it on to several friends, and they and their husbands are also very thankful. I am currently talking to my pastor's wife to see if she would read it.

My friend and I joke that when we are older, she will teach wives how to submit, and I will teach them to belly dance in front of their husbands. Smile! Oh, what a joy life is becoming in our house! I praise God for being so patient with me and for the many blessings we have. It always amazes me how great and vast the Father's love is. Well, enjoy your treats, because we are enjoying ours! Thank you, Thank you, Thank you!

His Help Meet,

Melanie

Exception: Sexual Perversions

Anal sex is a homosexual act, and no normal man or woman desires this. The use of pornography has increased this abomination. It is a filthy practice and medically dangerous. God, the master creator, made a "**natural use**" of the woman for sexual expression. Any man who practices anal sex is automatically suspect for other deviant activity. If your husband has been perverted in this manner, you must respectfully decline to participate. Explain to him why, and then give him a good time in all that is natural.

"For this cause God gave them up unto vile affections: for even their women did change the natural use into that which is against nature: And likewise also the men, leaving the natural use of the woman, burned in their lust one toward another; men with men working that which is unseemly, and receiving in themselves that recompence of their error which was meet. And even as they did not like to retain God in their knowledge, God gave them over to a reprobate mind, to do those things which are not convenient" (Romans 1:26-28).

If your husband ever sexually handles your children, call the authorities. Testify against him in court, and pray that he gets at least twenty years in prison, so that the children will be grown when he gets out. Visit him there, and be an encouragement to him. Get him books and tapes on good Bible teaching, and let him see the children three or four times a year in the prison visiting area. Children heal better from sexual assaults when they know the perpetrators (even their fathers) are punished for it. They're also less likely to follow in his steps.

"It were better for him that a millstone were hanged about his neck, and he be cast into the sea, than that he should offend one of these little ones" (Luke 17:2).

REFLECTING ON
To Love their Husbands

The physical union between a man and a woman is so beautiful, so otherworldly that God uses sexual intercourse to illustrate our relationship with him (Ephesians 5:22-33).

"This is a great mystery: but I speak concerning Christ and the Church" (Ephesians 5:32).

➤ *Traits of a Good Help Meet*
- A good help meet glories in answering her husband's needs.
- She learns to know his needs even before he is aware he has them.
- She empties her mind of the cares of the world so her body can respond to him with eagerness.

➤ *Traits of a Wife Who is in Danger of Blaspheming the Word of God*
- Accuses her husband of lust toward her because he wants sex more than she does.
- Accuses her husband of being insensitive when he needs sex and she doesn't feel the desire.
- Excuses her lack of wanting to satisfy him sexually on the grounds that _____. (You fill in the blank. The "Excuses List" can be very long.)

➤ *Make a new habit*
Make a list of personal plans of how you are going to love your husband. Be sure you come up with lots of bright ideas. I would suggest at least one special

➡️

date a week. Plan on a different addition to your "birthday suit" each week such as: ribbons, bows, furs, jewelry, lace, jeans, scarves, feathers, ragged T-shirt, a chain of wild flowers, or whatever! Just use your imagination.

➢ *Getting Serious with God*

The Song of Solomon is the 22nd book of the Bible. It is a love song/play that was written by Solomon about his wooing and wedding of a shepherd girl. All eight chapters tell the story (in graphic poetic detail) of longing for the lover, finding the lover, and what the lovers did when they were together. Most commentators find a need to turn the passage into a spiritual picture of Christ's love for the Church. I sincerely believe that old Solomon was thinking of the sexual expression of his love for her when he wrote it, and I think the same when I read it. What do you think? As you read "God's" novel about sex, ask yourself if you feel toward your husband the same hunger as the shepherd girl did for her lover. Make a written list of things you are going to do that will start a change in your actions. Your feelings will follow suit.

➢ *Several Good Reasons to be Sexy for Your Man*

- It's fun.
- It's healthy. Studies prove regular sex makes a person healthier.
- It provokes a man to appreciate you.
- It causes him to feel good about himself.
- It mellows a woman out and helps keep her hormones balanced.
- It safeguards your husband from wily, sinful women trying to mar his integrity.
- Children benefit from having a mother and daddy who are terribly in love.
- It is intended by God to be an earthly example of divine worship and intimacy.
- It makes sweet babies.

Chapter 17

3. To Love Their Children

Titus 2:4-5: "That they may teach the young women to be sober, to love their husbands, to <u>love their children</u>...."

Let the Children Lead Them

The most important thing a mother will do for her children is to create an atmosphere of peace and joy by deeply loving their Daddy and being satisfied with life. Several years ago, my husband did a Family Life seminar for homeschooling families at a large, very conservative church. The people were given age-appropriate questionnaires before we got there. Each homeschool child (from every child who could write, up to single adults still living at home) was asked two questions:

1. Is your home happy?
2. What one thing would you like to see changed in your home that would make you a happier person?

We were not expecting profound answers. We thought the children would say that they wanted name-brand clothes, or more freedom, or maybe more access to video games. We hoped we would get a few serious answers, like some kids saying they wanted to spend more time with their parents or they wanted to be trusted. Their responses shocked and saddened us.

Out of about 75 responses, only two or three kids considered their home happy. Nearly all 75 answers of the second question were basically the same. Ten-year-olds (who could barely spell) to single college-age adults had the same hopes and anguishes. They all said something to the effect of, "I wish Mama and Daddy would love each other." The younger kids wrote answers like these: "Our home would be happier if Mama and Daddy would not fight," "I would make my Mama and Daddy like each other," "We would have a happy home if Mama would not talk bad about Daddy" and "I wish Mama would not talk back and make Daddy get mad and yell." The older ones wrote along these lines, "Our house would be a more peaceful place if Mom did not walk around with this frozen bitterness. I feel like we live in a war zone."

How do **you** love **your** children? Let these 75 homeschool kids lead you to this important truth: Love their daddy. Honor their daddy. Obey their daddy. Forgive their daddy.

I Don't Want to Be Like Mama

Dear Pearls,

I would like to share my story with you. It is simple but probably common, and it needs telling. When I was a child, I was always aware that my mom was distrustful of my dad. If one of us children did a bad thing, she was quick to deal with us, "so Daddy will not whip you too hard." If Dad was going out to buy something, she would worry outloud that "he will be foolish in how he spends the money." When he got laid off, I remember her saying over and over, "I guess I need to learn a trade. Someone in this house has to work." I cannot fault her in any area of motherhood. She kept us fed, clothed, and warm. But when I think of my mother, I think of a worried, fretful woman who was always ticked off at Dad. <u>Our home was tense.</u> I have only a few memories of her smiling. I cannot remember a time when she sat in Dad's lap or danced around the room in playful fun. He was not a mean man. I remember hard whippings, but not any harder than the neighbor kids got. I remember him being interested in me. He taught me how to do simple, fun things, but because of her, I always avoided him. All of us kids are grown now.

My brother did great in life. His marriage has been good, and his children seem well adjusted. When he was growing up, he was gone to work with Dad all the time. Us girls never went with Dad, and so we were at home listening to Mom talk about how hard our life was.

All of us girls had terrible youths, and we have all had bad marriage troubles. Our kids have not done well. We don't talk about it much, but we know Mom played a big part in our misery. She still lays all the blame on Dad, although we all know he was just an average guy. **I always knew I did not want to be that kind of wife and mama. I wanted my children to remember me as loving their dad and enjoying life.** I did not care if we lived in the back of an old van and ate junk food, I wanted my children free of tension and the feeling that their dad was a dummy who had to be tolerated. My first marriage ended after a few short months. I determined when I married again that I would do it right. When I got married the second time, I lost my way and didn't even know it. When I realized that we would have  to move because my husband's company was down-sizing, and he was out of work, I packed in bitterness, while silently accusing him of not being a good provider and forcing me out of my lovely home. Then one day I looked up at him and saw the same lost look on his face that I had seen on my dad's face a thousand times when Mom was "taking care of the family." I was just like my mom. Something inside of me broke, and I hated the "wonderful person that I was." It was then I remembered my promise to myself to never be like my condemning mom.

I had bought your The Joy of Training DVDs and marriage tapes months before our move, but had not watched them. I knew the time had come. I settled down in the living room among the boxes, and before long the whole family had joined me. We laughed and laughed at the big old mountain man telling the funny stories.

*We sent the kids to their rooms and finished up the Wives Honor Your Husband tape. My laughter turned to weeping, and my kind husband held me in his arms while I begged for forgiveness. I cannot tell you how changed our family is. My husband is thinking of starting a business. He has wanted to for years, but my fear of failure has held him back. NO MORE. If we end up living in a van, that's OK. I am sad for lost ground with my children. **More than anything, for my daughters, I want to break this ugly chain of bitter, critical womanhood.** I have asked their forgiveness and found they were glad to be over the tension. They know that from now on, they are going to have a mama who thinks Dad is great, even when he is not what I think he should be. He really is a great guy. I am so ashamed when I think of all the earthly hell I have put him through. Our children are going to grow up secure in love, NOT insecure in a spotless house, insurance paid, and name-brand clothes. Life has never been so good. Better late than never. From all of us, a great big thanks,*
  Shelia

Shelia is obeying the words of God; she is loving her children by loving their dad. This next letter is typical of so many women who seek to <u>love self</u> more than loving their husband and children.

Seeking Something Higher Than God

Dear Mr. Pearl,

  I am a busy mother whose children go to a Christian school. I am realizing that without another close female in my life who could share house duties, it is harder on me than it should be. I meet with two prayer groups each week and have them pray for me and my family by name. My biggest need is for help physically in caring for the housework and someone to sit in quiet worship with me. I need at least 4 hours per week of meditation time, self-actualization time. It is 4 AM now and I'm up writing my friends to ask for prayer and see if they know of any gals with five children of their own who might be as stressed as I am. I am frustrated because of my culture and my isolation from regular and close fellowship with wise women. I have a heart desire to change my current lifestyle and to live a rich, full, and meaningful life, and I am motivated so because I want the best for God. I trust you will send me some good advice.

Love in Him,

T.P.

Dear Sister T. P.

Your divine calling is to serve your family. True worship of God is not dependent upon other people or special circumstances, nor does it require a time of meditation. The Spirit of God is present when you wash the dishes or pick up the dirty clothes, and he is there while you prepare meals for your family in the evening. God never intended for you to have intimacy with another woman, whether in worship or otherwise. **Stimulating your own inner feelings in the name of worship is selfish mockery, approaching idolatry.** Your seeking of "self-actualization" in the name of spirituality is a mixture of foolish psychology and emotional insecurity.

> God has honored the mother with the position of being the constant trainer of her young children.

You are part of a trend sweeping through church women's circles—a pursuit of intimacy and deep feelings apart from your husband. **This inner-self-stimulation is what my husband calls "spiritual masturbation". It has nothing to do with the God of the Bible.** It is spirituality more akin to Eastern mystic meditation. When <u>your</u> spirituality competes with your service to others (especially your husband and family), it is just that—"your spirituality." Jesus said to Peter, **"Do you love me"** . . . then **"feed my sheep."** God does not call women to be mountain-top gurus or to seek one out for their personal benefit. He commands them to be **"keepers at home,"** to **"obey their husbands,"** to **"render due benevolence** (give him good sex)," and **"reverence"** him. <u>Remember that the sin of Eve was to seek deeper knowledge and *to be like the gods*.</u> Independent of her husband, she sought to go deeper. <u>Her ambition was personal, spiritual fulfillment,</u> which is the most selfish drive that can possess a person and the easiest to justify, humanly speaking. It is the foundation of all sin and rebellion.

Learn to read the Scriptures just a few minutes here and there throughout the day, and meditate on what you read as you work. Sing unto the Lord. Don't allow the 'lonely women's club' mentality to sweep you away from your role as a wife and mother. Your time at church and prayer meeting is sufficient enough time with other women. Focus your life on your home, husband, and children.

There is a grave danger in becoming emotionally dependent on other women. Too many times I have seen this lead to something abnormal and sick. **Your husband and God should be the ones to whom you turn for emotional support and intimacy.** Women who seek higher spirituality end up feeling and acting spiritually superior to their husbands and others in the church, and it is a death knell to a healthy marriage relationship. Spend that "desired" spiritual time with your husband, where real growth and maturity with God will be found.

Seek to serve your family by tying your little one's shoe strings, reading a book to your toddler, telling a simple Bible story to the whole gang, and making sweet love with your husband. These are the things God counts as important in knowing and loving him.

-Debi

"A wise woman never expects anyone to serve her, and is therefore never disappointed. She is ready to help, always the giver. By her example, her children learn to cheerfully and energetically serve."

Raising Cows or Kids

"Train up a child in the way he should go: and when he is old, he will not depart from it" (Proverbs 22:6).

God has honored mothers with the blessed privilege of being the daily trainer of their young children. He did not place this responsibility in Grandma's hands or with good friends, teachers, or baby-sitters. All of us mothers will stand before God one day and give an account of how we trained our children. To love our children is to devote ourselves fully to their training. If we fail here, we fail as a help meet. Husbands go away to work and leave their young children in our care. They trust us to train them up to be all that they can be. If we fail our children, we fail our husband, and we fail God.

Some of the new commercial translations say, "Discipline up a child in the way he should go...." We will not put that text in bold because it does not deserve status as Scripture. Only someone who knows little about God and the Hebrew language and even less about children would translate what God said in such a way. God said **train up**, not discipline up. The Hebrew word translated "train up" appears only four other times, and each time it is translated "dedicate." *Parents train up their children by* *dedicating themselves, their time, and their children to that which God desires for them to become as an adult.* That is not discipline; it is a commission from God to train them as a full-time occupation. **Training up a child means showing them how to:** make corn tortillas, pedal a tricycle, make up a bed, put toys away, cook for forty people in one hour, read, demonstrate respect for others, and a thousand other wonderful things. For a mother who loves her children, training is not a chore, it is a full-time all-consuming passion. They are worth every minute of time and trouble to every "dedicated" mother.

Little Esther

Little Esther is only five years old. She is quite confident and competent in setting the table or folding the clothes. She knows the difference between the applications of cabbage and lettuce, because when she helps make salads and slaw, her mother discusses the whys and wherefores of all that they are doing. When she is asked to wash the broccoli and cauliflower, she knows both how and why.

> The woman who invests in a child's life will be the one the child loves and with whom the child bonds.

Esther helps fold the clothes and put them away. She knows all her colors, because from the earliest age she has helped separate dirty clothes into different color piles. When Esther takes a book off the shelf, she chooses carefully, because she wants books that have words she can read. She can read many words, not because she has been officially schooled, but because her mother has always taken time to read to her, occasionally stopping to point out words and how to say them. **All this has been fun.** When Esther "starts school," she will already know how to read many words. Therefore, learning will not be a tense, fearful exercise, but only a continuation of her first five years of informal learning. <u>Her mother spends all day stimulating her developing mind with intriguing ideas</u>.

Esther's mom has ten children, yet she is not too busy for Esther or her younger brother. Many little children are not so blessed as Esther. Some mothers treat their children as I treat my cows. I make sure they have good things to eat, clean water, and a place to exercise. If they show any signs of sickness, I attend to them immediately. This is good for cows, but if you raise kids like that, you're going to have a brood of little dummies. Unlike your care of the cows, the training of your children is the deepest expression of your love for them.

Mama, Why Am I So Dumb?

I have been around some real dumb kids. I ask them, "Did you see the eclipse last night?" Stare. "I heard your daddy is designing a new program for the flight school?" Stare. "Did your mom put whole wheat flour in these cookies?" Stare. Mama answers, "She doesn't cook yet, and he doesn't know his daddy works at the flight center. My husband and I enjoyed the eclipse, but it was too cold for the children to come out, besides, they were watching a video."

> In life, there are a few things that must be done right the first time around.

We visited a different family whose father also works at the flight center and spoke to a child who is two, almost three years old. "Donnie, did you see the eclipse last night?" "Yep, and the Milky Way, too. We looked through a 'telyyyscrope!'" "I heard your daddy is designing a new program for the flight school?" "Yep, my daddy is showing them how to build a better airplane 'cause he is smart, and I am smart, and I can make a airplane with my Legos, but it cannot fly because…" "Because, why?" I ask him, fully expecting an intelligent answer. After all, any two-year-old who can make an airplane out of Legos has to be brilliant. He didn't disappoint me. "It hasn't got a motor," he explained.

I decided to check out his knowledge of the kitchen, "Did your mom use whole wheat for these cookies?" Right on cue he responded, "Yep, they are sooooo healthy. Do you want to see my muscles? Mom let me mix up the cookies cause I'm strong."

Knowledge is something given bit by little bit. It sounds almost like computer-age learning: Lots of little bits make a big byte, and away we go to kilobytes and megabytes of information, all stored in little bits! The Scripture says it like this, **"Whom shall he teach knowledge? and whom shall he make to understand doctrine? them that are weaned from the milk, and drawn from the breasts. For precept must be upon precept, precept upon precept: line upon line, line upon line: here a little, and there a little"** (Isaiah 28: 9-10).

Will the REAL Mama Please Stand Up

Just because you happen to be the birth mother of a child does not make you THE mama of that child. If you hurriedly get up in the morning and rush your little one off for someone else to dry his tears, feed him lunch, and read him a book, please do not call yourself his *mama*. That child is being "adopted" out every day, with the added insult of being yanked around from one adopted mama to another. In order to bond properly and grow up emotionally stable, a small child must spend the vast majority of his time with his one true, permanent mama, whom God has ordained to daily pour knowledge and love into that little life.

Daddies are different from mamas in many ways. They provide security that is so vital to a child's emotional health, but no dad can take the place or fill the need that only the feminine personality can supply. A mother's constant presence—the same comforting, nourishing breast, the same room, the same blanket, the same sippie cup, and the same toys—makes a child feel secure. You cannot jerk a child around from one baby-sitter to another and expect him to be secure and well balanced at four years old. But you *can expect* a child raised in that manner to *not cherish* his mother later when he is 8, 10, 15 or 25 years old, just when she begins to need some cherishing herself! If your child is to later cherish you, you must cherish him every day, every hour of his development. There are no neutral moments in a child's life. Every moment is a time of continuous need and development.

For a moment, if we skip forward in the list of commands in Titus 2:5, we read that women are to "**love their children**" and to be "**keepers at home.**" There is a context in which we are to love our children *to the max*, and God says it is when we are **keepers at home**. Consider this your fair warning. You cannot improve upon God's design. In life, there are a few things that must be done right the first time around.

The Hall

There is no permanent cure for genital herpes and many other forms of STDs. Yet one in five young teens in the USA has a sexually transmitted disease. Many statistics also tell us that **one in four little girls will be sexually "messed with" by the time they are four years old.** One in five little boys will be victims of homosexual abuse. Our children are in grave danger in today's world, not only from emotional trauma, but also from many of these diseases.

How many times will your little toddler wander down the hall (while you sit in a roomful of friends engrossed in a video) before some young "trustworthy" teenage boy slips silently in behind him or her and maneuvers her into the bathroom for a four-minute "session"? When the four minutes are up, your little child will emerge forever broken and diseased. You cannot pray and expect God for supernatural intervention and protection. God has already provided for her through you. You can and must pray and ask God to make you a more attentive and sober parent, that you might better protect your children. **You are your babies' keeper. Please, keep them well.**

The book *To Train Up a Child* by Michael and Debi Pearl is a must-read for every mama who loves her kids and wants them to be happy, obedient, hardworking, and smart. Check it out at the _nogreaterjoy.org_ website.

Reflecting on
To Love their
Children

The woman who invests herself in a child's life will be the one whom the child loves <u>and</u> the one with whom he will bond when he is older.

> **"I have no greater joy than to hear that my children walk in truth"** (III John 1:4).

➤ *Make a new habit*

Look into your child's eyes and smile *many times* each day. Take a five-minute break every thirty minutes or so to just play with him or her. Never work alone; always have your "little buddy" helping you.

God has given your children guardian angels who watch them from heaven. You are their guardian angel here on earth.

➢ *Traits of a Good Help Meet*

- A good help meet soberly considers the needs of her children before her own interests.
- She invests time in training them to know and do many things.
- She schools herself in diet and medicine to be better equipped to keep them safe.

➢ *Getting Serious with God*

God directs us to train our children and, when necessary, to direct their path with correction. As women, we might feel we love our children too much to spank them. Our sentiment is silly and unloving. You cannot expect God's personal blessings on your life and on theirs unless you do it God's way. Study these verses and ask God to give you a heart of love and a backbone of courage to walk by his principles.

> **"He that spareth his rod hateth his son: but he that loveth him chasteneth him betimes"** (Proverbs 13:24).

> **"Foolishness is bound in the heart of a child; but the rod of correction shall drive it far from him"** (Proverbs 22:15).

> **"The rod and reproof give wisdom: but a child left to himself bringeth <u>his mother to shame</u>"** (Proverbs 29:15).

Chapter 18

4. To Be Discreet

Titus 2:4-5: "That they may teach the young women to be sober, to love their husbands, to love their children, <u>To be discreet</u>...."

To be discreet: Prudent; wise in avoiding error and in selecting the best means to accomplish a purpose; circumspect; courteous, polite, honest dealings.

We learned the practical side of marriage when we studied the word *sober,* the sexual side when we studied to *love our husband,* and that our job is to be instant in season and out of season when we learned how to *love our children.* The next word on God's list is **discreet**. One usually thinks of discretion as the ability to avoid saying or doing that which is inappropriate—to know when and how to conduct oneself so as not to offend. If this is all that is intended by the text, then a person intending to commit fraud would always attempt to do so discreetly, but much more is obviously contained in this word. The Greek word that is translated **discreet** is also translated, in the Authorized Version, *"taste"* several times. In other instances, it is translated *"behavior"* and *"judgment."* **Discretion, therefore is, having good tastes...good judgment...useful...to be of good understanding.** God says that a woman who lacks discretion is like a jewel in a pig's nose. She is ridiculous, out of place, embarrassing, a joke. Something otherwise lovely is rendered ridiculous in the context of <u>in</u>discretion. She might be pretty, a real jewel of a beauty, but if the jewel is in the nose of a pig, what good is it? **"As a jewel of gold in a swine's snout, so is a fair woman which is without discretion"** (Proverbs 11:22).

As I studied the word *discreet*, I realized how easy it is for us women to miss having the character trait of discretion, and I marveled that so many of us so often have been guilty of its lack in our character. Think about it. Let's carefully examine discretion in all its many aspects.

SEEK TO BE COURTEOUS *(Consideration of others)*

Prisoners Speak

If you read the life stories of prisoners who have been rehabilitated, you will notice one thing they all have in common. It doesn't matter if the man is God-fearing or not, they all write that the day they learned to be considerate of others was the first day they stopped being the kind of man that put them behind bars. Rehabilitated men write of learning to be considerate of other men's right to walk unharmed down the street, the right of the lady to live without fear, the old man's right to drive slowly through town without being reviled or teased, and the right of the young child to grow up unmolested. Consideration is just another way of saying, *"Do unto others as you would have others do unto you."* A child learns how to be considerate by watching his parents being considerate—the same way they learn how to be "good" hypocrites. If a parent exhibits a great deal of politeness toward a guest while he is present, but speaks ill of him when he is gone, this teaches the child to be dishonest and hypocritical. Being polite and being considerate are not necessarily the same—or even related. **Politeness is just performing in a culturally acceptable way. The motivation to be polite can be quite selfish.**

When you deal with insurance companies, when you return purchased goods, when you borrow or lend things, and even when you are reacting to other motorists, you must remember to consider the other person's welfare; you need to be mindful of the other person's perspective and weaknesses.

The Old Red Truck

The following two verses are examples of how the word *discreet* is used in God's word.

"*Now therefore let Pharaoh look out a man <u>discreet and wise</u>, and set him over the land of Egypt*" (Genesis 41:33).

"*And Pharaoh said unto Joseph, Forasmuch as God hath shewed thee all this, there is <u>none so discreet and wise as thou art</u>*" (Genesis 41:39).

Almost 20 years ago, my husband decided we would leave our lifetime home in Memphis and move to the country 170 miles away. At our new home, many of our neighbors were Amish or Mennonite-born. It did not take us long to realize that discretion was a character trait highly valued among these plain people. Our Amish neighbors never used anyone unfairly and would never cheat or steal. **"Let no man seek his own, but every man another's wealth"** (I Corinthians 10:24).

> A discreet person is one who handles another person's resources with grave carefulness and honesty.

We had an old red pickup truck that was pretty much a piece of junk, but it still ran. One of the young Amish men, who did not have a vehicle, needed to use a truck for a brief hauling project, and we told him he could use the old red truck. For years the very rusty floor was about to fall through. When he returned the truck, we were stunned, for the floor was fixed, and we noticed it seemed to run smoother than it had before he borrowed it. And, shock of all shocks, the boy had filled the tank with gas! We figured the gas that was in it now would outlast the old truck. We have had a lot of people borrow a lot of things over the years, but we never had anyone treat our old truck better than they would have treated their own. After that, we were ready to loan him anything we had. Like Joseph of old, this young man showed himself to be discreet and wise. He was careful, considerate, and watchful of our property.

When you are discreet, wise, and kind in your dealings with other people, you will reap the benefits throughout life. If you treat someone shabbily or unfairly, even when you have a good excuse, it will never be forgotten. Others will whisper your unjust deeds, adding their knowledge of your lack of honest dealings with them. Such a reputation is impossible to live down. An indiscreet person has to move often, leaving his tarnished reputation far behind. Honesty, kindness, integrity, and discretion pay dividends many times over.

Be kind in your dealings with others

SEEK TO BE HONEST *(Discretion is Good Judgment)*

The Fancy Pig

A person without discretion is without honor. Remember the jewel in the pig's nose? **"As a jewel of gold in a swine's snout, so is a fair woman which is <u>without discretion</u>"** (Proverbs 11:22). If a woman uses her friends by asking unnecessary favors or by borrowing and not returning, she is showing a lack of basic courtesy, which is an important element of discretion. When a woman manipulates people or situations, leaving others feeling used, all the while smiling in triumph at getting her way, she is the one actually losing.

Women who want the best food, clothes, chair, jewelry, car, etc., are fodder for Satan. **"...envy slayeth the silly one"** (Job 5:2). (Silly one: rude, simple, contemptuous of character.) Silly women are so easy to deceive into believing a lie. Satan will provide ample opportunities for her to use people. He wants to make fools of us all, but the woman without discretion is easy prey, making it easy for him to lead her astray.

The woman without discretion will go to the local eatery and get ten packets of sugar while sweetening her coffee, and use only one, taking the others home. She will use other's resources and think she is "cool" for pulling it off and then will brag to her "friends." Those who hear her might laugh, and she interprets it as admiration, but they go away knowing that there is something disgusting about their "friend." She is not considerate, courteous, or thoughtful. She uses others with no thought to the hurt it might cause. You can see why God calls her a jewel on the end of a pig's nose.

Men are aware that women are sometimes spiritually acute and sensitive, so unless the woman has proven otherwise, men tend to hold them in a kind of reverence. They like to believe their women are good, wholesome, and clean and that their consciences are pure. Many a fight has occurred over a woman's honor. Down at the prison where my husband goes each week to preach, all the men hold their mamas in high esteem, but few care about their daddies. If a man of integrity has the misfortune of having a wife who has a suggestion of dishonesty about her, that man will be ashamed, but it will be a silent shame, and it will eat away at him, at his soul and at his honor. **"...even the ornament of a meek and quiet spirit, which is in the sight of God of great price....Finally, be ye all of one mind, having compassion one of another, love as brethren, be pitiful, be courteous"** (I Peter 3:4,8).

SEEK TO BE GRACIOUS *(Discretion is good taste)*

The Stove

Dear Mrs. Pearl,

I know that joy comes from complete submission to God and to my husband. Does that mean I should not be frustrated and just plain tired? I have a question. Should one be quiet when you know your husband is making a poor decision? Doesn't being a helper mean that I need to help him make better decisions?

Last week my husband went to buy a new stove that we badly needed. He picked out a top-of-the-line stove and was willing to spend too much money in order to have the best. He called and asked me to go look at it and let him know what I thought. I shared my deep concern that it was simply too expensive. We do have the money, but I saw no need to buy the best, when the next scale down would do just as well. He called and told me he had canceled the order and bought the one I recommended. We both felt better with what I picked out. Should I have kept my mouth shut? I didn't tell him NOT to get it. I just thought it unwise to spend money unnecessarily. Do wives have to submit in everything? For example, what color to paint the walls or what kind of furniture to have? Are we to be just mindless robots?

He sent my two oldest children to public school against my better judgment, and I can now see some negative effects. I guess I have to live with that. I think I save him, myself, and my careless youngest daughter from many skirmishes. I really want to do the right thing. I battle this all the time.

I want genuine joy, but it is just not there.

Ruth

Dear Sister Ruth,

You wrote about a stove, but the thing that caused you to write to me was your lack of joy. The uneasy void you feel is your conscience testifying to you of your blame in many matters of life. You want to change, to be the kind of person who doesn't try to control, who is at peace and can let go of issues like this. But, there is

Value what he values ❤

another part of you that wants to hold on and justify the very actions that bring you such misery of conscience.

Your husband's choice of stoves is a statement that he is trying to express his great appreciation of you and to please and delight you. Your countermanding his choice, even if it were a better choice, speaks to him about how little you value him, more than it does about how you value the dollar. In effect, your actions said that, like so many times before, he was not even capable of making a choice as simple as purchasing a stove. Your history of "cautious leading" says to me that you see yourself as a wise woman, but you view him and your "careless" daughter as lacking good common sense. You feel your husband lacks discretion in spending money, raising children, and in many other areas, but it is not your husband's lack of discretion that troubles your conscience. It is yours.

Your lack of joy tells the true state of your soul. You don't like yourself, yet you don't know why. Most women could tell their husband which stove they wanted or what color paint they preferred, even debate with him over it, and it would never be an issue. It is an issue with you because it is not just a stove, it is the fact that you view your husband as inept. He knows this is how you feel. This is why life is a constant struggle, why you are unhappy, why your daughter is "careless," and why (just a guess) you do not have a good sex life. It is all tied together. Regardless of the issue at hand, your actions seem to say that you think of yourself as being somewhat wiser and him more of a fool. Your conscience speaks louder than the worldview you have adopted—louder than your logic, louder than your "wisdom" in "saving" the family from foolishness. **Your conscience, at least, is telling the truth, which is why you wrote to me.**

> You have forgotten the pleasure of having a man do something special for you.

You have forgotten the pleasure of having a man do something special for you. You have left off the important things in life. **"A gracious woman retaineth honour"** (Proverbs 11:16).

If you had been wise, gracious, and loving when your husband called to inform you of the stove he had in mind to buy, you would have laughed and been delighted with your husband's choice of stove. **If you had viewed the extra expense as one would a gift of flowers—a wonderfully beautiful waste of money, and an extravagant gesture of devoted husbandly love—yours especially, but his life also, would have been richer and fuller for it.** After all, it was just money, and you said yourself you had the means to afford the one he chose. He would have been so delighted that you were pleased with what he had picked out for you. Something that simple could have changed your relationship into something wonderful. Every time you stood at the stove cooking, it would have reminded you of your husband's love. And, whenever he saw you cooking on it, just imagine the deep satisfaction that he would always feel for having expressed himself so lavishly towards you. But now, every time you cook on the stove *you* picked out, you will feel your own wisdom and economy; he will remember your rejection and his foolishness, and the food will never taste as good. The stove that you must use will always be a constant reminder of what a fool your husband is.

Do you remember earlier in this book the girl who pulled her husband's arm from around her shoulders because he messed up her hair? In effect, that is what you did with the rejection of his choice of a stove. It is no wonder that you are frustrated and "just plain tired." I'm plain tired from thinking of the damage that you have done and what you have been missing. Your husband is probably tired, too...tired of this marriage.

You think in terms of this stove or that stove, this choice or that, whether you have to be silent or say your piece. **The real issue is your heart's perspective.** If your attitude were right in all the little areas, you could safely discuss with him about "which stove," and no one would feel rejected. It is just that issues like the stove become the point at which you recognize the problem that exists in your mind and heart about your relationship with your husband. It will not be enough for you to just force yourself into silence and start surrendering your will. It is time for you to start practicing reverence toward your husband. Go back and read the story found earlier in the book about the girl named Sunny, and ask God to do a work in your heart as he did in hers. I know you are seeking God. As you seek to do it God's way, he will help you establish a heavenly marriage. Read again the story of Jezebel found in the first section, and make a list of responses in your life that you are going to change. Read the section on joy and learn to practice joy and thanksgiving. Then, read the section on loving your man and **perhaps you both can cook up something really nice, without a stove of any kind.** *-Debi*

THE SKINNY SWINE

Lack of Judgment

> **"Every wise woman buildeth her house: but the foolish plucketh it down with her hands"** (Proverbs 14:1).

"A wise woman doesn't attempt to instruct her husband through feigned questions. Her questions will be sincere inquiries concerning his will."

The skinny woman who inspired this next list of questions doubtless saw herself as a kind person, wonderful mother, and first-rate wife, yet she was tearing down her house one question at a time.

Twelve Questions a Wife Can Ask That Will Tear Down Her House

1. **Do you feel comfortable spending that much money buying that _____?**
   He begins to doubt his ability to make wise decisions.

2. **Are you sure God wants you to work at that job and be away from us all the time?**
   He wonders about his reasons for working there, even though it is a good job. He remembers he has had opportunity to witness. Yet? He grows unsure of his own leading.

3. **Honey, I need to ask you something very important that really tears me up inside. Doesn't this activity you are engaging in grieve your spirit?**
   The Spirit of God had been prompting him concerning this, but he was trying not to hear; he almost brought the subject up himself last evening, but now she is disappointed with him. He suspects he is not spiritual, but somehow the whole thing makes him angry. He feels pushed. Now he resists her just to maintain control.

4. **Why don't you ever want to go with me to _____?**
   He doesn't feel comfortable around those people; they seem so artificial, and their kids are whiny. The man talks in a quiet, humble way, which grates on his nerves; it just seems so "put on," but his wife doesn't see it that way. He guesses he must be carnal. Somehow, he just doesn't care anymore.

5. **Before we were married, you read your Bible or at least you said you did. Why don't you ever read and teach me and the children?**
   He has a vague memory of enjoying reading and relating to how scared Moses was of the job God gave him, but somewhere he just lost interest. He supposes he is backslidden—at least his wife seems to think so.

6. **Why don't you spend more time with our sons?**
   The thrill of having boys has faded. The few times he has disciplined them, his wife later talked with him for being harsh. Maybe he was. He likes being with the men better; anyway, they are mama's boys. Not that they are sissies, they just have this close, talky, relationship with mama. He feels separated from them. He's just not that type. He can see the accusation in the boys' eyes; it is reflected from their mother's eyes. He sees the same questioning looks, which provokes in him the same feelings of condemnation he gets from being around her. He thinks, "I am a real loser. I wonder if I'm even saved."

Don't steal his confidence by being wiser

7. Do you ever think of just loving me in the spiritual way instead of always the carnal? I am so hungry for some deep spiritual understanding and communication.

Something deep inside him is so dissatisfied, so frustrated that she responds intimately only when she feels right about it. It speaks nothing of his manhood. His soul is sick all the way to its core. He falls asleep fantasizing about the woman he met in the store today. God, help his filthy soul.

8. Sweetheart, why won't you have devotions with us? We want you to lead us in prayer and help us grow spiritually. The Bible says you are our spiritual leader; why, why will you not lead?

He laughs inside himself, "Are you kidding? I can't do that. I would feel like a total hypocrite. I can't teach them about something I don't know. I'm out of here." He leaves, or works, or watches TV all the same; it is his escape.

9. Why do you think the pastor said that about Charles? Don't you think it was cruel? Sometimes I wonder if we should go to church somewhere else.

Angry bile seethes in him as he listens to her tell the story for the fourth time. He silently contemplates, "The pastor's a hypocrite. He's not any better than anyone else. I don't know what makes him think he's so righteous."

10. Poor Charles, it is so sad to see what the preacher's mean words have done to that family. Don't you think we should do something about it, like call and let them know we love them and don't agree with the pastor? Besides, I am so hurt at the pastor myself.

Frustrated at his own failures, and being full of bitterness for others has run its course and is now bearing fruit as he silently surmises, "All those self-righteous people make me sick. I don't care what they do, but they will not do it to me."

11. Honey, it's church time. You need to get dressed. What! You're not going? But you always go to church. Do you think you should let a silly thing like that business with Charles keep you from worship? Besides, you know, the pastor was right, that Charles was up to no good all along! You have to go to church. What about the boys? You'll be a bad influence on them. Don't you care?

12. Jane, I want you to know that without your close, loving friendship, which I turn to every day, I would never be able to get through this loveless marriage. He is so cold and distant. He doesn't care about the children. I don't know how I could have been so deceived into thinking he was a fine, Christian man when I married him. Will you ask the girls to pray for him this week at our women's meeting?

REFLECTING ON
❧ Discreet ❧

"But the fruit of the Spirit is love, joy, peace, longsuffering, gentleness, goodness, faith, Meekness, temperance: against such there is no law" (Galatians 5:22-23).

Temperance is a fruit of the Spirit.

➢ *Traits of a Good Help Meet*

- A good help meet grows in grace and knowledge.
- She is gracious and honest.
- She is without guile toward her husband.

➢ *Getting Serious with God*

Do not be deceived. If you regularly use people as baby-sitters, visit around too often, ask for rides here and there, or frequently borrow other people's things, they might tolerate your selfishness, but they will never really like you. You will be secretly spoken of as a nuisance instead of a friend. **No one ever really likes a user. A wise woman always gives more than she takes.**

$\longrightarrow$

➢ *Words God uses to describe a Godly Woman*

Locate in a concordance every time the following words are used. Mark the words that describe you. Beside the words where you know you are lacking, put an X. Write out beside each word what you are going to start doing that will bring you closer to becoming what God desires.

- Chaste
- Sober
- Modest
- Shamefacedness
- Meek

- Quiet spirit
- In subjection
- Obedient
- Kind
- Virtuous

- Prudent
- Good
- Discreet
- Keeper at home
- Gracious

"A wise woman knows how her words can color her husband's perspective. She can subtly move him to the negative or the positive."

Chapter 19

5. Chaste

Titus 2:4-5: "That they may teach the young women to be sober, to love their husbands, to love their children, To be discreet, <u>chaste</u>...."

We aged women are to teach the young women to be **chaste:** *pure* in thought, word, and act, <u>and</u> to be modest and honorable in all things.

"Likewise, ye wives, be in subjection to your own husbands; that, if any obey not the word, they also may without the word be won by the conversation of the wives; While they behold your <u>chaste conversation</u> coupled with fear. Whose adorning let it <u>not be that outward adorning</u> of plaiting the hair, and of wearing of gold, or of putting on of apparel; But let it be the hidden man of the heart, in that which is not corruptible, even <u>the ornament of a meek and quiet spirit, which is in the sight of God of great price</u>. For after this manner in the old time the holy women also, who trusted in God, adorned themselves, being in subjection unto their own husbands: Even as Sara obeyed Abraham, calling him lord: whose daughters ye are, as long as ye do well, and are not afraid with any amazement" (I Peter 3:1-6).

The English word *chaste* is found three times in the Holy Bible (KJV). The Greek word translated *chaste* is also translated *pure* in four verses, and once it is translated *clear*. Read Philippians 4:8 and James 3:17 to get a more complete definition.

Looking for a Hidden Treasure

Dear Mr. Pearl,

I am a 24-year-old male and looking for a wife. It is not as easy as it seems to find a decent girl. **I want one who not only says she is decent, but LOOKS as though she is.** *A friend of mine married one of the girls of the church. She wasn't the most chaste dresser, but he was sure that once they were married she would sober up.* **She says she does not feel convicted about how she dresses, and he can only push so far to change her.** *I avoid him since he married, because I got aroused the whole time I was around them due to the way his wife dresses.* **It leaves me disgusted,** *frustrated and angry that a stupid, silly girl can cause so much trouble. Sometimes I feel my own body betrays me, but I know I am a normal male with a normal need, and the problem lies with females dressing so godless. Talk about dishonoring a man, all the rest of the younger females in church dress as bad or worse. I had rather not get married than end up with a silly wife like her. Seeing Jacob embarrassed by his wife scares the rest of us unmarried men, because, as much as we want to get married, we sure do not want to end up being dishonored as he has been. I want a girl who has not encouraged a thousand other guys to commit sight adultery with her by how she dresses.* **I want a woman I can be proud to call MY OWN little hidden treasure.** *How could a man ever trust a woman who, before she got married, "let it all hang out" for everyone to see? I guess the big question for me is, how do we single men find chaste girls to marry, girls who are not interested in how sexy they can dress?*

James G.

Dear James,

The Bible asks, "**Who can find a virtuous woman?**" The question implies, *"Not an easy find."* It will be worth the search to find a chaste, virtuous girl. Until then, here is your letter advertising your concerns. I pray that the married ladies and

♥ Who can find a Virtuous Woman? ♥

mamas raising girls who read your letter will know and care how you godly men are thinking. I wish I had room to print 25 more letters like this, but one will have to do.

She who has ears. . .LET her hear!
-Debi

Modesty

A chaste woman is a modest woman. God speaks of a woman maintaining her chastity and purity by the clothes she wears. **"In like manner also, that women adorn themselves in <u>modest apparel</u>, with <u>shamefacedness</u> and <u>sobriety</u>; not with broided hair, or gold, or pearls, or costly array; But (which becometh women <u>professing godliness</u>) with good works"** (I Timothy 2: 9-10). God says that a woman's apparel should profess godliness. Her clothes, hair, and adornments—not just her mouth—make a loud profession to all who see her that she is modest and godly, <u>or</u> that she is immodest and ungodly. Our Heavenly Father has dress standards! Would you employ the standard argument and dismiss God as "legalistic" when he tells us that *there is a proper way to dress* **and** *there is an improper way?* Clothes speak to all who see us. Clothes make a constant profession. That is, they declare out loud—drowning out our words—our true heart condition and our attitude toward ourselves and toward those who see us. When I want to tease or entice my husband, a slight change in my clothes, hair, or demeanor is all that it takes to arouse him. Men are very much different from women. Jesus warned men, not women, when he said, **"Whosoever looketh on a woman to lust after her hath committed adultery with her already in his heart"** (Matt. 5:28). Then God tells a man what to do about it if he cannot keep from looking and lusting. **"And if thy right eye offend thee, pluck it out, and cast it from thee: for it is profitable for thee that one of thy members should perish, and not that thy whole body should be cast into hell"** (Matt. 5:29). This is very serious business!

It is impossible for a woman to understand a man's visual drive. She can only believe what an honest and candid man tells her, but few men are willing to admit to their weakness. A woman's body, moving within visual range of a man, unless it is modestly covered in a way that says to the man that you have no interest in him taking pleasure in your appearance, can be as stimulating to him as disrobing completely. He may be a better man than the woman who is dressing immodestly and may have the fortitude to deny his eyes the stimulation you offer, but it makes you a source of temptation to sin, rather than someone to whom he can relate.

> Our Heavenly Father has dress standards!

If you find pleasure in being a source of temptation to men, you are definitely an ungodly woman and are in desperate need of repentance.

Jesus said that a lusting man commits adultery WITH a woman, not against her, meaning that the woman is included in the lusting adultery. Women have told me that they are "not convicted" about the way they dress, as if God has to chase them down and torment them about it before they will obey his Word. Many are offended when their "style of dressing" is called into question. They say they are not going to be legalistic about it, even when God has clearly stated his will. The Holy Spirit convicts according to the will of God. If you are not convicted by the Holy Spirit for your immodest dress, then you are not being led by God. **"For as many as are led by the Spirit of God, they are the sons of God"** (Romans 8:14). If you are God's child in more than just name, you *will* be led by the Spirit of God. If God is not leading you consistent with his Word, then you must face the fearful truth that you do not have that Spirit indwelling you. **"Now if any man have not the Spirit of Christ, he is none of his"** (Romans 8:9).

God gave us ladies bodies that men desire as much as they desire life itself. It is a precious gift that keeps us "pretty" and desirable to that husband, that man of our youth who loves us, long after our youth is gone and our skin looks like alligator boots. We have a power that could cause many men to sell their souls and blindly run down the path to hell. Or, we can use that power to soothe, heal, minister, and act out the intimacy that exists between Christ and his bride. As my husband said in his book, *Holy Sex*, "The devil didn't invent erotic pleasure, God did." But God also placed boundaries upon the exercise of sexuality. All of life is living within boundaries. The world sometimes provides boundaries that prevent us from acting the fool or from suffering in our pursuit of pleasure, but it never provides boundaries that are as strict or as reasonable as God's. This aged woman is telling you ladies that *it is the will of God for you* to always be modest in public. It is your profession of godliness.

What About Pants?

We cannot leave this subject without dealing with an issue that comes up over and over again. Is it permissible for a woman to wear pants? Deuteronomy 22:5 is cited as a prohibition against a woman wearing pants: **"The woman shall not wear that which pertaineth unto a man, neither shall man put on a woman's garment: for all that do so are abomination unto the LORD thy God."** To

God expects us to be modest

cite this verse as prohibition against women wearing pants, one must assume several doubtful concepts. Do pants pertain to men? What verse? According to the Bible, the common garment for a man is a **skirt** or **cloak**. Seventeen times the Bible speaks of men wearing skirts, such men as Boaz, King Saul, and Aaron. One time, the Bible speaks of a woman's skirt, and another time it speaks of God's skirt. So, even God wears a skirt, as did the Scottish men and the Roman and Greek men of old. American Indian men wore mini skirts. During Bible times, as far as secular history reveals, the only people who ever wore pants were Eastern women.

We want the Bible to be strictly our guide, but there is always a danger of reading something into it to suit our personal sense of propriety. Anyone with an open mind knows that the passage is speaking against transvestitism—cross-dressing so as to appear as the opposite sex. The manner of dress would differ from one culture to another and from one era to another. Men and women are not to pervert and besmear the Creator's designation of their sexuality, which essentially challenges God's "and it was very good" declaration of the distinctiveness of his crowning "male and female" creation. **It is disturbing to see women blurring gender distinction in the way they dress, and it is absolutely disgusting to see a man dress effeminately. Males and females dressing out of their gender is clearly troubling to God,** which is why he addressed the subject in his Word. It is an abomination to him, an affront to his sovereignty in the creation of mankind. Keep that in mind as you choose your wardrobe. **Modesty is the principal rule of female dress.** If you want to get provocative, do so in private with your husband. In fact, I recommend it, but when you come out of the bedroom and go to church or to the local store, dress as you would dress for the Judgment Seat of Christ.

> *Dear Pearls,*
>
> *I am sick of looking at fat. Females dressing with short tops and low-riding pants or skirts with a roll of fat around the middle remind me of 'pop and serve' biscuits that busted open. Gross. I'm a pig farmer, and when I see these "biscuit" females, it makes me see what the Scriptures mean about pigs with jewels in their noses. They are just about as desirable as one of my sows! Ugh! It is not so much the fat as it is the way they sport it around—like it's hot stuff. I am profoundly thankful my wife dresses like a lady, a virtuous lady. Everytime I go to town, I come back home so glad to have a good woman who knows how to dress like one. If you print*

my letter, be sure to include my name because I want to go on record as a grateful husband.

Jonathan Beachy

Bad Bob

In the following story, the characters, Bob and Lydia, are composites drawn from counseling sessions of two different couples. We have heard the same basic story many times over while ministering to countless married people.

Bob had an upset stomach and was not hungry, so his family dropped him off at the motel where they would be staying, and then they went to get something to eat. His dad never let them watch the motel TV, but Bob knew they would be gone for at least an hour, and he was bored. The first scene that he saw held him riveted. The music was sensual. Bob stared, trapped in his own shocked silence. There before him in slow motion was a woman walking up steps. All he could see was the woman's butt encased in a short leather skirt with a slit up the backside. The camera slowly shifted down her long slender thighs until he could see the backless high heels. Then it traveled slowly up her long legs focusing on the open slit as she climbed. He watched as she reached the top of the stairs and stepped into a room; still the camera stayed on her legs. Bob's heart pounded in anticipation. The soft music began to swell as the camera climbed. A sound on the outside of the motel door jerked Bob back to the present. He hit the off button with such force as to crack the remote and then flung it across the room as if it were a poisonous spider. False alarm, no one was there, but after only two minutes of a mere introduction to soft porn, Bob would never be the same. That day was the first day that Bob masturbated. He was 13 years old.

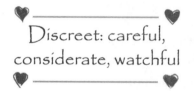

Discreet: careful, considerate, watchful

Two years later, Bob was sitting in church when Lydia, the youth director's wife, stood up directly in front of him to take her youngest child to the bathroom. His mouth got terribly dry as he stared at her round butt encased in a tight leather skirt with a slit up the back. It is true that Lydia's skirt was several inches longer than the one that was now part of his daydreams, but when Lydia bent over to pick up the child, several of the young men sitting behind her slowly covered their laps with their songbooks. **Bob almost hated Lydia after that day.** She was responsible for his torment and

Chaste = Modesty

temptation. The force of those few seconds of soft porn 2 years earlier, along with the stretched material pulled dangerously high as Lydia leaned over, caused him to empty his semen into his pants, right there in church, resulting in a large wet spot. He found a use for his Bible that day after church. It covered his shame as he rushed out to the van to take the back seat. A week later Bob dropped out of the youth group. His sudden departure puzzled and saddened the earnest youth director. He went to Bob to ask him if there was anything Bob wanted to talk about. Bitter bile filled Bob's mouth at the memory of the youth director's wife slowly walking up the church steps with her tight skirt and high-heeled shoes, just like the woman on the TV. Lydia, with her sanctimonious smile, did not deceive him; how could she be so dumb as to not know exactly what she was doing to him? No, he had nothing to talk about, he told Lydia's stupid husband.

Chaste: pure in thought, word and act; modest, honorable

Lydia never knew she had shamed her husband, hurt his ministry, and caused a young man to smolder with bitter hatred and almost falter on the edge of quitting the faith. She would not have believed me (or perhaps she would have been secretly pleased at what she thought was her beauty) if I had pulled her aside and explained how the young men at church were reacting to her and why several treated her with such disdain. She would have explained to me that her style was just "her style," and *they* needed to get a grip. I know this because I have talked to many Lydias.

Bob had not looked at porn since that first night, but his mind was in a constant struggle, and his battle with masturbation was never-ending. Opened or low-cut shirts were a misery to him. Bare midriffs were bad too, but a girl who had long slender thighs coming to the meetings in mid-length shorts or skirts made him miserable beyond belief.

When Bob was 22 years old, he met a sweet, little peach of a girl with soft, warm eyes and a good, clean heart. They married, and Bob was relieved that his miseries were finally over. For the first three years she was sexually exciting, and he was able to fully enjoy what before had shamed and frustrated him in his youth. He now knew blessed relief from his old enemy, lust, which was finally brought under control in his pure marriage relationship.

Life never seems to roll out easy, and after Bob's wife had her second child, she stopped being so responsive to Bob in the bedroom. **Her excuses were exhaustion, sickness, didn't want to get pregnant, didn't feel like it, it hurt because**

God expects you to protect your brother ♥

"something seems wrong inside me now," etc. She knew she had to give him sex once a week, but she came to him half-heartedly, which caused him to never really get total satisfaction. The women at work always dressed sexy and had tried to provoke Bob, but he saw them as a bunch of diseased animals, so although they provoked him, he resented it.

Church was different. Church ladies seemed clean and wholesome. At 25 years old, Bob was in his prime, and he needed his woman. God had designed his body with a sensitive trigger that needed release at least 2 or 3 times a week. He had developed certain habits in order to avoid unexpected temptations. His wife had no idea why he had such strange habits, like picking the spot where they would sit in the church, but she just sat where he led her. Lydia was not a problem anymore. Thankfully, the few years that had passed had played havoc on her beautiful butt and thighs. Bob smiled and said "hi" when he saw her walk by. She still tried to put on that stupid "what did I do" look, like she really didn't know why he had always disliked her. It was true, he still did not like her and found a certain sense of gratification at the demise of her beauty. Seeing her made Bob remember when her husband, the youth director, was teaching a small group of the young married men, explaining to them that all women go through times of total disinterest in sex, including his own wife, and how important it was to be vigilant against lust during those times. He had felt sorry for him at the time, but now Bob's own little honey had turned off her water spigot of sweet loving.

"Vigilant, I must be vigilant." Bob was scanning the church building looking for a safe place to sit when he felt his wife pulling on his arm. "I want to sit over behind the Chandler family." Bob's alarm went off. Three tall, long-legged, beautiful teenage girls, who liked tighter, shorter skirts, were members of the Chandler family. He groaned with irritation. His wife caught the groan and took offense. He wished he could explain all this complicated mess to his wife, but she would only get jealous and spend the rest of his life watching where and who he was looking at. He looked down at her, whom he loved with all his heart and wished she were a little more sober-minded and not so quick to get hurt feelings. **He wished she loved him the way he needed to be loved, he wished she would be his *help meet* when he needed her most. He wished she had enough wisdom to be discreet and discerning and would look out for him at times like this.** He wished she would just obey him, not because she understood, but because she cared for him enough to obey. He wished she knew how much he needed her and how in a way, she held the power of heaven or hell for him in her hands. He allowed her to lead him into the row of temptation. If anyone could see his mind while he sat behind the Chandler girls, they would have had him arrested. He knew he was Bad Bob, full of lust, anger, frustration, and defeat. Somehow he always thought bitterly of Lydia when he was feeling defeated: "What a fat cow, no, not a cow, she's a pig."

Bob, Frank, Tom, and Your Pastor

Bad Bob is the story of a thousand Bobs and Franks and Toms. If you think that Bob is some kind of freak or deviant, you don't know men. Listening to these struggling men pour out their stories and their bitterness is a counselor's job. It is our duty to "help" them overcome. Over the years, my husband and I have wished we could tell all the young women who, by their immodest dress and unladylike behavior, cause the lust of countless men to explode into participation in visual adultery. Bad Bob is intended to inform you and warn you of your complicity. Bad Bob is the regular guy at your church. He is your preacher and your daughter's Sunday School teacher. He sits behind you in church, or, just maybe, he is the one who avoids sitting behind you and your daughters.

I Am My Brother's Keeper

Because Bathsheba was indiscreet, she caused great calamity, resulting in the bloodshed and suffering of many. **Her lack of discretion** cost her husband his life, his comrades-in-arms their lives, her baby son his life, and the integrity of one whom God upheld as a man after his own heart. By simply doing what she thought she had a right to do, she was complicit in bringing ruin on an entire family line, including rape, incest, rebellion, and murder. David should have been with his men, but he was not out looking for a woman. She provided the opportunity for him to lust by her lack of discretion in where she chose to bathe. Her beautiful body won out in a contest between his flesh and his love for God. Generations have associated the name of Bathsheba with a wicked woman, yet she was the wife of a fine military man. All she lacked was modesty and discretion. Too often in life, many tragedies would never have taken place, if only....

Your life is not your own. You are bought with a price, the blood of our Lord Jesus Christ. We will all stand before God for acts of the flesh, even the ones we are responsible for in a careless way. Remember the warning in Matthew 5:28: the woman is part of the adultery when she puts herself into a place that causes a man to lust after her.

REFLECTING ON
Chaste

> ### The appearance of a Good Help Meet

Think with me one moment about the last time you went to church. In your mind's eye, scan the room and reflect on how the women, including yourself, were dressed. Now read what God says:

> **"In like manner also, that women adorn themselves in <u>modest apparel</u>, with <u>shamefacedness</u> and <u>sobriety</u>; <u>not with broided hair, or gold, or pearls, or costly array</u>; But (which becometh women professing godliness) with good works. Let the woman learn in silence with all subjection. But I suffer not a woman to teach, nor to usurp authority over the man, but to be in silence. For Adam was first formed, then Eve. And Adam was not deceived, but the woman being deceived was in the transgression. \<A Promise\> Notwithstanding she shall be saved in childbearing, if they continue in faith and charity and holiness with sobriety"** (I Tim 2:9-15).

> ### Getting Serious with God

II Samuel 11 tells the story of how David sinned with Bathsheba. The last verse of that chapter reads, **"But the thing that David had done displeased the LORD."** Read the story found in II Samuel 11 & 12 and David's cry of repentance found in Psalm 51. Let the story of the misery of sin instruct you, change you, and cause you to desire to dress in a way that would never cause a brother in the Lord to lust.

Chapter 20

6. Keepers at Home

Titus 2:4-5: "That they may teach the young women to be sober, to love their husbands, to love their children, To be discreet, chaste, <u>keepers at home</u>...."

Keepers: Being on guard, watching, caretaker.
Home: Seat of domestic life.

The Keeper

According to the words of God, I, one of the aged women, am commanded to teach the young women to be **keepers at home**. This is the sixth of eight mandates for young women. *It is not a suggestion; it is God's will for wives.*

You will remember that I wrote earlier about how I asked God to teach me why he used the word *blaspheme* to describe the consequences of young women not obeying God in these eight areas. This is how God taught me this lesson.

The morning after I prayed and asked God to give me wisdom concerning the word *blaspheme*, I walked into my office and started wading through my e-mail. I came to one written by a young man whom I know quite well, having spent a lot of time with his wife. Tears streamed down my face as I read the tragic words written by a young man who had been sacrificing to take the gospel to people on a foreign field. He told how their little baby girl, not yet one year old, had been molested, most likely by someone with a terrible disease. It was as though God spoke to me and said, "Is the word *blaspheme* too strong?" Then I could see so clearly why God chose the word *blaspheme* for all eight things listed. For a mother to leave her command post, even though the need at another post seems greater, the Word of God will be blasphemed.

This young couple's tragedy could easily have been my own. I remember when my oldest daughter was about two years old, I found a baby-sitter so I could more easily do my shopping (lack of sobriety). I remember so clearly, even though it was over 28

> ♥———————♥
> A home is not
> a home unless
> the lady is there
> making it a home.
> ♥———————♥

years ago, walking into that home and putting my daughter down, then looking up into the eyes of an old man, who was the baby-sitter's husband. Something in my spirit stirred fear, and I picked my daughter back up and walked out. I wonder if I had left her there that day when she was two years old: would she have had the moral courage when she was 22 years old to live alone on a mountain top in Papua New Guinea, translating for a primitive tribe (read *Rebekah's Diary* found at <u>nogreaterjoy.org</u>). Eternity will tell. This missionary couple didn't drop their child off so they could go shopping or go to a movie. They left their baby behind for less than ten minutes when the wife was needed to help with "ministry." The Word of God is the same yesterday, and today, and forever, and speaks the same truth for all families today. **A young mother's place is in the home, keeping it, guarding it, watching over those entrusted to her.** To do otherwise will surely cause the Word of God to be blasphemed. Even if you could disobey God and it not produce visible ill consequences, it would prove only that God is long-suffering as he was with Israel, but the judgment will assuredly come. The Word of God speaks to what is true and right. If you ignore what God says by ignoring the words of God written in Scripture, you are blaspheming, speaking evil of his words.

Whom Do I Obey?

What if your husband tells you to go to work and leave your children at day care or with a baby-sitter, in conflict with God's command for you to be a keeper at home? It is God's will for a woman to love and obey her husband, and it is God's will for her to be a keeper at home. Whom do you obey? This is where firm conviction of faith in God becomes vital. God can make a way for you to obey both. **The important thing is attitude**. If you have a heart of surrender to your husband's will and a heart to obey God, it becomes God's responsibility to resolve the conflict. We are going to talk about

Not being a keeper at home is blaspheming God's word

how to present an appeal later, but for the moment, understand that if you are willing to obey in all areas and you do not build a spirit of rebellion toward your husband or God, your appeal is more likely to fall on sympathetic ears.

Commit your way to God, and tell your husband that you will do as he says. Then express your concern for the children, showing to him the Scripture that constitutes your dilemma. Tell him that you want to help with the finances and you also want to protect and train up the children. Ask him how you can do both. Your attitude must be trusting, not accusatory or judgmental. There can be no hint of an ultimatum or a pending rebellion. **Trust is the key word. Depend on your husband's wisdom and guidance.** Ask him if there is a way you can stay at home while you and the children engage in some work that will bring in an income. Ask him if there is a way you can cut back on expenses so the family can get by on his salary alone. Ask for a trial period. Show him how you can save on unnecessary expenses. Shop at secondhand stores. Move to a less expensive house, if necessary. Have one less automobile. Don't buy new furniture. When the refrigerator quits, buy a used one out of the local paper. Don't go on expensive vacations. Use your vacation time for the whole family to paint the house instead of hiring someone to do it. Ask an older friend to help you see where you waste money.

It was as though God spoke to me and said, "Is the word 'blaspheme' too strong?"

Most men would allow their wives to stay at home if the wife could show that it was her heartfelt, Spirit-led desire to be obedient to God in the matter of child training **and if she could learn to be more frugal and content.** Pray, and ask God to change your husband's heart <u>and</u> your financial situation. Be prepared for an extreme change in your lifestyle. God will rescue a trusting heart.

Leaving Home by Phone, E-mail, and Chat Rooms

"I will therefore that the younger women marry, bear children, guide the house, give none occasion to the adversary to speak reproachfully" (I Timothy 5:14).

God's will for a young woman, according to the verse above, is that she **guide the house** and provide **no occasion** to bring reproach upon the family from Satan. In the previous verse, the apostle Paul tells what the young women were doing that enabled

Satan to bring reproach upon the family. **"…they learn to be idle, wandering about from house to house; and not only idle, but tattlers also and busybodies, speaking things which they ought not."**

The sum of their sin was being **idle** instead of being industrious, visiting from **house to house** (phone to phone), **tattlers** (just talking about people) and repeating everything they heard, and giving their "righteous" opinions about everyone's business. The Scripture tells young women to be keepers at home because of their natural tendency to loaf around doing nothing except seeking entertainment.

Modern inventions have provided a way for a woman to stay at home and still **not be a keeper at home**. We can sit at home in body while traveling in spirit by means of the telephone and the computer. You cannot keep *your* home and everybody else's at the same time. More churches and individuals have been destroyed over the knitting table, the telephone, and now the computer, than by any other means. **"A virtuous woman is a crown to her husband: but she that maketh ashamed is as rottenness in his bones"** (Proverbs 12:4).

> The sum of their sin was being idle, visiting from house to house (phone to phone), tattlers (just talking about people), and telling things they should not.

"Keeping the home" is more than staying at home; it is having a heart that is fixed on the home. A help meet will be engaged in creative enterprises that challenge and inspire the children. She will guard the home against outside influences, and she will always be on watch to protect the children from their own inventions of evil. *She will not be idle and neither will her children.* She will ease her husband's load by painting the hall and cutting the grass. She will be frugal in all her endeavors, and she will teach the children to love serving Daddy. She will keep the home so that when Daddy comes home, it is to a sanctuary of peace, love, and order.

A real help meet will make herself useful to her man instead of wasting her time. ☺

It was God's command, not his suggestion

Reflecting on Keepers at Home

➤ *Traits of a Good Help Meet*

- A good help meet can be found *at home*.
- She takes her responsibilities seriously.
- She maintains safety for her children in the refuge where God has put her.
- A help meet fears blaspheming God's Word. She knows that whatsoever you sow, you will reap.
- A good help meet is at home being an earthbound guardian angel to her children.
- A good help meet makes valuable use of her time at home, creating a clean and pleasant haven.

Look up the word blaspheme. It appears 10 times in God's Word. It is a fearful thing to blaspheme! Look up these verses, and ask God to teach you to fear being guilty of blaspheming his Word by not obeying the eight mandates given to young women in Titus 2.

➤ *Hospitality*

Hospitality is one way that a keeper at home can minister to others. Four times in his Word, God admonishes us to use hospitality in service to others. Look up those four verses, and seek ways to show hospitality to others.

"Use hospitality one to another without grudging" (I Peter 4:9).

Chapter 21

7. Good

Titus 2:4, 5:"That they may teach the
young women to be sober, to love their husbands,
to love their children, To be discreet, chaste,
keepers at home, <u>good</u>...."

A **good** woman is genuine, joyful, <u>virtuous</u>, valuable, competent,
ready, kind, benevolent, merciful, hardworking, agreeable,
pleasant, congenial, honorable, faithful, gracious, and wise.

Good is as Good Does

James Hamilton described goodness like this, "Goodness is love in action,
love with its hand to the plow, love with the burden on its back. Goodness is love
carrying medicine to the sick, food for the famished. Goodness is love reading the Bible
to the blind and explaining the gospel to the felon in his cell. Goodness is love to the
Sunday School Class, or in the school, or on the away-from-home mission assignment—
whenever and whatever, still the same love, following His footsteps who went about
(continually) doing good." Hamilton's words are formed around the admonition found
in Titus 3:14: **"And let ours also learn to maintain good works for necessary**
uses, that they be not unfruitful." A person is what he does.

The Crown

"A virtuous woman is a crown to her husband: but she that maketh ashamed is as rottenness in his bones" (Proverbs 12:4).

A good woman is a crown to her husband. She can make a mediocre man be as honored as one wearing a crown.

➤ A good woman might be married to a man who is lazy or just does not make much money. Yet, because she is a wise shopper and does not waste her time or their money foolishly by eating out or indulging in expensive entertainment, and because she is a keeper at home, she makes his "little money" go a long way. As a result, he appears wiser and wealthier than he really is and is looked upon with honor because of it.

➤ A good woman may be married to a man who is not an attentive father or a patient child trainer. Yet the good wife never shows dishonor to him, and she trains the children to be obedient and resourceful. When people see their children, they assume that the father must be a good man to have such fine children.

➤ A good woman could be married to a man who is a poor example of a father and husband. He may be selfish and self-centered, possibly not even honest, yet because she is submissive and honoring towards him, he treats her with kindness. People look at their relationship and think he must be a good man since he has a good woman and because they seem to be happy together.

By now you are likely saying, "Why should she carry the load and make a lazy, impatient, selfish man look good?" Why should she not? **By being a crown to her husband, she is raising children who will rise up and call her blessed.** By the time they are teens, they will know their dad is something much less than he should be, but they will honor him because of the example of their mother. **By being a crown to her husband, she is winning his love and appreciation**, thus she gets treated much better than if she stood against him. And, **by being a prudent woman** in how she uses the meager funds given to her, **she is gaining a comfortable place to raise her family.** In the final analysis, **she is doing exactly what God says will cause her husband to come to God.** And most of all, she is bringing honor to God by fulfilling her calling as a help meet. In the end, people who know her will know the truth.

The Ball-and-Chain Woman

"…But she that maketh ashamed is as rottenness in his bones" (Prov. 12:4).

➢ **A ball-and-chain woman** is one who spends her husband's modest wages, five dollars here and ten dollars there, on things of **no permanence**. At the end of the day, she is "too tired to cook" or "there is nothing in the house to eat," so she wants to eat out. There just never seems to be enough money to get ahead. He appears to be a poor man, and she makes him feel the lack of every penny. He gets discouraged easily, because no matter how much he makes, it never seems to stretch far enough. When it appears that they might be getting ahead a little, a vacation or new furniture that she buys eats up their reserve. Others often look upon him as a loser. Rather than being a crown to him, she brings him shame and is as rottenness to his bones.

➢ **A ball-and-chain woman** can also be married to a man who is an attentive father and a patient child trainer. Yet, because **she wants to run around during the day** while he is working, his children are left behind with baby-sitters. God's Word is blasphemed because she, not being a keeper at home, allows bad seed to be sown in her children, which will reap a bitter harvest for them both. When the children "go bad," people will say, "Well, *he* sure didn't do something right." This wife will also bring shame and great sadness on her husband. Ball-and-chain…ball-and-chain…ball-and-chain…dragging him back every good step he takes forward.

➢ **Some ball-and-chain women** are married to honest men of high integrity, yet because their wives use other people's time or resources in an irresponsible manner, neither of them are highly regarded. The man is judged by his wife's actions, yet a woman is seldom looked down upon because of her husband's actions. He knows something is wrong, and he spends his life repairing broken images and relationships and never moves forward. He loves her, yet she is as rottenness in his bones.

Although a **good woman** can lift up a poor husband, a good man cannot make up for the deficits of a poor wife and create a family with a good reputation. A man married to such a wife usually becomes a lifetime loser, no matter how hard he tries to win. At first he has hope, but over time, deep down in his bones, he feels the rottenness, and despair consumes all his hopes.

♥ A Good Woman is a helper ♥

Ridin'-the-Line Lady

➢ "I admit that I buy prepared foods that are expensive and not healthful for us, but at least we don't eat out all the time."

➢ "I don't run around leaving our children at sitters, but I do sit them down in front of a video now and then while I read a romance novel instead of investing that time teaching them how to cook or make doll clothes." **"…A child left to himself bringeth his mother to shame"** (Proverbs 29:15).

➢ "I would not dare be dishonest, and I think it is wrong for people to accuse me of wasting my time gabbing on the phone or sitting in front of the computer."

A Good Woman is Prudent

God tells us in Proverbs 19:14, **"… and a prudent wife is from the LORD."**

Dear Mrs. Pearl,

I am so tired and discouraged. I feel as though my husband just doesn't love me or care for his family as he should. The house is falling apart. The yard is full of trash. The last straw is that the sink is leaking so badly that the floor under the sink always stays wet. He is quick to help anyone who calls for help, but to get anything done around here is impossible. Last night we had a big fight because of the screen door. It has a big hole in it that I asked him to fix months ago, and it is still not fixed. Then some old lady called and needed her car started, and he up and left to help <u>her</u>. What is wrong with him? Why can't he see his family should be first? What should I do?

Vicky

Dear Vicky,
Before I answer your question I want you to take the following test.

A Standard Dumb-Cluck Test

♦ Does natural healing not grab your attention?

♦ Have you neglected to check out what vaccinations might do to your child's health?

♦ Have you considered what store-bought, prepared cereal has in it?

♦ Do finances and business matters confuse or bore you?

♦ Are you satisfied with knowing who's who in Hollywood but really don't care a fig's worth who is deciding the fate of your children's future in world events?

♦ Do you love fiction romances but find books that will teach you practical knowledge a drag?

♦ Have you ever checked the oil in your car?

♦ Can you use a hammer, saw, tape measure, and screwdriver?

Well, are you a dumb-cluck? You might be asking what that has to do with your "lazy" husband. More than you think!

Vicky, you asked me, "What should I do?" You should get off your easy chair and learn to do a thing or two. **Any good woman should be able to fix a screen door.** Plumbing is not so hard, either. I have fixed several broken pipes in the dead of winter and replaced at least two toilets. There are some good books at the library that you will find helpful for those things. If a man can do it, why can't a woman? It doesn't take great strength. You are the keeper of the home, are you not? The yard is certainly not his job. Get off the couch, go outside with the children, and start cleaning the yard. You will be shocked at how much good training the children will acquire, and he will appreciate you when you show some initiative.

Furthermore, you are missing many great opportunities to teach the children some practical skills, as well as to provide them with character-building experiences. Do the home projects one at a time, discussing each step with the children. Let them do what they are capable of. Have fun doing it!

A man works all day long and comes home to a messy yard, dirty house, leaky faucet, and a lazy, complaining wife. He sees so much that needs to be done and just feels overwhelmed that he is apparently carrying the whole load himself. He feels as though he became a slave when he married. He doesn't have a help meet pulling her share of the load; he has a cranky, demanding leech sucking him dry. So, when a call comes from the little old lady in distress, of course he will drop everything and run. She will smile sweetly at him and tell him how much she appreciates him. When

♥ You were created to be his helper ♥

he gets her car running again, it will be a job finished, and he will feel good about himself. If he stayed at home and fixed the screen, the faucet would still be leaking, and you would still be unhappy.

He was not created to be your servant. You were created to be his helper, so get to it. Learn to make yourself useful. I have found that when there is a job too big for me, if I at least start it, my husband will see that I am in over my head and will step in and finish the job. Then I can brag on how smart he is, and he doesn't even realize that I just manipulated him. (I am sacrificing a lot to put this in print.) *-Debi*

> In the end, it is a woman's work that speaks of her worth.

A Good Woman is Crowned With Knowledge

A good woman has a lot to offer the marriage. A man is wiser and more successful in his endeavors because his wife has a great deal of informational resources and a lot of hard work to add to the mix. God tells us that a prudent wife is from Him.

"The simple inherit folly: but the <u>prudent are crowned with knowledge</u>" (Proverbs 14:18). Prudence is growing in knowledge. It is making the effort to learn something new and using that information or skill, whether you enjoy the new skill or not.

God describes the prudent when he writes to us in Proverbs 18:15, **"The heart of the prudent getteth knowledge; and the ear of the wise seeketh knowledge."**

"The wise in heart shall be called prudent: and the sweetness of the lips increaseth learning" (Proverbs 16:21). I love that phrase, "The wise in heart." We have already studied wisdom, and we know that wisdom starts with fearing God in regard to the consequences of our actions. Fear causes us to pay attention to what God says, knowing that he is quite serious in his blessings and his cursings.

God is pleased with our learning. He calls it being prudent. Learning how to cook healthy, low-cost meals is a prudent thing and would certainly qualify us as a *good woman*. For us to learn how to bring natural healing to our children instead of taking them to the doctor (which would mean high medical bills and unnecessary risks, as well) would be a prudent thing to learn and would also make us a good woman.

A Good Woman Is *a Prudent Woman.*

Consider this:

- ♦ A prudent wife is not dumb.
- ♦ A prudent wife is not lazy.
- ♦ A prudent wife does not waste her time.
- ♦ A prudent wife is a learner.

Men value hardworking women who are eager to learn how to do new things. No man wants to be saddled with a slow, incompetent wife. I have often heard my sons and their friends talking about what they wanted in a wife. They all agreed that they did not want to marry "a high-maintenance chick." No young man wants to marry "a lazy, visiting, 'gotta eat out' gal."

All men agree on this one point: **A good woman is a helper, not a hindrance.** A help meet works, learns, and helps with the daily tasks of life. When a man gets home from work, there should be an obvious, visible, tangible difference in his house, his children, his food, and even his income, which she has helped generate. He knows his lady makes things happen, gets things done, and is not just a sweep-the-floor and wash-the-dishes gal. She is a true entrepreneur, an initiator.

Perhaps you have heard a man say on occasion about some other man's wife, "He's got a good woman." If you ask that man to define the woman he referred to as *good,* he would be describing a Proverbs 31 woman. It is a general blueprint of how a woman seeking to honor God should fashion her life. It is the kind of woman a man most admires.

A Good Woman *is Virtuous*

Proverbs 31 is a record of a king reflecting back on some important things that his mother had taught him. He called this wisdom, **"the prophecy that his mother taught him."** His mother admonished him to refrain from certain lewd women. She warned him of the evil of the use of alcohol and how it would pervert a king's judgment. She encouraged him to speak for the man who cannot speak for himself, and to plead the case of the poor and needy. Then, his mother expressed her concerns that he find a good woman for a wife. She started by telling him that a virtuous woman is rare and precious. And, so he would know what to look for, she described at length how a really good woman spends her time and what she gets accomplished. It was as if she were telling her son, who would soon be king, "You will know her, son, by what she DOES." You may have already guessed—the King was Solomon of Israel.

A Good Woman is a Doing Woman

All the key words in Proverbs 31 are **action** words. She is a creative merchant. She is a worker. Almost every verse describes daily chores or a new enterprising task she is involved in. No one, not even her enemy, would call this woman lazy or slothful. She is diligent in her work, both when it is convenient and when she does not feel like working. In the end, it is this woman's work that speaks of her worth.

How does God rate one wife *good* and the next wife bad? The opposite of diligence is slothfulness, and **"He also that is slothful in his work is brother to him that is a great waster"** (Proverbs 18:9). A great waster is a loser. A slothful woman is wasteful by not taking care of things in a timely manner, therefore causing her goods to be damaged. A slothful woman wastes her time and often the time of her friends. A lazy woman puts off a job, saying it can be done tomorrow. God chose to add to his written Word the description of a virtuous woman so we would clearly know one when we meet her. The portrait painted here of this good woman, whom God says is worth much more than priceless jewels, far above the value of the average wife, is that of a diligent **worker.**

A virtuous woman is busy doing constructive activities. She explores business opportunities. She is saving money, making money, and investing money. I came to greatly admire this woman as I studied through her day-to-day activities. I stopped and asked myself over and over, "What could I start doing that would make me more of an active help meet for my husband?"

A Good Woman is Not a Fool

As you read this, don't decide to get on the web and order $100,000 worth of stock, all in the name of being a good woman. You would be portraying a fool instead of a wise, virtuous wife. Don't think you have to go out and buy $40 worth of cloth to learn to sew or $170 worth of health-care products to sell part-time. Be wise, prudent, and first consider your husband's desires, your options, and your gifts. Remember our letter from Vicky? She could have been cleaning up her yard, fixing the screen door, and tightening up her leaking pipes. It would not have cost anything but her labor. I suggest we all start "being good" with things that are less glamorous and more practical.

Traits of a Good Woman

(Proverbs 31:10-31)

Vs. 10—A good woman as described here is very valuable. There are not many like her.

"Who can find a virtuous woman? for her price is far above rubies."

Key words: *far above*

Rare, uncommon, unusually excellent, unique, precious, matchless.

Vs. 11—A good woman is honorable, faithful, and chaste. She doesn't do anything or say anything behind her husband's back.

"The heart of her husband doth safely trust in her, so that he shall have no need of spoil."

Key words: *safely trust*

Trustworthy, dependable, inspires confidence, reliable, honest, deserving.

Vs. 12—A good woman is trustworthy, genuine, and wise. She does not explode one day and apologize the next. She is good to him every day.

"She will do him good and not evil all the days of her life."

Key words: *will do*

Constant in her love, unshaken, unmoved, faithful, ceaseless, enduring, unchanging, loyal, permanent.

Vs. 13—A good woman is a willing, eager, hardworker. She LOOKS for tasks that will be an asset to her family.

"She seeketh wool and flax, and worketh willingly with her hands."

Key words: *seeketh, worketh willingly*

Industrious, hardworking, busy, diligent, patient.

Vs. 14—A good woman is prudent. She is a capable, wise shopper.

"She is like the merchants' ships; she bringeth her food from afar."

Key words: *is like, bringeth*

Frugal, not wasteful, using economy and good management.

Vs. 15—A good woman gets up early and serves others.

"She riseth also, while it is yet night, and giveth meat to her household, and a portion to her maidens."

Key words: *riseth, giveth*
Self-starter, energetic.

Vs. 16—A good woman is enterprising. She buys property, plants a cash crop, and multiplies her investments. She is not afraid of getting her hands dirty.
"She considereth a field and buyeth it: with the fruit of her hands she planteth a vineyard."
Key words: *considereth, buyeth, and planteth*
Enterprising, daring, yet cautious, resourceful.

Vs. 17—A good woman does physical labor and thus is strong.
"She girdeth her loins with strength, and strengtheneth her arms."
Key words: *girdeth, strengtheneth*
Physically strong, hard worker.

Vs. 18—A good woman is competent; she takes stock of her work and is satisfied that she has done things right. She is dependable.
"She perceiveth that her merchandise is good: her candle goeth not out by night."
Key word: *perceiveth*
Willing to work long hours.

Vs. 19—A good woman is willing to do repetitive, boring work.
"She layeth her hands to the spindle, and her hands hold the distaff."
Key words: *layeth, hold*
Willing to do monotonous work.

Vs. 20—A good woman is benevolent; she gives to those in need.
"She stretcheth out her hand to the poor; yea, she reacheth forth her hands to the needy."
Key words: *stretcheth, reacheth*
Compassionate, merciful, generous, easily moved by the distresses and sufferings of others.

Vs. 21—A good woman is confident of how she has provided for her household. It is well-outfitted due to her management and hard work. She doesn't wait until the last minute to prepare dinner. A good woman plans and prepares ahead.

"She is not afraid of the snow for her household: for all her household are clothed with scarlet."

Key words: *not afraid*

She made preparation for the future.

Vs. 22—A good woman is a craftsman. She is a skilled worker who creates beautiful wall and bed coverings for her house, as well as beautiful clothes for herself.

"She maketh herself coverings of tapestry; her clothing is silk and purple."

Key word: *maketh*

Has mastered skills of crafts and sewing, makes dresses with beauty.

Vs. 23—The good woman's husband has the time and honor to be a ruler. She brings honor to her husband by the way she keeps his domain.

"Her husband is known in the gates, when he sitteth among the elders of the land."

Key words: *is known, sitteth*

Her support helped bring him to this place.

Vs. 24—A good woman is a merchant. She makes, sells, and delivers quality goods.

"She maketh fine linen, and selleth it; and delivereth girdles unto the merchants."

Key words: *maketh, selleth, delivereth*

Organizes, manages, does not pass the work off on others.

Vs. 25—A good woman is known for her honor and strength of character. Her hard work and good attitude will pay high dividends.

"Strength and honour are her clothing; and she shall rejoice in time to come."

Key words: *shall rejoice*

Not swayed or upset by circumstances, steadfast, valiant.

Vs. 26—A good woman studies and shares her wisdom and knowledge in order to help others. She uses her information in an agreeable and pleasant manner.

"She openeth her mouth with wisdom; and in her tongue is the law of

A good woman is not lazy

kindness."
Key word: *openeth*
Discerning, thoughtful, gentle.

Vs. 27—A good woman is conscious of responsibilities. She does not waste her time or other people's time.

"She looketh well to the ways of her household, and eateth not the bread of idleness."
Key words: *looketh, eateth not*
Duty-conscious, reliable, not idle.

Vs. 28—You will know a good woman by how much her children and husband appreciate her and truly enjoy her company.

"Her children arise up, and call her blessed; her husband also, and he praiseth her."
Key words: *arise, praiseth*
She reaps her pleasant fruits.

Vs. 29—God describes a virtuous woman as one whose own hard work proves her value. She has won the right to be where she is and to have what she has acquired—honor, appreciation, esteem, and love.

"Many daughters have done virtuously, but thou excellest them all."
Key word: *excellest*
Day in and day out, in season and out, she puts forth her creative labor; for that effort, she was named the most worthy of all.
Virtue means "acting power." It has the strength to affect or improve that which is around you.

Vs. 30—A good woman is not caught up in looking good. She is conscious of the fear of God in her life. She has lived every day as though she believes she will reap what she has sown.

"Favour is deceitful, and beauty is vain: but a woman that feareth the LORD, she shall be praised."
Key word: *feareth*
Fear of God is the beginning of wisdom.

Vs. 31—A good woman reaps what she has sown, and it is good fruit. The enterprises and business ventures she has put her hand to are profitable. The crafts, goods, and clothes she has made are known to be of excellent quality. Her dwelling and her services are well-managed, efficient, and tidy. Her children are honorable and seek God. Her husband has the time and heart to invest in other people's lives because of her being a good help meet. A good woman has lots of good fruit.

"Give her of the fruit of her hands; and let her own works praise her in the gates."

Key words: *give, let*

Praiseworthy, complimented, approved, deserving, admired, applauded, worthy

"A gracious woman retaineth honour" (Proverbs 11:16).

"A wise woman is not pitiful, puny, or whiney. She makes herself confident, capable, useful, and thankful."

God's estimation of a Virtuous Woman?

Virtuous Woman is a Hardworking Lady

Pr. 18:9 **"He also that is slothful in his work is brother to him that is a great waster."**

A Slothful Person is a Waster

REFLECTING ON
Good

"But the fruit of the Spirit is love, joy, peace, longsuffering, gentleness, goodness, faith, Meekness, temperance: against such there is no law" (Galatians 5:22-23).

Goodness is a fruit of the Spirit. Our goodness should first be directed toward our family.

➤ *Traits of a Good Help Meet*

- A help meet **helps**.
- The good lady is a doer. She is busy serving others.
- She serves her husband first, her children second, others next, and herself last.
- She is genuine and well-disposed.

"She looketh well to the ways of her household, and eateth not the bread of idleness" (Prov. 31:27).

➤ *Make a new habit*

Keep on hand informational books on health, gardening, cooking, child training and other teaching aids. For every hour you spend watching a film or reading a novel, spend the same amount of time reading something that will help you grow as a person. You will be amazed at how soon you come to enjoy the "real" stuff over the "make-believe."

$\longrightarrow$

➢ *ABCs of being a Help Meet*

A - Admit when you are wrong

B - Be positive

C - Cuddle

D - Do it his way

E - Encourage him

F - Fix his breakfast

G - Give back rubs

H - Hug often

I - "I love you" should be said many times daily

J - Joke around in a playful manner

K - Know his needs

L - Listen to him

M - Manage your home well

N - Never hold grudges

O - Open your eyes in the morning and smile

P - Pray for him

Q - Quit nagging him

R - Reminisce about good times

S - Show respect and honor

T - Trust, and earn his trust

U - Understand his need for reverence

V - Vulnerability is a feminine trait; cultivate it

W - Wink at him

X - X is for private times

Y - Yearn to please him

Z - Zealously guard him with your love

8. Obedient to Their Own Husbands

Titus 2:4-5: "That they may teach the young women to be sober, to love their husbands, to love their children, To be discreet, chaste, keepers at home, good, <u>obedient to their own husbands</u>...."

Obedient: Yielding, willing and eager to accomplish injunctions or desires, abstaining from that which is forbidden.

By now you should be fully aware of what the text means when it says that aged women should **"teach the young women to be obedient to their own husbands, that the word of God be not blasphemed."** However, a quick review of some of these Scriptures is in order.

"Unto the woman he said, I will greatly <u>multiply</u> thy sorrow and thy <u>conception</u>; in sorrow thou shalt bring forth children; and <u>thy desire shall be to thy husband, and he shall rule over thee</u>" (Genesis 3:16). According to God's very words, apart from any cultural context, it is a woman's nature to place her full attention and interest upon her husband, and she is to be under her husband's rule. That is the will of God, no matter what the women preachers and the modern Greek and Hebrew scholars say to the contrary.

"But I would have you know, that the head of every man is Christ; and the <u>head of the woman is the man</u>; and the head of Christ is God" (I Corinthians 11:3).

There can be no cultural context that nullifies this verse, for it says that the basis of a man's headship is rooted in the very essence of the woman's created nature. Just as God is the head of Christ and Christ is the head of the man, so the man is the head of the woman (his wife). My husband does not lose any dignity by being in subjection to Christ, nor do I lose any dignity by being in subjection to my husband. And, just as my husband finds security and meaning in submission to his head, so I become the person God created me to be in submitting to my head—my husband.

> ♥———————♥
> I do not submit to any other man as I submit to my husband. There is no pastor or minister higher than my husband.
> ♥———————♥

"Wives, <u>submit</u> yourselves unto your <u>own husbands,</u> as unto the Lord. For the <u>husband is the head</u> of the wife, even as Christ is the head of the church: and he is the saviour of the body. Therefore as the church is subject unto Christ, so let the wives be to their own husbands <u>in every thing</u>" (Ephesians 5:22-24).

Here again—a second witness in Scripture—we wives are informed that our submission to our husband should be viewed with the same love and fervency as our submission and love for Christ. The text says that we submit **"as unto the Lord,"** as if we were submitting to the Lord. Since my husband's authority is delegated by God, when I submit to my husband, I am recognizing God's authority, and I am indeed submitting to God.

It also says that our submission is unto our **own** husbands. I do not submit to any other man as I submit to my husband. There is no pastor or minister higher than my husband. My husband is my head, in the same way that Christ is his head.

Many women have written, telling me that their pastor told them to tithe, to go to church, to put their children in the church school, to make their children part of the youth group, or a hundred other things, against the will of their husband. The pastor claims that he is the head of the local church and is, therefore, the highest religious power on earth. My husband's response to a man's claim to ecclesiastical authority over the family is to call him a liar and a deceiver. The Scripture clearly teaches that a woman is to obey her **own** husband.

When our first daughter was just two months away from getting married, she asked her daddy a theological question. Remember now, she was a graduate of Bible college and had spent three years on the foreign field as a missionary. But, rather than answer her, as he had been doing for the previous 26 years, he told her, "I cannot answer your Bible questions, for you now believe what your husband believes. He will be your head, and you will follow him. It is time to get adjusted to your new role. Ask him what he believes about it."

That is what it means when you **"give** your daughter in marriage." It is the passing on of the torch to a new one-flesh family unit.

"Nevertheless let every one of you in particular so love his wife even as himself; and the wife see that she reverence her husband." (Ephesians 5:33).
As wives, we are to reverence our husbands as God's divinely appointed head. In I Peter 3:6, we are told, **"...Sara obeyed Abraham, calling him lord."** If that is a shock to your religious system, take heart, because God thought it might be a shock to us. He went on to tell us wives **"not** [to be] **afraid with any amazement."** Don't be amazed at what God commands, and don't be afraid to submit to your man as God commands.

"Wives, <u>submit yourselves</u> unto your <u>own husbands,</u> as it is fit in the Lord" (Colossians 3:18).
The text says that a woman obeying her husband should do it as it **is becoming, or is fitting, in the Lord**—the fitting thing for a Christian woman to do! Think about it. This is not another culturally unique situation. It is timeless. From God's perspective of marriage here on earth that he instituted, it is the fitting thing to do. It is the way His Son responds to Him.

"Likewise, ye wives, be in <u>subjection to your own husbands</u>; that, if any obey not the word, they also may without the word be won by the conversation of the wives" (I Peter 3:1).
This is the third time that God has emphasized that our subjection to our *own* husband is not rooted in the superiority of the male over the female. God is not setting up one gender to be superior to the other. It is only in the context of a marriage union that a woman is to be in subjection to her man. It is her God-appointed office that renders her second in command in the family.

This passage in I Peter 3:1-6 addresses another issue that comes up regularly. What if my husband is unsaved, and does not recognize Christ as his head? Am I still to obey a man who does not follow Christ? The following letter is typical of many I receive.

How to Win Your Lost Husband

> *Dear Pearls,*
>
> *My husband is lost. He is full of anger. I feel hopeless of ever having a heavenly marriage. Has anyone ever emerged from the gloom and doom I am now in and achieved a heavenly marriage? Does God in his grace and mercy have a plan and promise on how to win my godless husband to saving grace? How long? How long? I want to believe there is hope. I want to trust and obey God, whether my husband ever gets saved or not, but I would love to have a little hope and direction on how I could win my husband to Christ. I have prayed and cried out to God. I have been faithful to Bible study and church. I have given tithes and offerings, and I have seen nothing in the way of repentance from my husband. I do not want to leave him. I want to love him, but it is hard. Is there any hope left?*
>
> *Amy*

God Gives Us Hope and a Plan in I Peter 3

"Likewise, ye wives, be in subjection to your own husbands; that, if any obey not the word, [lost husband] **they also may without the word** [not won with Bible teaching and preaching] **be won by the conversation of the wives; While they behold your chaste conversation coupled with fear. Whose adorning let it not be that outward adorning of plaiting the hair, and of wearing of gold, or of putting on of apparel; But let it be the hidden man of the heart, in that which is not corruptible, even the ornament of a meek and quiet spirit, which is in the sight of God of great price. For after this manner in the old time the holy women also, who trusted in God, adorned themselves, being in subjection unto their own husbands: Even as Sara obeyed Abraham, calling him lord: whose daughters ye are, as long as ye do well, and are not afraid with any amazement"** (I Peter 3:1-6).

In those six verses, God reveals his plan for a wife to win her lost husband to faith in Christ. The following true story, a part of my own experience, illustrates a woman applying this passage and winning her husband by her chaste conversation—without preaching the Bible to him.

My Friend, the Queen

When I was a young wife, my best friend had an unsaved husband. She always reminded me of a queen. She had a certain presence about her, in addition to her beauty, poise, and intelligence. She was a pastor's daughter, raised very religiously and with high standards. But when she was seventeen, she crossed paths with a young man of charm, the first guy to ever show interest in her. She "fell in love" at first sight, and they ran away and married. She soon learned that her husband was hardworking, *when* he worked. But, he had several bad habits which included use of tobacco in various forms, cursing, screaming at her when he was mad, and pornography. By the time I met her, she had come to repentance and was trying to make a go of this unequal marriage. Through God's grace and her growing fear of the Lord, she was able to live out the "love" chapter of I Corinthians 13.

> **"Charity suffereth long, and is kind; charity envieth not; charity vaunteth not itself, is not puffed up, Doth not behave itself unseemly, seeketh not her own, is not easily provoked, thinketh no evil; Rejoiceth not in iniquity, but rejoiceth in the truth; Beareth all things, believeth all things, hopeth all things, endureth all things"** (I Cor. 13:4-7).

It wasn't going to church or having a quiet time with God that won him. She won him by responding to him with honor and affection.

When he was rude or insensitive, she did not get **puffed up** with righteous indignation. When he was mean and cussed at her, she was **kind** and **suffered long**. She **bore** with his sloppiness and **believed** he would bring home the paycheck instead of spending it on the way home. Most of the time, she was able to **endure all things** with cheer and thanksgiving.

When she came to me for advice, I hid my sick feelings and told her what the Bible said, (not what I felt) which was, **"To honor God, you must honor your husband."** Everyday I felt as though I were watching a heavenly battle, and God was winning. Other than his use of pornography, the vice that repelled her the most was his physical uncleanness. He often required "things" of her that were repulsive because he had not bathed. I felt truly ill when I thought of her in this situation. Yet she submitted and responded to him. Of course, she would tell him how happy she would be and how happy he would be, if he would bathe. She believed I Peter 3:1-2,

"Likewise, ye wives, be in subjection to your own husbands; that, <u>if any obey not the word</u>, they also may <u>without the word be won</u> by the conversation of the wives; While they behold your chaste conversation coupled with fear."

It wasn't going to church or having a quiet time with God each day that won him. **She won him by responding to him with honor and affection.** It never occurred to her to shame him or impress him with her "religion," which was real. And she did not honor her husband because she was raised to honor him. It was a day-to-day miracle for her. Witnessing her experience built faith in me like nothing ever had before. I had seen thousands of people saved during the "Jesus movement" of the sixties. I had seen devils cast out, and I had watched people get healed of terrible diseases, but to see an eighteen-year-old pregnant girl walk before God in pure obedience to Him was truly a miracle of miracles.

♥ —————— ♥
Honoring God
gives a woman
power to change
her man.
♥ —————— ♥

Her husband worked all night at a factory. All his fellow workers were drunks and whoremongers. One early morning near closing time, some of the men started complaining about their wives, telling each other how lazy, no account, dishonest, disloyal, cheap, sorry, fat, and ugly their wives were. My friend's husband, Jim, said nothing. Finally, one of the men asked Jim about his wife. It was the first time he had ever really thought about his wife in comparison to the other men's wives, and he was suddenly deeply thankful, "Oh, I am not going to tell you about my wife, because it would make you all mad." The men insisted, so he told them, "She's beautiful, with long, pretty blond hair. She is always so sweet; she will do anything for me. She thinks I am one hot-dog." They all were highly irritated and thought he must be telling a big lie. He told them, "When I go home this morning, she will be prettied-up and cooking my breakfast, and, she will meet me at the door with a very sexy kiss." Since all the men had already given descriptions of their wives sleeping in and never fixing their breakfast, they simply would not believe Jim. After a heated conversation with a great deal of cursing and swearing, Jim boasted, "I bet I could take all you guys home for breakfast and she would cheerfully fix you the best breakfast you ever ate—and all with a smile." "No way," they said. After more bragging, he ended up taking five of them home with him that morning, without calling to warn his wife.

Now, his unsuspecting young wife at home knew nothing of their argumentative conversation and had no idea that her husband's integrity was at stake. The Bible

She won him with honor ♥

says, **"A virtuous woman is a crown to her husband: but she that maketh ashamed is as rottenness in his bones"** (Proverbs 12:4). This young woman was about to become either a crown to her husband or rottenness. Unworthy though he was, he knew her and trusted her. She had earned his trust.

"The heart of her husband doth safely trust in her, so that he shall have no need of spoil" (Proverbs 31:11).

(Trustworthy: dependable, worthy of confidence, reliable, honest, deserving)

"She will do him good and not evil all the days of her life" (Proverbs 31:12). *(Constant in her love, unshaken, unmoved, faithful, ceaseless, enduring, unchanging, loyal, permanent)*

At 6:30 that morning, she met him at the door with a radiant face of love, her hair freshly brushed, and a pretty dress on. But instead of one smelly tobacco-chewing man, there were six—five of them looking rather embarrassed and apprehensive. Although surprised, she responded with delight, "Oh, sweetheart, I see you brought your friends home." In front of these men, this statement in itself was a great victory and an honor to Jim. He ushered his co-workers into his home and in a gruff manner said to his wife, "Fix breakfast for my friends." This was asking a lot, since those men would eat all the food she had bought for the next week's breakfasts. Jim made a poor-man's wage, and he was not careful with his money. What was left was hers to make do. She went into the kitchen and prayed quietly, "Lord, you know I have to feed six men this morning. Please help me." She cooked all the bacon, every egg, fried all the potatoes, and baked a huge pan of biscuits, plus, she made "country milk gravy." Her whole week's worth of breakfast supplies she graciously served on a snowy white tablecloth. The dirty men sat in strained, embarrassed silence as she served them. It was Jim's crowning moment. <u>All the men knew instinctively that nothing between them would ever be the same. Jim's wife *did* treat him with honor.</u> He *was* different from them. The men ate, then got up and filed out. They must have noted that Jim never thanked his smiling wife.

He would never again be just one of the guys. They would always feel he was just a little smarter; he wasn't the jerk they thought him to be. The next night at work, the men were still subdued. <u>She had honored him when it meant the most</u>—in front of the guys. She honored him because she believed God and chose to obey God by honoring a man who did not deserve her honor. She put down her feelings of revulsion, hurt, and of being used, and put on a chaste conversation. She was a crown to her husband.

Can you see how her chaste conversation would win her husband—any husband? Gradually, over the years, he came to treat her with respect. Her queenly manner made him see himself in a different light. The other guys were married to a bunch of dirty, clamorous, partying, base women, but <u>his wife had class</u>. He came to think of Christians as a more worthy class of people—kind, longsuffering, loving, respectful, giving, honest, and frugal. What a testimony she had to the world! The rough and repulsive things fell away one by one, changing to loving kindness, not because she demanded it, but because she won him to herself by her chaste conversation. Even as an unsaved man, he came to honor her because she was so gracious. When he looked into her eyes, he saw a man better than what he knew himself to be. Love made him want to be worthy of her belief in him. The moral of this story is that I Peter 3 is true. <u>By treating her husband like a king, she became a queen whom God used to win him to Jesus Christ</u>. The **"goodness of God leadeth thee to repentance"**; so does the goodness of a good wife.

Years later, he finally came to true repentance and made Jesus the Lord of his life. When we went back to visit them recently, their children were all grown, and he was praising the Lord and rejoicing in God's goodness to his family.

Dignity Befitting a Queen

My friend responded to her husband with dignity befitting a queen. He was proud of her beauty. He was proud of her dignity and poise. He was honored that such a woman would treat him with such reverence.

A man will resist with all his might those who come against him. Most women spend their whole married lives in conflict with their husbands, trying to change them. It is a battle of the wills that no woman has ever rightly won, for even if she gets his compliance, she loses his heart, and he loses his self-respect.

While we women tend to reduce everything to the issues of "who is right and what is just," God authoritatively points us to the real issue— "Whom did I place in charge, and whom did I create to be a help meet?" When a woman resists or tries to change a man, she makes him more stubborn, and her own heart will be filled with bitterness. If a woman obeys God, a man does not have anything to come against, to resist, to dominate, to conquer, or to beat down. A woman's greatest power is in obeying God through obeying and honoring her husband. When she departs from God's order, she is setting herself up to create a life of turmoil, bitterness, and defeat—for both of them.

I have received many letters from women saying, "By the way you write, you would think all men are like your husband." No, and my husband wasn't always like he is now. He is now a work of art, and I don't mean his body. God has changed him over the years, and if some of you were married to him, even now, you would be writing me letters asking for advice on how to find the grace to endure. I have come to like the bear in him—sometimes teddy bear and sometimes real bear, but he is always my bear!

I have seen women come through some rough times to arrive at a heavenly marriage. They did not start out with a righteous man, but <u>God is a master at making heavenly marriages</u>. I know one young woman who had a husband so violent, vile, and unrepentant that she asked the church to pray, "Lord save him or kill him as soon possible." In two weeks he was dead. I don't recommend that kind of prayer meeting, for if God killed all the husbands who *deserved* to die, we ladies would be fighting over the few who remained. Furthermore, if God decided to be fair and took to killing all the ladies who deserve it, well…you can see we would be better off pleading for grace and mercy for our husbands.

> You cannot become his conscience or his accuser, expecting that pressure is going to push him into repentance.

How to Minister to a MAD Husband

It is common for men to react with sudden anger when things do not go their way. They can get mad over a lawnmower, a faulty appliance, or a child talking too much. It is unregulated testosterone seeking a conflict. It is not usually conflict-induced, and seems totally irrational to us ladies who must have a reason to get mad. Come to think of it, men are rather irrational sometimes—something they regularly accuse us of. Women are led by their emotions to be sentimental, and men are led by their emotions to be aggressive, even to the edge of violence. Men, instead, should be expending their male drives on the challenging hardships of life and on a little evening romp. It is sin for them to have no more self-control than boys in day care, but it is *their* sin, not yours. There is not a thing we ladies can do to change this tendency—the expression of it, yes, but not the tendency. God can give a man total self-control. The man who walks after the Spirit will be as meek as Christ, but let's face it, most marriages start off with a man who is not Christ-like. That is the way of Adam's sons.

The question is, how should we wives respond to make our own lives better and to provide a window of opportunity for our husbands to respond to God and improve in this and other areas? **Lesson number one**, above all else: you cannot become his conscience or his accuser, expecting that pressure is going to push him into repentance. It will work the exact opposite—hardening his resolve, making his fighting instinct kick in, and then, for him, it becomes an issue of him winning in a contest against a challenging female. Furthermore, you would be competing with the Holy Spirit in convicting him of his sin.

   The wisest way to handle the aggressive husband is by not taking personal offense. Always avoid "provoking" him, except, of course, to provoke him to love and good works. Most women know what causes their man to lose his cool. Give him time to cool down; he will feel ashamed soon enough. Although this explosive anger is emotionally upsetting and certainly not pleasant, it is a man-thing that a smart woman can learn to deal with in a wise manner.

   The kind of anger we have been talking about is not directly caused by the relationship of the wife to her husband. Faced with that kind of anger, a wife needs to take care to respond impersonally to it, recognizing that although she can exacerbate the problem by an incorrect response, his anger is not caused by their relationship.

Another Kind of Anger

   However, there is another kind of anger that is deeper and more personal. It is caused by bitterness. It is rooted in the very essence of the spirit. It is the constant seepage of an ugly soul. You will remember that we discussed how some women practice being mad (bitter), like angry musicians practicing the piano until their very souls, without any thought or effort, strike notes of discord. This bitter-mad kind of anger is not as common in men as it is in women, but it is dominant in some relationships, and it is important for you as a wife to learn how to respond to your man if he shows tendencies toward it. To respond correctly, you need to keep in mind the two different kinds of anger: the causeless anger that we just discussed and the anger that springs from bitterness over issues.

   It is common for wives to be the cause of their husband's bitter anger. They talk and talk about some problem in the family, community, or the church until their husband finally gets stirred up and becomes very angry with them. To the normal, talkative wife, it was just something to discuss, but suddenly the man becomes angry, and the whole thing gets out of hand and scary. I write about this because it is

Chapter 22 ~ 8. Obedient to Their Own Husbands

so common to find the wife complaining about her husband's anger, even while **her words are stoking the fires of his wrath**.

If your husband is quick to take offense at his neighbors or at the people at church, or if he assumes everyone is out to get him or they are talking bad about him, then he has an anger problem rooted in bitterness. Your first concern should be to ascertain your part in the problem. Only then can you help your husband to think clearly about it by ceasing to fuel the flames of his anger.

Once you are able to recognize the source of his anger and the contribution you make in words and attitude, you can make changes that will stop fanning the flames and allow him to cool down. Learn to think and speak well of all people. Practice looking at the good in people. Print Philippians 4:8 on a card and put it in a conspicuous place where you can read it frequently.

Do not confuse sympathy with encouragement.

"Finally, brethren, whatsoever things are true, whatsoever things are honest, whatsoever things are just, whatsoever things are pure, whatsoever things are lovely, whatsoever things are of good report; if there be any virtue, and if there be any praise, think on these things."

Do not allow your mind to consider the evil of others. Love **"thinketh no evil"** (I Corinthians 13:5). Remember the 40,000 thoughts a day? Don't think critical and judgmental thoughts about others, and never speak derogatorily about others in your husband's presence. It can be the trigger to flare up his wrath toward them, toward you, and toward the kids. It is also destructive to the peace that ought to pervade your home.

Never let your mind be carried away by reacting in criticism when he is telling and retelling a story of what someone said about you. When you see he is getting worked up, remain calm and objective, and encourage him to see the good side. Don't lecture. Just be an example of how to respond in forgiveness and peace.

Do not confuse sympathy with encouragement. If you feel sorry for his hurt feelings and sympathize with him, you will only add fuel to his emotional fire. I have seen many couples' relationships develop into something sick. They become partners in persecution, welcoming outside rejection so they can draw closer in their bitterness, shutting the cruel world out, until they even become suspicious of each other and fight to their emotional death.

In almost every church you will find couples dropping out from time to time, because the wife got her husband worked up over small issues, until his bitterness and anger drove him out of the company of "those hypocrites." They complain about the pastor or his children or something a deacon's wife said. The wife runs to her husband with every real (and sometimes imagined) report of gossip about them. The wife sometimes complains that, "No one bothered to greet us Sunday," or "When I was in the hospital, no one came to see me," or "There is a clique at the church, and they don't like us (or our children)." The husband is made angry enough to do something just to get some peace.

This road leads to the destruction of the children. In time, the wife becomes a martyr, speaking in quiet tones of her suffering at her husband's hands. She resists his "discipline" of the children and protects them from his anger. The children grow up embittered and withdrawn from Christian fellowship. The wife goes to women's groups and seeks prayer for her husband, where she is honored as a woman who must endure much. She has made her bed of self-pity and has learned to enjoy its sick pleasures.

The Wife Does Make a Difference

I once knew a young man who was well respected in the community, a strong leader both in his family and in the church. His young wife died and left him with several small children. In time, he married a very nice widow lady. By all appearances, they were happily married, but in a short time, the man began to demonstrate a weaker and withdrawn personality. He became defensive and took offense where there was none intended. He lacked the attitude of authority he once had and was never again a leader. More and more, he separated himself and his children from people and eventually from the church, although he never did leave the faith. In fact, he thought himself more righteous than others. I think the thing that shocked me the most was the difference in his posture and walk. During his first marriage, he had a cocky walk—almost arrogant. After he married the second wife, his walk became hesitant and uncertain. He kept his shoulders down and never looked challenging. He seemed withdrawn. With the first lady, he was always early to church and took charge; with his second wife, he showed up late and left early.

Encouragement Versus Sympathy

Could a woman make that kind of difference? From my perspective, both ladies were as good as gold. It was clear that the first wife was an *encourager*. I can almost hear her say, when he felt knocked down or offended, "Get up, you can do it. It doesn't matter what they say. You're the man." The second wife was gentle, loving, tender, and sympathetic. She would have responded, "Sweetheart, you know I love you, and I am so sorry those awful people treated you so badly. You come over here, and let me hold you. I just want you to be happy."

It reminds me of how Ahab lay on his bed and put his face to the wall when he was upset because he could not have the vineyard he wanted. **Jezebel was full of sympathy, too.** This second wife meant well. She found comfort and fulfillment in comforting. She likely nursed her husband into infantile responses. They drew close together and shut out the cruel world. He stopped being "the man." It was an amazing example of the power a woman has to be the wrong kind of help to her husband.

If you see your husband moving in the direction of taking offense or being suspicious of the motives of those around him, *never* be sympathetic and supportive of his hurts. Make your life's verse Philippians 4:8. And remember, I Peter 3 says we can even win our lost husbands with our chaste conversation. A chaste conversation has greater power with a man than does sympathy.

Is There Yet Hope?

There is hope. We can hope in God's Word when circumstances and counsel are all to the contrary.

I once heard about a sweet and godly lady named Teresa, married to a godless, dope-head criminal who made his living dealing heroin. Her church prayed and prayed for him, to no avail. Finally, he was busted for his crimes and given many years behind bars. In the same church there was a fine man of God who had a wife totally disinterested in the things of God, and not very interested in her husband. When Teresa's husband was locked away, Ben was counseled to divorce his wife and marry Teresa, whom he had greatly admired for many years. He followed their counsel, and the church had a grand, happy wedding for this new union.

The lady who was telling me the story would periodically stop to exclaim, "Look what God hath done! Isn't it wonderful?" When I had heard the whole story, my heart was broken, and I told the teller to stop blaming God. People see only the here and now; we look only for ways that will make us happy today. God sees so very much more, which is why he gave us his Word as a light to direct our path when we cannot see clearly.

I knew that God was dishonored by the whole mess. If sweet, little Teresa had believed and trusted God and had been willing to suffer being alone, she could have devoted herself to visiting her husband in prison, sharing books and tapes with him, and taking her little ones to see Daddy. He would have finally begun to treasure his faithful wife and family, and he would have come to know that only the power of God could cause a woman to love the rotten, lowdown sinner he knew himself to be. Mr. Dope-Head then would have been open to God. Who knows how many men in that prison would have heard the old, old story of how a Savior came from glory just to save them from their sins, all because one little lady was willing to live her life for Jesus by honoring and reverencing the man who was her husband? He was her hope, and she was his. If only wise men and women could have helped Teresa see the miracle God could have given her.

> **"And unto the married I command, yet not I, but the Lord, <u>Let not the wife depart from her husband</u>: But and if she depart, let her remain unmarried, or <u>be reconciled to her husband</u>: and let not the husband put away his wife. But to the rest speak I, not the Lord: If any brother hath a wife that believeth not, and she be pleased to dwell with him, <u>let him not put her away</u>. And the woman which hath an husband that believeth not, and if he be pleased to dwell with her, <u>let her not leave him</u>. For the unbelieving husband <u>is sanctified by the wife</u>, and the unbelieving wife is <u>sanctified by the husband</u>: else were your children unclean; but now are they holy. But if the unbelieving depart, let him depart. A brother or a sister is not under bondage in such cases: but God hath called us to peace. For what knowest thou<u>, O wife, whether thou shalt save thy husband</u>? or how knowest thou, O man, whether thou shalt save thy wife?"** (I Cor. 7:10-16).

Is there hope? Yes, there is hope! It is not always the way we think hope should be. God gave us a plan by which, through our submission and reverence, he could change the heart of any man to some degree. In the end, the Scriptures teach that there is something bigger and more important to God than our happiness. It's not about our happiness; it's about our holiness. Regardless of how much it hurts, whether or not we see results, even if our man does not get saved, God is worthy of our obedience, which in His eyes is worship.

> **"Behold, the eye of the LORD is upon them that fear him, upon them that hope in his mercy"** (Psalm 33:18).

Children Need an Example

You are not your own. You are bought with a price, the precious blood of Jesus. We are lights to this world, and this world desperately needs to see heavenly marriages. Our kids need to see heavenly marriages, marriages where they can see that God is making a real difference in the lives of their parents. If your children don't see it lived out in the daily reality of the home, no amount of preaching will make them believe. If God cannot provoke you to honor your man and cause your marriage to be full of love, then how can your children believe that God is anything more than all the other "make-believe" characters they read about?

Three Key Issues
(Remarriage, Birth Control, and Head Coverings)

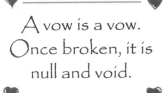

A vow is a vow. Once broken, it is null and void.

1. But I'm Already Remarried

Dear Mr. and Mrs. Pearl,

It is sad to know you have missed God's will for your life. I want God's will and with the help of my church, I am willing to lay my life down for Christ.

My first husband left. He filed for divorced (I never would, of course) and offered to give me everything, including the children, as long as I did not push for child support. If I did, he would fight for the children. I let him off, in order to save my children. He was not a Christian and lived a selfish, self-centered life. When two are unequally joined, it is so hard. He had no interest in church or reading the Bible, and he was a bad influence on the kids. I was not sad to see him go.

Three years later, I met and married Fred. We had both been divorced and both of us brought children into the marriage. For the last 12 years we have had our ups and downs. I started feeling like something was not right about our sexual union and asked him to give me time to think it through. Sex just seemed wrong, and I did not want to dishonor God again. God led me to a lady who went to a very conservative church an hour away. I asked Fred to take us to her church, but he did not want to leave our church, plus he refused to drive that far "just for church." I went just to see how it was, and that is where I finally saw what God was trying to tell me. I now know that before God, Fred and I are not really married. It is just terrible to think of all those years I lived in adultery. God forgive me! Anyway, I told my husband how I felt and moved upstairs.

At this time in my life, I do not have an income or a home, other than our home we share. I know I cannot live as a wife to Fred, but he is telling me to either be his wife or get out. I have prayed and prayed, and God has not given me direction. I only want to be the pure bride of Christ. Eternity is more important than the here and now. What can I do?

Sue Ann

Dear Sue Ann,

You said that your first husband was not a believer and that he left you. God tells us, **"But if the unbelieving depart, let him depart. <u>A brother or a sister is not under bondage in such cases</u>: but God hath called us to peace."** I Corinthians 7:15.

You also state that your first husband married again, thus joining himself with another. Matthew deals with this in two different chapters.

"But I say unto you, that whosoever shall put away his wife, <u>saving for the cause of fornication</u>, causeth her to commit adultery: and whosoever shall marry her that is divorced committeth adultery" (Matthew 5:32).

"And I say unto you, Whosoever shall put away his wife, <u>except it be for fornication</u>, and shall marry another, committeth adultery: and whoso marrieth her which is put away doth commit adultery" (Matthew 19:9).

"What? Know ye not that he which is joined to an harlot is one body? For two, saith he, shall be one flesh" (I Corinthians 6:16).

You cast doubt on your marriage to Fred being a "real marriage," yet Jesus gives us a clear example of what he considers a "real marriage" when he spoke to the woman at the well.

"Now Jacob's well was there. Jesus therefore, being wearied with his journey, sat thus on the well: and it was about the sixth hour. There cometh a woman of Samaria to draw water: Jesus saith unto her, Give me to drink. (For his disciples were gone away unto the city to buy meat.) Then saith the woman of Samaria unto him, How is it that thou, being a Jew, askest drink

of me, which am a woman of Samaria? for the Jews have no dealings with the Samaritans. Jesus answered and said unto her, If thou knewest the gift of God, and who it is that saith to thee, Give me to drink; thou wouldest have asked of him, and he would have given thee living water. The woman saith unto him, Sir, thou hast nothing to draw with, and the well is deep: from whence then hast thou that living water? Art thou greater than our father Jacob, which gave us the well, and drank thereof himself, and his children, and his cattle? Jesus answered and said unto her, Whosoever drinketh of this water shall thirst again: But whosoever drinketh of the water that I shall give him shall never thirst; but the water that I shall give him shall be in him a well of water springing up into everlasting life. The woman saith unto him, Sir, give me this water, that I thirst not, neither come hither to draw. Jesus saith unto her, Go, call thy husband, and come hither. The woman answered and said, I have no husband. Jesus said unto her, Thou hast well said, I have no husband: For thou hast had five husbands; and he whom thou now hast is not thy husband: in that saidst thou truly" (John 4:6-18).

Jesus clearly distinguished between a live-in and a husband. Jesus recognized the legal contract of marriage. If Jesus recognized all five of her husbands as legal husbands, do you think he does not recognize your marriage contract and vow with Fred?

Lest you think you might have some religious reason to go back to your first husband, it is important for you to read the passage in Deuteronomy.

"When a man hath taken a wife, and married her, and it come to pass that she find no favour in his eyes, because he hath found some uncleanness in her: then let him write her a bill of divorcement, and give it in her hand, and send her out of his house. And when she is departed out of his house, she may go and be another man's wife. And if the latter husband hate her, and write her a bill of divorcement, and giveth it in her hand, and sendeth her out of his house; or if the latter husband die, which took her to be his wife; Her former husband, which sent her away, may not take her again to be his wife, after that she is defiled; for that is abomination before the LORD: and thou shalt not cause the land to sin, which the LORD thy God giveth thee for an inheritance" (Deuteronomy 24:1-4).

I Corithians 7 deals with marriage, separation and divorce. It's conclusions are:

"Art thou bound unto a wife? seek not to be loosed. Art thou loosed from a wife? seek not a wife" (1 Cor. 7:27).

"Let every man abide in the same calling wherein he was called" (1 Cor. 7:20).

2. My Husband said I had to use Birth Control

Dear Mr. and Mrs. Pearl,

Our family is in despair. I have stood on the promises of God against all counsel, and it appears it was not enough. I have six children and one on the way. My husband told me if I got pregnant again, he would leave me and I would never hear from him again. I guess he meant it. We have not heard from him for three months, and he left us without any means of support.

My oldest two boys were caught stealing bad magazines at the local country store last night. They are only 10 and 11 years old! This is not the first time the boys have been in trouble with the law. Since the Child Protection Services got involved, the neighbors have come forward complaining about my other children running wild and unsupervised. It is just because I homeschool. It is like the Devil will not be satisfied until he steals them away!

I thought my husband was a good man when we married. He worked hard and went to church and loved choir. I was careful to marry a man whom my parents approved of. Right from the first, he said he only wanted two kids at the most. He is not very tolerant and cannot stand noise or mess. It was fine with me until I heard from the Lord in the sweetest way about how precious little children are to the Lord. I knew I could not use birth control any more when I learned how many of the so-called birth controls cause murder! I begged my husband to listen to the Lord and consider his seed, but every time I got with child he seemed more distant and remote. He went for months without having intercourse with me, and I think he just did not want another child! How could a man who says he is saved leave his own family? I love all my sweet babies. I truly believed my husband would repent.

I need help. Except for the state, I have no income and no one to protect me and my precious children. Where do I go from here? How can God have forsaken us? All I ever wanted to do was obey him. Please pray for us. If you have any counsel or place where we could go to find a sure refuge, please write me soon.

Diana

The Question of Birth Control

God tells us in I Timothy 5:14, **"I will therefore that the younger women marry, bear children, guide the house, give none occasion to the adversary to speak reproachfully."** It is clearly the will of God for young women to get married and have children. There is nothing more precious to my husband and me than our five children. They are all married adults and are now having their own children. When I hear little feet running in the house and then hear the glad call, "Big Papa.... Mama Pearl," my heart just melts with joy and gladness. When I see my children carefully training their little ones to cheerfully obey, or when I see the light in their eyes as they hand me their newest baby, it stirs a deep well of pleasure. God tells us in III John 4 **"I have no greater joy than to hear that my children walk in truth."** I hope all my children have a house full of children. My husband says, "I would like to hold forty grandchildren on my lap before I become just an occasional memory in a three-dollar picture album."

We have noticed that big families are more likely to produce children who are emotionally stable and less self-centered, with a better-than-average probability of growing up to be dependable, balanced adults. The most selfish people I have known were an only child, or a last child who came along ten years behind the other children and grew up like an only child.

I know that I grew as a person with the birth and training of each of my children. The burden of caring for a child, worrying, praying, and training them will cause maturity in young mothers and fathers. Without children, teenage brides often remain immature, with little thought about the needs of others. They will never enjoy the pleasures afforded that special class of women referred to universally as grandmothers!

Husbands and wives are not always in agreement on this issue of family size. Sometimes, as in the letter above, husbands express to their wives that they do not want to have a great number of children. His wife is keenly aware that the purpose of the family is to produce godly children, and so she takes what she sees as the high ground in believing that using birth control (a form that does not abort a fertilized egg) or spacing their children through careful planning is not trusting God. She doesn't come across a passage in the Bible that commands her thus; she reads

> When a woman takes what she believes is the high ground (as Eve did), and disobeys her husband, she is blaspheming the written word of God.

literature and listens to other teachers who encourage her to "obey God" rather than her husband in this important matter.

Diana refused to follow her husband's leading, essentially becoming the head of the household on this one issue. When a woman takes what she believes is the high ground (as Eve did) and disobeys her husband, **that woman is blaspheming** (speaking evil of) the Word of God. There is no command in Scripture concerning family size, only the strong promise of God to bless the "man" whose quiver is full of children. God clearly states that the man is the head and that a **woman is to submit** to her own husband.

I have no answer for Diana, whose husband left her with an overflowing quiver of children to rear alone. There is no sure refuge for all the families who have split over this issue—and judging from the vast amount of letters like this that we receive, there are many. I can only tell her that God did not forsake her; **she forsook God, his written Word, and his clearly spelled-out plan for a woman**. This is what happens when the Word of God is blasphemed.

On occasion, it will be the wife who hesitates having more children. She is usually concerned with her health. This issue looms large in a woman's mind, but is really minor compared to eternal issues. In any event, the answer is the same. The husband is the head. He decides, although the woman is free to appeal (not nag) to her husband to reconsider. A woman stands before God for her willingness to honor her husband; a man's place is one of much greater gravity. He will stand before God for the way he has led his family and the decisions he has made. Be thankful you are a woman with an uncomplicated, clear-cut command.

3. What About the Head Covering?

Dear Mr. and Mrs. Pearl,

I wonder if you would explain to me just what it means when Scripture says that a woman should wear a covering. A good friend sent me a booklet called "Should She Be Veiled." God has convicted her about wearing a covering, and she wanted to share the joy of the covering with me. My husband thinks I am silly and refuses to even talk about the issue. He told me I could do what I wanted, but if I did what he wanted, I would not "wear the silly rag." He did ask me to write you, because he knows that I read your child-training literature. He also knows you are well known for telling women to honor their husbands, and he thinks you will stand with him on the matter. I am writing, as I do, wondering why some of the women I have seen in your No Greater Joy pictures have head coverings on and some do not. Either you stick by your convictions or you don't. Which is it?

Darlene

Dear Darlene,

The reason you see some women wearing extra coverings on their heads and some are not is because the church is not the head over the wives—the husbands are. If a man wants his wife to have an additional covering, she should do so; but if not, then she shouldn't. The convictions belong to the individual men, not the women and not the church. God's Word clearly states that the church has "**no such custom**" (I Corinthians 11:16).

The Scriptures to which you refer are I Corinthians 11:2-16. As you read the passage, you will note that <u>the subject is the spiritual chain of command</u>. This spiritual chain of command is called an *ordinance*. God says "keep the ordinances". The text makes two things clear: the head covering is a <u>custom</u> that is not part of the church, and the headship of man over his wife is an <u>ordinance</u> that God commands us to keep.

> **"Now I praise you, brethren, that ye remember me in all things, and keep the ordinances, as I delivered them to you. But I would have you know, that the head of every man is Christ; and <u>the head of the woman is the man</u>; and the head of Christ is God"** (I Corinthians 11:2-3).

These verses introduce the subject of this chapter. The subject is not head coverings, which verse 16 calls a <u>custom;</u> it is the chain of command. The woman has a head—her husband. The man has a head—Christ, and Christ has a head—God. That is God's chain of command set forth from the beginning. This chain of command is an <u>ordinance</u> that God commands us to follow.

> **4 Every man praying or prophesying, having his head covered, dishonoureth his head.**

A man is dishonoring Christ (his head) if he prays with his head covered.

> **5 But every woman that prayeth or prophesieth with her head <u>uncovered</u> dishonoureth her head: for that is even all one as if she were shaven.**
> **6 For if the woman be not covered, let her also be shorn: but if it be a shame for a woman to be shorn or shaven, let her be covered.**

A woman dishonors her husband (her head) if she prays uncovered. It is a shame (disgrace) for a woman to shave or cut her hair short. Therefore, cover it.

> **7 For a man indeed ought not to cover his head, forasmuch as he is the image and glory of God: but the woman is the glory of the man.**

Verses 7, 8 and 9 give a summation of the matter. God is reminding us of how he, God, reached into the clay of the earth and molded Adam into his (God's) own image. God says he made Adam like himself and for HIMSELF. Adam was created for God's glory. God made a person like himself—someone who could enjoy the things God enjoyed. Verse 7 finishes by reminding us that woman was created as a glory to the man. God looked at his friend, Adam, and knew that Adam needed someone for his own glory, someone to be his supporter, helper, and friend. So God reached into the body of man for a rib and made of it a woman. Bone of his bone, cell of his cell, RNA of his RNA, in the image of the one from which she came.

> **8 For the man is not of the woman; but the woman of the man.**

> **9 Neither was the man created for the woman; but the woman for the man.**

God is giving us the foundation of his creation plan. HE set up the chain of command. This plan is in the genetic code; it is in the very essence of who and what we are. To re-create ourselves to be the head of the man is an affront to God's original creation. The angels know and understand this created plan—they were there, watching and waiting. God says it is for their sakes (angels) that a woman should honor her husband as her head.

> **10 For this cause ought the woman to have power on her head because of the angels.** (The Greek word for "power" is: *exousia*, meaning authority).

The Bible says in Ephesians 6:12,

> **"For we wrestle not against flesh and blood, but against principalities, against powers, against the rulers of the darkness of this world, against spiritual wickedness in high places."**

This is a spiritual issue put in place at creation. The woman who remains under her husband's authority with the outward sign of the long hair, or some other head covering that stands in for the long hair she does not have, is saying to the rulers of darkness of this world, "I belong to this man, and I am under his safe spiritual headship; you can not mess with me."

When a man prays or prophecies with long hair or a cloth covering his head, it could be sending strange messages to spiritual wickedness in high places.

> **11 Nevertheless neither is the man without the woman, neither the woman without the man, in the Lord.**

12 For as the woman is of the man, even so is the man also by the woman; but all things of God.

Paul recognized that if these verses were misunderstood, they might leave women feeling unimportant, so the Holy Spirit moves upon him to interject the assuring fact that there wouldn't be any men if God had stopped with Adam. It takes men **and** women in God's creation plan.

Paul continues by appealing to our very nature.

13 Judge in yourselves: is it comely that a woman pray unto God uncovered?

Is it comely (Greek: *prepo*, means proper or suitable) for a woman to pray uncovered?

Again Paul appeals to our innate understanding of human nature. He says it is not comely for a woman to pray uncovered, but for a man to pray covered is a downright SHAME. Note that the covering that is a shame on the man is his long hair.

14 Doth not even nature itself teach you, that, if a man have long hair, it is a shame unto him?

The same covering that brings a man shame is a glory to a woman.

15 But if a woman have long hair, it is a glory to her: <u>for her hair is given her for a covering</u>.

<u>The covering God gave a woman is her hair</u>. No second covering is ever mentioned. For the Kumboi woman in the mountains of Papua New Guinea, a treasured piece of cloth will be used to cover her baby from the cold, not to place on her head, because God gave her hair for a covering.

Paul concludes his messages with a simple reminder concerning the issue of hair, coverings, and a church's authority. He commands churches to not strive over the issue of hair (long or short) and not to treat it as a divinely-sanctioned custom.

16 But if any man seem to be contentious, we have no such custom, neither the churches of God.

Whether you have short hair, long hair, or wear a scarf, God's rule is still for all women (married or single) to keep silent in the church, which includes praying and prophesying. This is not hard to understand, but many find it hard to accept.

"Let your women keep silence in the churches: for it is <u>not permitted unto them to speak</u>; but they are commanded to be under obedience, as also saith the law. And if they will learn any thing, let them ask their husbands at home: for it is a shame for women to speak in the church" (I Cor. 14:34-35). The church, of course, is <u>not</u> the building (I Cor.14:23a). It is the assembly of believers for the purpose of worship, preaching of the Word, and ministry of the gifts. The 14th chapter of I Corinthians discusses the church and its functions.

The head of the woman is man ♥

To *answer your question:*

Now to answer your question, Darlene, "Do we stick by our convictions, or not?" Yes, we do. The Scripture clearly teaches that the only safe place for a woman is under her *husband's authority.*

As I sit here typing, several really "bad wife" examples come to my mind. They are "older-wiser-spiritual" women who have run their husbands off, or, for all practical purposes, have shut the bedroom door to them. Most have long hair and wear headscarves and pious dresses, and they are the most rebellious, cantankerous women who ever tormented a man. I have seen them in many places in the country; some denominations breed more than others. Many claim to be the "bride of Christ" or a prophetess, and spend their lives "helping" others. **Scripture clearly teaches that they will not be any better as brides for Christ than they are as wives to their husbands.**

Today, women rebel against their husbands so they can express their submission to God. Strange indeed! But nothing new.

God told you what he meant for women to do concerning hair and left it up to you to honor his will. Without being commanded by the church, since it has no customs regarding these things, if you want to fall in line with God's will as revealed in this passage, ask your husband, "May I grow my hair out long?" Watch his eyes light up. He will say something like, "I've been asking you for years to grow your hair long; I would love it."

However, neither long hair nor a scarf on your head are necessary for a heavenly marriage. I know of couples who are bathed in love for each other, and the lady's hair is shorter than my husband's.

Oh, but I would be remiss in not telling you: long hair casts a spell on men that is unparalleled. When the veil of my long hair falls about my body and hips, my old husband loses his mind. We have counseled enough men to know that this is a fantasy they all have in common.

For the very few ladies who have husbands who want them to wear a scarf, but they do not want to, I say this: "Stop being rebellious. Get under your husband's authority and cheerfully, thankfully wear what your husband requires, knowing that by wearing it you are obeying God—and pleasing your husband."

-Debi

Learning to Make an Appeal

There were a few times in our early married life when I had differences with my husband that I felt had to be resolved. I felt I had to speak to him and that <u>he must listen</u>. At first, he had a tendency to brush me off, attributing my "irregularities" to female hormones. If I got upset over something, the first thing he would do was to ask me if I was "on my period." I usually was, but I resented his attributing *everything* I did to female hormones. It seemed as though he was not taking my issues seriously. When I did voice my hurt or concerns, I would, of course, be emotional and, according to him, somewhat irrational. My emotions and his cold, male logic couldn't speak to each other. It took me a while, but I eventually learned to make an appeal that he would respect, and he learned to stop asking me if I was on my period—he just quietly continued to assume I was.

We decided early in our marriage that when something was so important to me that I <u>had</u> to have it resolved, he would take a step back, stop all his ministry and business, and listen with grave concern and consideration. **I had to be willing to let go of the issue after he considered it, even if his decision did not suit me**. Together, we made a pact that I would never misuse my "liberty" of appealing to him as a ploy to control him, but only use it when he was blind to my needs, and that he would listen when I did appeal. We decided that I would raise my hands and speak in a serious, unemotional way, "This is an issue that I must have resolved." As it turned out, I have only used it 4 or 5 times in our entire marriage.

If you knew my husband, you would be surprised at the few times I have had to fall back on my "appeal." He was born with an extreme amount of drive and dominance, and what seems to some, a deficit in gentleness. I say that in a complimentary way. He is a leader. He expects to be served. When he walks into a crowded room, whether in a church building or at a gas station, people are aware of his presence. Where most men walk miles in their lives, he has traveled galaxies. He has expected me to do the same. My life was never my own; every minute of every day, I have been on call.

What I learned when we decided on this "appeal policy" is that most of the daily issues were not that overwhelming after all. And, once I knew I had a forum that could gain a fair hearing, I discovered that I was now willing to tolerate much more. The few times I have needed to use my "appeal" were primarily centered on his inability to see a woman's side of an issue. Once he heard my appeal, he was willing to take my word about a woman's perspective. He carefully reviewed the case and came up with a compromise that was satisfactory to us both. **The key was, I never misused my liberty; he therefore respected my voice**.

REFLECTING ON
Obedient to their own Husbands

➢ *Getting Very Serious with God*

Emphatic Statements from God concerning Women

Look up the verses that contain the statements below, and mark them in your Bible. Will you obey God? Mark the emphatic statements that indicate you have been dishonoring to God, and ask God to help you as you start your path to obedience.

- Younger women, bear children.
- Younger women, guide the house.
- Wives, give none occasion to the adversary to speak reproachfully.
- Wives, submit to your own husbands.
- Wives, love your own husbands.
- Wives, love your children.
- Women, be discreet.
- Women, be chaste.
- Women, be keepers at home.
- Women, be sober.
- Women, be good.
- It is a shame for a woman to be shorn or shaven.
- Woman's long hair is her glory.
- Woman's long hair is given her for a covering.
- Women praying uncovered are not comely.
- Let the woman learn in silence.
- I suffer not a woman to teach.

- Women, do not usurp authority over the man.
- Wives, reverence your own husbands.
- Wives, have chaste conversation.
- Women, adorn yourselves in modest apparel.
- Women, have shamefacedness and sobriety.
- Let your adorning be the hidden man of the heart.
- Wives, have a meek and quiet spirit.
- Wives, render due benevolence to your husband.
- Wives, care how you may please your husbands.
- Women, keep silence in the churches.
- Women are not permitted to speak in church.
- Wives, be not idle.
- Wives, do not wander about from house to house.
- Wives, do not be tattlers or busybodies.

Chapter 23

To Obey or Not to Obey ?

(That is the Question)

Throwing Rocks

Dear Pearls,

About 6 months ago, I noticed that every evening my husband started going to our spare room to "work" on his computer. One of our younger daughters often cried when he was around, and so he said he was giving her space and trying to avoid upsetting her. Besides, he was tired and wanted some peace after working all day. I inwardly wondered, but let it pass.

His evenings in the "room" started earlier and earlier and lasted later as time passed. I would ask what he was doing, and he would say it was research for work or that he was trying to build a web site. On occasion, I tried to get in the door to see him about something, but it was locked, and my husband would call out that it was because the kids would not leave him alone, so he had to keep it locked while he was in there.

One day a friend came over, and I asked her if she would show me some things on the computer since I knew nothing about it. She was surprised because part of the wiring had been removed so it could not turn on. It was then I finally admitted to myself that my wonderful homeschooling, church-leading husband was into porn.

I fixed the window shades to where there was a tiny crack and moved the computer screen and desk a little so that I could see the screen when I looked in through the shade from the outside. All day my blood boiled hotter and hotter. **I was so mad it scared me**. My husband went into the computer room right after dinner. I waited until I knew for sure the children were asleep, and then I went outside to peer into his office. What I saw on his screen was shocking— I will never forget it as long as I live. I am disgusted such a thing attracts him. I backed up in confusion and anger, and I just wanted to throw the **wrath of God** at him. That is when I remembered the big stones around the flower bed I was standing in. I picked up one about the size of a kitchen plate and threw it through that window just as hard as I could. It busted right through that recently installed Andersen window. My husband was running out to stop the bad guy by the time I got into the house. I passed him and ran straight into his room carrying a rock with me and **finished the job**. Of course, when he heard the smashing inside he figured out he had been caught. I was screaming like a crazy woman and bleeding from a few superficial wounds where glass had flown back at me. The kids woke up and came in crying, so it was the worse possible scene.

My husband tried to pretend like I was a hysterical woman and that I had not seen any porn, **but I was past his self-righteous nonsense**. I told him that tomorrow I was going to call everyone we knew, including his mother, and tell them exactly what I saw. Then he started saying it was his first time. This only made me madder. He finally saw his act was up, and he began to break up with fear and shame of being exposed. I do not regret my actions at all. I felt God was at least as mad as me that this man who expected his wife and children to exemplify Christ was hiding behind a door looking

The Wrath of God

at filthy pictures. I did not tell on him, but he knows if he ever goes in and shuts a door or shuts himself off from his family again, I will assume he is into his evil trade, and I will talk and talk and talk. I don't consider it blackmail; **it is accountability**. He has proven he is not trustworthy, that he uses his authority and religious clout as a cover for his sin. So the doors will be open and the children and I will have access to him at all times, and he will not have a job where he is free to play on the computer, and he will not go out at night without one of the children with him, and he will come straight home from work and not stop over for an hour or so anywhere to do whatever. I expect him to act like a husband and a father. I will forgive him and love him and honor him, but he will know there are some things that I need from him that will be a surety to me that he is remaining faithful and true. His openness to us will give me peace and cause me to believe in him.

> Drastic times call for drastic measures.

I write this as a testimony to you to share with others. I know you talk against religiously controlling women, yet somehow I believe you will understand and approve of what I did. Drastic times call for drastic measures. I believe if I had stored up my suspicions and tried to reason with my husband, he would have never confessed his sin, and **I would have grown old and bitter** knowing he was an unfaithful deceiver. I know I would have come to hate him, and this would have destroyed us as surely as his porn was destroying us. He is thankful now that I threw the rock. He told me his first thought was that God had just broken into the room, and it scared him bad. He said he needed to see how mad the porn made me for him to see how really evil it was. We are rebuilding and know it will take time. I feel like we have been through a terrible battle, and we are both weary but relieved it is over.

I know there are thousands of women in my same shoes. Pray for us. Pray for my husband.

Shannon

When NOT to Obey—Exception Clause

The Bible gives us an example of a circumstance under which it is inappropriate for a wife to obey her husband.

Acts 5:1-10

"1 But a certain man named Ananias, with Sapphira his wife, sold a possession,

2 And kept back part of the price, his wife also being privy to it, and brought a certain part, and laid it at the apostles' feet.

3 But Peter said, Ananias, why hath Satan filled thine heart to lie to the Holy Ghost, and to keep back part of the price of the land?

4 Whiles it remained, was it not thine own? and after it was sold, was it not in thine own power? why <u>hast thou conceived this thing in thine heart</u>? thou hast not lied unto men, but unto God.

5 And Ananias hearing these words fell down, and gave up the ghost: and great fear came on all them that heard these things.

6 And the young men arose, wound him up, and carried him out, and buried him.

7 And it was about the space of three hours after, when his wife, not knowing what was done, came in.

8 And Peter answered unto her, Tell me whether ye sold the land for so much? And she said, Yea, for so much.

9 Then Peter said unto her, How is it that ye have <u>agreed together to tempt the Spirit of the Lord</u>? behold, the feet of them which have buried thy husband are at the door, and shall carry thee out.

10 Then fell she down straightway at his feet, and yielded up the ghost: and the young men came in, and found her dead, and, carrying her forth, buried her by her husband."

This book would not be complete without addressing the subject of what a woman should do if she knows her husband is breaking the law of God and man, or that his sin may bring imprisonment to her, or that his sinful actions may bring death to her or the children—as in contracting AIDS from him. In short, is there ever a time when a woman should disobey her husband? Since this is a doctrinal issue, I have asked my studious **husband** to help me out on it. He contributed to the section on **When Not to Obey**.

Michael Pearl Contributes:

All Authority Belongs to God

Paul taught that we are to obey the higher powers, and yet there were times when he and the apostles obeyed God instead. We know that when the Jewish or Roman government commanded the early church to act contrary to Scripture, Peter said, **"We ought to obey God rather than men" (Acts 5:29).** This and other examples establish the fact that there can be exceptions to obeying the authority that you are under. Many women disobey their husbands on grounds that they are obeying God instead. They get into a **habit** of always doubting his judgments and of second-guessing him. They let him "lead" when <u>they think</u> he is right, effectively reversing the male/female roles. When is it appropriate for a wife to refuse to obey her husband? Is there a point at which she is no longer under his authority? Yes, but not as soon or as often as most women suppose.

Spheres of Authority

All authority is derived from God and must answer to him, but he has delegated some authority to angels, some to government, some to the church, some to husbands, and some to wives. Angels have authority that prophets don't have, and husbands have authority that governments don't have. Likewise, governments have authority that neither angels nor husbands have. God has defined the jurisdiction of each authority. For example, neither governments nor husbands have the right to legislate belief or morality. God retains that right. The church does not have the right to intrude into family matters, unless false doctrine or immorality is involved. A husband does not have the right to break the just laws of man or God, nor does he have the right to constrain his wife and children to do so.

In those areas where God has delegated someone to be in authority, he has relinquished a certain amount of control to that authority—for better or for worse. God does not micromanage all spheres of authority. He allows certain latitude for the authority to be wrong and still retain the office.

Our entire lives are bound up in a chain of command. We must answer to others, who, in turn, must answer to God.

Jesus Taught Spheres of Authority

Jesus emphatically confirmed that God has established different spheres of authority when he said, **"Render therefore unto Caesar the things which are Caesar's; and unto God the things that are God's"** (Matt. 22:15-22). Which is to say, government has its jurisdiction, and God has his jurisdiction; there is no conflict in regarding each in its sphere of authority. When God granted government the power to rule in carnal areas, he relinquished to them the power to tax as they might choose. God does not step in and stop a government from unjust taxation. That is a sphere of influence that belongs to government alone—even if they abuse the power.

The principle would apply to all delegated authority: police, judges, governors, presidents, kings, husbands, churches, and parents over their children. Only within the realm of authority that God has granted each entity, does he allow them to use or abuse that power without interfering. If any authority abuses its power beyond that which God has allowed, it becomes subject to a greater power—as when a husband physically assaults his wife and becomes subject to the power of the state.

God will allow government to license its citizens, to act unjustly, and to abuse its regulatory powers, and its subjects are still obligated to act obediently, but if government attempts to regulate belief, as in commanding parents not to teach their children that homosexuality is sin, then it has stepped outside the sphere of authority that belongs to government. **The secret is to know from Scripture the extent of the jurisdiction God has delegated to each authority.**

The Husband's Sphere of Authority

A wife does not have to choose between God and her husband. **Render therefore unto your husband that which is your husband's and unto God the things that are God's.** The authority God gave to your husband is his alone, and God will not interfere and take back to himself that power, even if your husband abuses his powers within certain permissible parameters. We will discuss those exceptions directly. But first, know that a husband has authority to tell his wife what to wear, where to go, whom to talk to, how to spend her time, when to speak and when not to, even if he is unreasonable and insensitive, but he does not have authority to command her to view pornography with him or to assist him in the commission of a crime.

In the same way, a parent's authority does not extend to the right to command a child to participate in immorality, abortion, or anything that may defile the child's conscience before God or that causes him to violate the just laws of the land. Yet a child must continue to honor the **office** of FATHER, even if the father is immature and verbally abusive. Wives are to obey an unreasonable and surly husband, unless he were to command his wife to lie to the Holy Ghost, as did Ananias, in which case, the wife should obey God, not her husband. A husband has the authority to have natural sex with his wife, but he does not have the authority to command her to participate in unnatural (anal) sex. The wife, as well, has authority to access her husband's body for sexual gratification.

This principle seems obvious and simple enough when stated in theory. There are two sides to this marital coin. On the one side, the wife is to obey her husband in all things, reverencing him, serving him, as unto the Lord. On the other side, if he steps outside his sphere of authority and attempts to command her to do the illegal or immoral, she is to obey God or government, as the case may be.

Now, if husbands always ruled their homes in holiness and justice, there would be no need for exceptions to obedience. But, of course, that is not the case, nor has it been the case for centuries on end. In truth, **"For there is not a just man upon earth, that doeth good and sinneth not"** (Ecclesiastes 7:20). Yet God, while acknowledging the fact of man's sinfulness, nevertheless commands the wife to reverence and obey her husband— in the Lord. The key, then, is for the wife to have the wisdom to know what is within her husband's sphere of authority, the government's sphere of authority, the church's sphere of authority, and God's sphere of authority—a daunting task for the carnal mind.

If all wives were inclined by nature to submit to authority—be it God, government, church, or husband—I am sure that it would all work out smoothly. Wives would cheerfully obey their husbands from day to day, and only in those rare exceptions, when a husband commanded his wife to do evil, would she take the reluctant step of refusing to obey him in violating the laws of God and man. But, alas! Wives are also fallen children of Adam and not prone to be balanced or wise.

Most "Christian" divorces are religious. Her religious convictions and narrow-minded insistence drive him to leave her. As a divorcee, she maintains the image of the persecuted and abused victim, but in many cases, it was her "standards" that created the rift that led to divorce. **The devil laughs, the children cry, and the church's Singles Class grows**. Isn't it ironic that the teachings of Christ should be blamed for a woman disobeying and dishonoring her husband?

God does not override a man's authority when he uses it unjustly.

Where Is the Line?

God does not step in and divest a father of his authority when he proves to be short-tempered and neglects his children, or when he is excessive in his corporal punishment, <u>as long as</u> it does not cross the line that would violate the just laws of the land or slip into the category of violence against another human being. Children are still required to obey an unreasonable and surly father. Likewise, wives are to obey unreasonable and surly husbands, for they retain their headship until they cross the bright red line of criminal acts or imposing immoral behavior on the family, bringing God or government to intervene. This is Scriptural in every way. Consider the following text as it deals with this principle of authority.

Enduring Suffering Wrongfully

The text of I Peter will eventually come to a discussion of wives obeying their husbands, but it begins, just as we did in our discussion of the subject, by covering the general concept of spheres of authority.

I Peter 2:13-23

"13 Submit yourselves to every ordinance of man for the Lord's sake: whether it be to the <u>king, as supreme;</u>

14 Or unto governors, as unto them that are sent by him for the punishment of evildoers, and <u>for the praise of them that do well.</u>

15 For so is the will of God, that with well doing ye may put to silence the <u>ignorance of foolish men:</u>

16 <u>As free,</u> and not using your liberty for a cloak of maliciousness, but as the <u>servants of God</u>.

17 Honour all men. Love the brotherhood. Fear God. Honour the king."

The Bible is so clear. We are commanded to submit to every ordinance of the government that we are under—even to ignorant and foolish men. Verse 16 points out that we are actually free from the laws of man, for we are under the higher law of God. We have a liberty, but we are warned to not use our liberty as a cloak of maliciousness. That is, we are not to cloak (disguise) maliciousness in the garments of our liberty in Christ. In other words, don't rebel for selfish reasons, while claiming to be serving a higher, more just law—the excuse of every rebel.

> Most "Christian" divorces are religious. The standards and pride of a Christian woman will destroy the marriage.

The text continues with the same principle, but now discussing servants under the authority of their masters, or, in modern terms, employers and employees.

18 Servants, be <u>subject to your masters</u> with all fear; <u>not only to the good and gentle, but also to the froward.</u>

19 For this is thankworthy, if a man for conscience toward God <u>endure grief, suffering wrongfully</u>.

20 For what <u>glory is it</u>, if, when ye be buffeted for your faults, ye shall take it patiently? but if, when ye do well, and suffer for it, ye take it patiently, this is acceptable with God."

This is where the issue is resolved. Servants are to be subject to their masters whether they are **good and gentle** or **froward** (crooked, perverse, wicked, unfair, surly). Even if a person in authority causes the one under him **unjust suffering** and **grief**, God commands the servant to **endure** it, and take it **patiently**. The servant is not given the option of deciding that the master is not acting within the will of God and therefore should not be

Exceptions by Michael Pearl

obeyed. It is **acceptable with God** (God's will) for the underling to **suffer wrongfully** and **take it patiently.**

You will surely wonder, "Why is it the will of God for the underling to suffer at the hands of an unjust and perverse authority?" Two reasons are obvious, one of which we have already stated. First, the chain of authority must remain intact, even to the point of allowing some abuse. The other reason is introduced in verse 20—**glory.**

We were created by God and placed upon this earth to express his glory (Ps. 8:5; Is. 43:7; Rom. 2:7; Heb. 2:7). Jesus did not live his life in ease for his own pleasure. He lived and suffered for the glory that was to follow (I Pet. 1:11). Lady, you were created to give glory to God. When God puts you in subjection to a man whom he knows is going to cause you to suffer, it is with the understanding that you are obeying God by enduring the wrongful suffering. And when you suffer wrongfully, as unto the Lord, you bring great glory to God in heaven.

The text of verse 21 says that you were called by God for the very purpose of suffering for him, just as he suffered for you.

21 For even <u>hereunto were ye called</u>: because Christ also suffered for us, leaving us an example, that ye should follow his steps:

22 Who did no sin, neither was guile found in is mouth:

23 Who, when he was reviled, reviled not again; when he suffered, he threatened not; but committed himself to him that judgeth righteously:

Has your husband reviled you and threatened you? You are exhorted to respond as Jesus did. When he was reviled and threatened, he suffered by committing himself to a higher judge who is righteous. You must commit yourself to the one who placed you under your husband's command. Your husband will answer to God, and you must answer to God for how you respond to your husband, even when he causes you to suffer.

My interpretation is not out of context or fanciful, for the text of I Peter continues to develop this principle of authority and submission by discussing it in relationship to wives obeying their husbands. The first word in chapter 3 is **"Likewise,"** connecting this chapter to the former discussion of chapter 2—the verses we just covered.

I Peter 3:1-6

1 <u>Likewise</u>, ye wives, be in <u>subjection to your own husbands;</u> that, if any obey not the word, they also may without the word be won by the conversation of the wives;

2 While they behold your chaste conversation coupled with fear.

3 Whose adorning let it not be that outward adorning of plaiting the hair, and of wearing of gold, or of putting on of apparel;

4 But let it be the hidden man of the heart, in that which is not corruptible, even

the ornament of a meek and quiet spirit, which is in the sight of God of great price.
5 For after this manner in the old time the holy women also, who trusted in God, adorned themselves, being in subjection unto their own husbands:
6 Even as Sara obeyed Abraham, <u>calling him lord</u>: whose daughters ye are, as long as ye do well, and are <u>not afraid with any amazement</u>.

The passage is clear to all who have eyes to see. Just as we are to obey government in every ordinance, and servants are to obey their masters, even the ones who are abusive and surly, "Likewise, ye wives, **be** in subjection to your own husbands...", even the ones who obey not the Word—have no regard for God. The text goes so far as to suggest that a wife should have the same reverence for an unsaved husband as to call him "lord," as did Sara. You can freely call your husband "lord" when you know that you are addressing the one who put him in charge and asked you to suffer at your husband's hands just as our Lord suffered at the hands of unjust authorities. Did Jesus reject the will of God and flee to safe ground just because it involved suffering? Jesus said, **"For I came down from heaven, not to do mine own will, but the will of him that sent me"** (John 6:38). Women who do their own will may flee from a marriage that is no fun, but women who do the will of God enter into a plane of blessedness known only to the obedient.

I know that this must be an amazing doctrine to many of you. Nonetheless, it is no less radical than Jesus was radical, and it is God's way. The text says to not be **afraid with any amazement** (3:6). The teachings of Jesus are so contrary to human nature that sometimes they will make you afraid and amazed. No one in the psychology department would ever think this one up. You will never hear this from Dr. Laura or from most of your modern preachers, but it is the path to glory, the path to a miracle that may change your husband after it has finally changed you.

God is seeking your glory. **Glory comes from doing the unusual, the brave, the wonderful, compared to what is normally done**. When a Christian wife does what a woman of the world would never do—cheerfully obey an unworthy man simply because God commands it—God in heaven is glorified. Children are to obey their parents "as unto the Lord," and wives are to obey their husbands as if they were obeying God. Read the text as it continues, and be amazed at your calling, not afraid of it.

I Peter 3:9-17

Not rendering <u>evil for evil, or railing for railing</u>: but contrariwise blessing; knowing that ye are <u>thereunto called</u>, that ye should inherit a blessing.

When you endure evil and railing without returning it, you receive a blessing, not as a martyr, but as one who worships God.

Contributions by Michael Pearl

10 For he that <u>will love life</u>, and see good days, let him refrain his tongue from evil, and his lips that they speak no guile:

11 Let him eschew evil, and do good; let him seek peace, and ensue it.

12 For the eyes of the Lord are over the righteous, and his ears are open unto their prayers: but the face of the Lord is against them that do evil.

13 And who is he that will harm you, if ye be followers of that which is good?

If you love life and want to live to a ripe, old age in peace and contentment, then refrain from returning evil words. For the eyes of the Lord see all that takes place. His ears are open to your prayers when you obey him and obey your husband. And then comes the promise: if you are following God, no harm will come to you by doing what is good.

14 But and if ye <u>suffer for righteousness' sake</u>, happy are ye: and be not afraid of their terror, neither be troubled;

You will receive a blessing when you suffer for righteousness' sake, that is, when you obey God by obeying your husband and not returning evil for evil. You will be happy, so don't be afraid or troubled by the things you must endure.

15 But sanctify the Lord God in your hearts: and be ready always to give an answer to every man that asketh you a reason of the hope that is in you with meekness and fear:

16 Having a good conscience; that, whereas they speak evil of you, as of evildoers, they may be ashamed that falsely accuse your good conversation in Christ.

17 For it is better, if the will of God be so, that ye <u>suffer for well doing</u>, than for evil doing.

If not for your husband, at least for God, be willing to suffer for your well doing.

If you are not at least moderately versed in Scripture and in the will and ways of God, this doctrine of suffering abuse in silence for **the glory of God will amaze you**. It is a pity that so many today are so ignorant of God's ways. This is the normal Christian life that we are advocating. God's way is the way of abounding joy and peace. Suffering for him brings **joy unspeakable and full of glory** (I Peter 1:8). On the other hand, we are not suggesting a long-faced, "poor me, look how I suffer" attitude that so many seem to manifest. You will never win a lost husband if he thinks you are accepting misery as part of your faith, and I wouldn't blame him. If your responses to him are making you miserable, you can be assured that you do not have God's heart in the matter. You must be a worshiper of God and enjoy his presence if you are going to suffer for his sake and it result in great glory.

–Michael Pearl

Practical Examples

You may still be confused as to when you are to obey and when not. We will list some of the questions and issues that we receive in the mail and discuss them one by one.

Sodomite Predator (E-mail that was answered immediately)

> Dear Pearls,
>
> Something terrible is happening, and we do not have any friends for me to turn to. I have to have HELP NOW! PLEASE read this letter and answer TODAY. A week or so ago, my son turned 13 years old. About that same time, my husband started wanting him to go out with him in the evenings to build man-to man relationships. I was glad. After the first time out, my son (from a previous relationship before my marriage to Dan) privately begged me not to make him go. My husband gets really mad if I or the children speak against him, but he is nice if we do what he says. He likes to brag on our obedience. I told my son he needs to obey Dan. Today my son told me that Dan takes him to interstate rest stops, where homosexuals hang out to "do" each other and watch for other boys using the bathrooms. My son said my husband makes him participate with him and other men. He knew too much to be lying, and besides, he was crying and begging and threatening to run away if I didn't do something. I am scared. I have strongly suspected Dan was doing porn for a long time, but tried to mind my own business. Now this terrible thing is happening. I am praying, PLEASE, dear God, I am begging, make them write me back today. I told my son to play sick tonight until I knew what to do.
>
> Jean, the mother of 7

Here was a clear example of a father and husband overstepping the bounds of his jurisdiction. Neither the wife nor the son were under obligation to obey him in this matter. We told her to call the law, so that they could set up a time to catch the sodomites at the rest stop, including her husband. She did. Her husband is in the slammer for a number of years, and the kids are growing up without a pervert for a daddy. Sometimes, it is a grave sin NOT to stand against your husband.

Chapter 23 Exceptions Examples

> AIDS is now a factor that must be considered, both for your own health and the health of your children.

Cross-Dressing

Dear Pearls,

My husband has started dressing in women's night gowns at night and wants me to pretend he is a woman when we have sex. He reminds me that what happens in our bedroom is OK because the bed is undefiled. He is a teacher at Church and well thought of. I know he is the head of the home, so I have gone along with him a few times, but it makes me sick. What is the right thing to do?

Anna

God did not delegate to a man the authority to induce his wife to participate in mental lesbianism. If she obeyed him, she would be committing sodomy in her heart—a clear violation of the moral law of God. The husband—or whatever he/it was—was taking to himself a sphere of authority that belongs to God only (Deuteronomy 22:5). **We instructed the wife to refuse to participate in his perversion and to express her disgust for his cross-dressing.** If she treated his sin as a preference, she would normalize his behavior. She must make it known that he is an unsaved man, on his way to hell, and that she is not going to dishonor her Lord.

Thievery

Dear Mrs. Pearl,

I have tried very hard to obey God and my husband, but I am afraid I will end up in jail if I keep helping him. He makes me stand "watch" at truck stops, while he breaks into semi-tractor trailer trucks parked at the stops. How can I honor him and still refuse what he expects?

Betty

We told her to report his crime to the law, to assist them in catching him in the act. She did, and he is in jail. She goes to visit him and brings him goodies and talks of the day when he can be back with the family. He knows he was wrong. He didn't need a dictionary to spell it out. If your husband tells you to break the law of God and man, and you know you will go to jail or others will be hurt, then you can respectfully refuse to comply, for God did not grant the husband unregulated power.

False Tax Returns

We have many letters from wives who tell us that their husband files false income tax returns, and she refuses to sign it with him, making him very angry. The wife sticks to her guns and takes the higher ground. When we question her and get the details, in most cases, the wife is upset because her husband did not report a little cash money that he made cutting grass or fixing several automobiles for friends and neighbors. We have never had a woman write whose husband was committing major fraud. It has been petty things that stick in her craw. She gives careful attention to every detail and

♥——————♥
God does
not appoint
a wife to be
her husband's
conscience.
♥——————♥

reminds him of the few things that he conveniently forgot to mention when declaring his income for the year. This puts great stress on the marriage. The husband senses that there is more to this than her "religious convictions." **He feels that she is using this opportunity to reject him, to take the reins in her own hands, and he resents it far more than any loss of revenue.**

In most cases, we are dealing with a man who would never steal. When he reads the Bible, the passage about taxes that stands out to him is the statement Jesus made when the tax collector came looking for him and his disciples. Jesus said in regard to taxes, **"Then are the children free"** (Matthew 18:26). That is, they are free from paying taxes to a government that is not representative. However, for testimony sake, he paid the taxes. Many men feel no moral obligation to stimulate their memories when it comes time to "voluntarily" contributing to a tax system that is illegal thievery. They do not feel any duty before God to contribute money to support abortions, the homosexual agenda in public schools, family-planning programs, the distribution of condoms to children, needles to dope addicts, support of the so-called arts, and so-called public radio with its socialist agenda. We are not advocating this position or justifying any dishonesty, but it helps a wife to understand a man's perspective.

God does not appoint a wife to be her husband's conscience. A wife has no right to make judgments concerning the way he interprets his compliance. However, she does have a duty to her own conscience. If she is required to sign her name to a document that declares, "This is how much we made in income, and not a penny more," then she has a duty to God and herself to tell the truth as she knows it. Furthermore, when you sign a tax form, you do so on penalty of perjury. Yet, from reading thousands of letters on this subject, we have come to the conclusion that IRS issues seem to be a convenient way for a wife to be her husband's conscience and still maintain her feeling of being a virtuous woman. She will have her day in court in front of the SUPREME JUDGE, who will judge the true intents of the heart.

As a Christian you have a desire and a duty to be honest in all things, but you must honor your husband as you do so. So, if you cannot sign your name to a document that would make you a liar, you must refuse to do so with grace and humility. There may be other ways to deal with it. Perhaps you could file separate tax returns, whereby you wouldn't be required to sign his returns, and then you wouldn't be involved in how he conducts his business.

My Husband Doesn't Want Me to Go to Church

Dear Debi,

My husband says I can't go to church in the evening anymore. I feel if I do not have this sweet time of fellowship, I will not be able to continue to walk faithfully before God. God's Word says not to forsake the assembling of yourselves together, so it would be direct violation of God's Word to not go. My husband told me to write and ask you.

Carla

Dear Carla,

It is common for unsaved or discouraged husbands to forbid their wives from going to church. In almost all cases, the husband's objections are not based on a desire to prevent her from worshiping God. Rather, he views her affiliation with the church as a second lover, maybe the preferred lover, and himself as a jilted spouse. He is jealous. He is unfulfilled as a husband and believes that the church is somehow getting your first love. Now, a wife with no wisdom might take satisfaction in his jealousy, thinking of herself as putting God first, but true worship of God is never neglectful of relationships. Loving God and serving him should make you a more attentive wife, a better lover to your husband.

The bottom line is that, if your husband does not want you to go to church, then stay home and paint the house with him. Go fishing or shopping, whatever he wants to do, and make sure you are having fun. To obey him with disappointment and reluctance is not obedience; it is revenge.

-Debi

The Bottom Line

If a wife has an attitude of rebellion, she can find a thousand different exceptions to obedience. But if a woman is really seeking God and asking for wisdom from on high, she will be able to discern the **difference between her own controlling spirit and those rare instances that a husband may command outside his sphere of authority—requiring legal intervention**. Women who threaten to "report him to the law," or women who refuse to answer the phone any way other than, "He is here, but will not talk," are rebellious. They will never make it to the hall of fame found in Hebrews 11, where Sara was listed, nor will they make it into a heavenly marriage here on earth. They will go to their graves unloved and uncherished, a total failure as the woman God called them to be. Wisdom allows us the ability to use our minds and spirits to handle small problems with grace and honor.

To those of you who are enduring verbal and physical abuse, we realize that statistically, you are likely to remain with your husband. It is therefore important that you understand how to speak and conduct yourself in a way that will maintain your physical and emotional safety and ultimately win your husband.

The Bible gives us several examples of wives in terrible circumstances coming up with different ideas to show honor and still obey. For instance, Esther, who was given as a bride to a godless, divorced man, diverted disaster and death by quick wit and courage when her husband made a foolish decree. (Read the book of Esther for the whole story, and check out *www.nogreaterjoy.org* for the *Esther Study*.)

Abigail's Story

The Scripture records one "exception" story, where a woman was forced by the law of the land and the preservation of her people to act contrary to her husband's will. It is the famous love story of David and Abigail.

When David, the anointed king of Israel, was living in exile, fleeing from King Saul, he created an army of men and trained them as a police force to protect

Abigail's wisdom & rewards ♥ ♥ ♥

the people of the land in which they were living. This militia depended upon the farmers and ranchers to supply them with food—remuneration for the protection they provided. On this occasion, David sent a message down to one of the local ranchers named Nabal, requesting the foodstuff he needed to be sent back with his messengers. Nabal refused to give them any food. In anger, David prepared to avenge this unrighteous man's affront to God's mercy and justice (David was God's "arm" of mercy, his anointed one), by destroying Nabal and all his innocent people.

I Samuel 25:13-38

13 And David said unto his men, Gird ye on every man his sword. And they girded on every man his sword; and David also girded on his sword: and there went up after David about four hundred men; and two hundred abode by the stuff.

14 But one of the young men told Abigail, Nabal's wife, saying, Behold, David sent messengers out of the wilderness to salute our master; and he railed on them.

15 But the men were very good unto us, and we were not hurt, neither missed we any thing, as long as we were conversant with them, when we were in the fields: [The men were David's soldiers protecting the farm hands from thieves.]

16 They were a wall unto us both by night and day, all the while we were with them keeping the sheep.

17 Now therefore know and consider what thou wilt do; for evil is determined against our master, and against all his household: for he is such a son of Belial, that a man cannot speak to him.

> To obey him with disappointment and reluctance is not obedience; it is revenge.

The servants of this man called him a "son of Belial", which means *son of Satan*. The workers left behind to keep the home place feared that their selfish, evil master was going to get them all killed, so they appealed to Abigail to save their lives. Abigail took the advice of the men her husband had left in charge of overseeing his home.

18 Then Abigail made haste, and took two hundred loaves, and two bottles of wine, and five sheep ready dressed, and five measures of parched corn, and an hundred clusters of raisins, and two hundred cakes of figs, and laid them on asses.

19 And she said unto her servants, Go on before me; behold, I come after you. But she told not her husband Nabal.

Then Abigail got on the ass and rode down to meet David before he had a chance to come up and kill her servants and the people who lived and worked on their huge ranch. It was her only hope of saving the people who were in her care.

23 And when Abigail saw David, she hasted, and lighted off the ass, and fell before David on her face, and bowed herself to the ground,

24 And fell at his feet, and said, Upon me, my lord, upon me let this iniquity be: and let thine handmaid, I pray thee, speak in thine audience, and hear the words of thine handmaid.

Abigail was willing to suffer for her husband's sins in order to save the people of her charge. Notice that she does not cover her husband's sin or pretend his character is wonderful or that there has been some misunderstanding. He is known to be a devilish man, and so she states the facts. It was her husband's selfishness that caused the problem, and she is forthcoming in her appeal to David.

25 Let not my lord, I pray thee, regard this man of Belial, even Nabal: for as his name is, so is he; Nabal is his name, and folly is with him: but I thine handmaid saw not the young men of my lord, whom thou didst send.

26 Now therefore, my lord, as the LORD liveth, and as thy soul liveth, seeing the LORD hath withholden thee from coming to shed blood, and from avenging thyself with thine own hand, now let thine enemies, and they that seek evil to my lord, be as Nabal.

David's gratitude for Abigail's courage and willingness to risk her life to stop him from killing many innocent people, which would have caused him grief when he discovered his error, was evident.

32 And David said to Abigail, Blessed be the LORD God of Israel, which sent thee this day to meet me:

33 And blessed be thy advice, and blessed be thou, which hast kept me this day from coming to shed blood, and from avenging myself with mine own hand.

After Abigail had to face David in a life-and-death situation, she turned around and went back to face her wicked husband's wrath. She knew her husband could have her killed without any fear of recompense, yet she returned to him. When she got to him, he was having a drunken party, so she waited until he had slept off his drunkenness to tell him. The next morning she told him what she had done in feeding David and his men. Then look what God did.

Abigail's Rewards

36 And Abigail came to Nabal; and, behold, he held a feast in his house, like the feast of a king; and Nabal's heart was merry within him, for he was very drunken: wherefore she told him nothing, less or more, until the morning light.

37 But it came to pass in the morning, when the wine was gone out of Nabal, and his wife had told him these things, that <u>his heart died within him,</u> and he became as a stone.

38 And it came to pass about ten days after, that the LORD smote Nabal, that he died.

What a gracious thing God did to give that mean old man a heart attack or stroke. When David hears that the wicked man is dead, he sends his men to bring Abigail to him to become his wife. She first washes David's servants' feet, then hurries off with them to meet David. **Abigail was one tough lady**.

REFLECTING ON
To Obey or Not to Obey

➢ *Traits of a Good Help Meet*
- An obedient wife is yielding, willing and eager to accomplish injunctions or desires, and abstains from that which is forbidden.
- She looks for ways to obey and reverence her husband.
- She channels her mind into positive ways of saying "yes."
- She never considers herself to be an exception to the rule of being a help meet.

➢ *Getting Serious with God*

Go through your Bible and find all the Scripture that we covered on the subject of *authority*. Ask God to give you a heart willing to cheerfully do his will, regardless of the immediate benefits.

➢ *Reality Check*

"But the fruit of the Spirit is love, joy, peace, longsuffering, gentleness, goodness, faith, Meekness, temperance: against such there is no law" (Galatians 5:22-23).

If the Spirit of God abides in you, you will show forth fruit, first, at home in your relationship to your husband and children, then also in social settings outside the home. Your true self is manifested at home and is known by those who know you best.

Chapter 24

Heirs Together in the Grace of Life

Sarah the Beautiful

If I had been the one authorizing exceptions, I would have released Sarah from obeying her husband on at least two occasions, but I would have been wrong. Sarah chose to obey Abraham even when he lied and told her to lie because he was afraid of what could happen if the king knew she was his wife. Hebrews 11 presents Sarah and Abraham as examples of faith. **In I Peter 3, she is honored as being the woman who called her husband *lord*.**

Abraham was God's man. God had called him out to be the father of a great nation. Yet Abraham, out of fear for his own life, told his wife to lie, a lie that would put her in danger of sexual advances from another man. Do you remember how Sarah responded to these situations? It happened twice. Once when she was young and beautiful, and once when she was quite old but still a very lovely and desirable woman.

One day Abraham came in and announced to his wife that God had told him to move far away from both their families to a distant land. When asked which land, Abraham couldn't say, because he didn't know. Abraham spent much of his life traveling around looking for a city whose builder and maker was God. He never found that city, and there were many trials and hardships along the way. How would you like that type of life? Would you have stood by your husband as a man of God in the face of such lack of evidence?

Genesis 12:10-17

"10 And there was a famine in the land: and Abraham went down into Egypt to sojourn there; for the famine was grievous in the land."

As the city in Egypt came into view, Abraham looked over his shoulder at his beautiful, smiling wife, and his heart melted with fear—a carnal response to a God who promised to bless him and keep him.

> ♥ ———— ♥
>
> I am thrilled when I see God delivering a woman from her husband's folly through dreams, plagues, wrecks, sickness, and even death.
>
> ♥ ———— ♥

11 And it came to pass, when he was come near to enter into Egypt, that he said unto Sarai his wife, Behold now, I know that thou art a fair woman to look upon:

12 Therefore it shall come to pass, when the Egyptians shall see thee, that they shall say, This is his wife: and they will kill me, but they will save thee alive.

13 Say, I pray thee, thou art my sister: that it may be well with me for thy sake; and my soul shall live because of thee.

What a terrible burden to put on a woman. Make her feel that she had to lie in order to save her husband's life. She must have also known that she would be in a danger of being taken by another man. Of course, Abraham was right about the Egyptians, who, when they saw Sarah, were very impressed with her beauty.

"16 And he entreated Abram well for her sake: and he had sheep, and oxen, and asses, and menservants, and maidservants, and she asses, and camels."

Sarah was taken to special quarters reserved for "brides in waiting." What a state of mind Sarah must have been in! Her husband was supposed to love, cherish, and protect her. Where was he now? Abraham was out getting gifts in return for his lovely wife. But Sara obeyed. If she had come to me for counsel, I would have had a hard time telling her to obey her husband and keep quiet, but God honored Sara's obedience.

"17 And the Lord plagued Pharaoh and his house with great plagues because of Sarai Abram's wife."

Since Abraham was fearful, God had to come to Sarah's rescue in a supernatural way. Do you let God be God in your life? There will be times when your husband is dead wrong, as was Abraham, and you will need to obey your husband and commit your way unto God.

Chapter 24 ~ Heirs Together of the Grace of Life

If this were the only time Abraham reacted like this, we could say, "Oh well, he learned his lesson." But no, he did the same thing again. Genesis 20 finds Sarah as an old lady, but she still must have been a desirable woman. The Bible tells us that Abraham journeyed to the south country. The king of Gerar got a look at Sarah and asked Abraham about her. Good old macho Abraham said, **"She is my sister."** So this King took Sarah in anticipation of her becoming his bride. Again Sarah went along and obeyed her husband. If it had been I, you would have seen me giving Abraham a little "spiritual" training—something like, "Abraham, why can't you just believe God will take care of us? Please don't put me in this position again." The Bible only records that Sarah simply did as she was told.

Do you grieve over the situations your husband puts you in? Tell me, how would you react if he pulled this one? Would you refuse to obey? Take authority into your own, "more spiritual" hands? This time the Bible tells us that God sent the king a dream, saying, **"Behold, thou art but a dead man, for the woman which thou hast taken; for she is a man's wife"** (Gen. 20:3). God cared for Sarah and kept her pure.

I am thrilled when I see God delivering a woman from her husband's folly through dreams, plagues, wrecks, sickness, and even death. How could Abraham, such a man of faith, do such a faithless thing? How could Abraham, who believed God for great and mighty things, not take better care of his wife? We know he loved her dearly.

Abraham was just that—he was a man.

All men make mistakes. A woman's place is simply to obey for God's sake, not for right's sake. If you wait until you feel that your husband is right before you obey him, then you will seldom obey him, and you will never enjoy the miracles of God.

God Chose a Woman

While Abraham was learning to obey God, **Sarah was learning to obey her husband**, and God was busy doing miracles for both of them. God chose Sarah as surely as he chose Abraham. **It took an obedient woman to become the mother of a great nation**. Sarah wasn't Abraham's only wife; nor was Isaac Abraham's only son. Hagar, Sarah's maid, who bore Abraham's son, Ishmael, was treated with very little regard by Abraham. When Sarah, in jealous anger, demanded that Abraham cast Hagar and her son out into the desert alone, God told Abraham to do as she said, thus fixing in Abraham's heart that only through Isaac's seed would come all the blessings he had promised. Abraham married again after Sarah died, yet you never hear anyone mention this wife. The six children Abraham had with Keturah merit just one little verse in Scripture, recording the fact that he had additional children.

I know that for Abraham to be the man he was, Sarah had to be a powerful *encourager*. There must have been times when Abraham became discouraged. "I look and I look for the city whose builder and maker is God, and still no city!" "Well, Abraham," Sarah might have laughingly told him, "Our life has been a lot more rewarding for the looking, and we have nothing better to do, so we'll try again tomorrow."

Who and what would my husband be if he had married another woman? Have I made it possible for him to be a strong, confident, aggressive man of God?

Have I allowed <u>God</u> to direct his life and work? Have I appreciated his calling and interests? Have I been a help meet for my man? Is he a better, stronger, more capable man for having had me as his wife? **If God were creating the perfect lady for him,** *would it have been me?*

> If God were creating the perfect lady for him, would it have been I?

Over the years, I have on many occasions seen what appeared to be a good woman married to a man who seemed to be a worthless, no-account slob. Finally, after years of abuse, the "good" wife divorces her drunken husband, with everyone agreeing that it was the only thing she could do. Within a year, the worthless drunk marries again. A few months after his marriage, he stops drinking—without the aid of a twelve-step program—and then spends the rest of his life working steady, enjoying his new family, loving his new wife, and never touching another drop of liquor. I have enough sense to know that some men are addicted to alcohol, porn, and laziness, regardless of their wives, but I have witnessed the above scenario too many times to dismiss it as insignificant. This is by no means advocating divorce and remarriage. Rather, it says that if some "worthless" men had wives who were more _____ (you fill in the blank), they would not be so worthless.

God chose this one special man and this one special woman to become the father and mother of a great nation. Sarah wasn't commended for being a wonderful mother. She spent most of her life childless, being an old woman before her only son was born, and then she died before Isaac was grown. **She was commended because she believed God and called her husband** *lord*. She was the kind of wife God needed to make *the kind of man* God chose to bring forth a great nation.

God says of Abraham, **"For I know him, that he will command his children and his household after him, and they shall keep the way of the LORD, to do justice and judgment…"** (Genesis 18:19). Are your children rebellious? Is your home in shambles, and you cannot get help from your husband? Perhaps the problem lies in how you respond to your man. **"Even as Sara obeyed Abraham, calling him lord: whose daughters ye are, as long as ye do well, and are not afraid with any amazement"** (I Peter 3:6).

When Two Become One

Dear Friends in Christ,

I am a minister. I recently listened to a tape a pastor recorded about a woman learning to honor and respect her husband. It was a message to women, but I thought I needed to learn how to better help married couples, so I listened carefully.

*I noticed myself strangely moved by the message. I have a great wife and kids who love and respect me. **Yet, I realized that I long to be respected and honored by them in ways that are not happening**. Although it was difficult (I am not given to emotionalism much, but could not deny the intensity of my longings and feelings), I shared with my wife my need to be respected by her and our children. I also shared my desire to have the companionship with her that the tape described as something very much needed by men from their wives. I know I could never have told her that before I heard the tape. My wife was responsive to this and said she did not realize how important this was to me. She was pleased and even blessed to know how important her involvement in "my" ministry was.*

*Interestingly enough, I shared the tape with a couple of men, and they felt similarly and had similar responses from their wives. Again, **the realization that this man she married felt incomplete without her involvement and respect gave these wives a real sense of purpose**.*

I realize now how much I need her. I really need her! Not just to cook my meals and warm my bed, but to be the encourager of my soul. Without her there, ever present with me, I know I would feel empty. Now we both realize how precious it is for us to finally understand how it feels to be one.

> Pastor Ben

*"**A wise woman** seeks to be part of her husband's life. His interests become her interests. She looks for ways to help him in all his endeavors. When he needs a helping hand, it is her hand that is there first."*

Heirs Together of the Grace of Life

Pastor Ben was hungering for his wife to be an heir together with him. **His unfulfilled need to be the king of his kingdom**, and his failure to receive the deference and reverence that comes with that position, caused him to feel alone. He had a need for his queen to support him. **No doubt, she was so busy being a GOOD wife and mother that she forgot her most important purpose for existing**.

He did not want his wife to be a performer for the church or to win the best housekeeping award; he wanted a woman to tell him he was wonderful.

"Likewise, ye husbands, dwell with them according to knowledge, giving honour unto the wife, as unto the weaker vessel, and <u>as being heirs together of the grace of life</u>; that your prayers be not hindered" (1 Peter 3:7) In our modern culture, we women push to accomplish so much outside the home. Most of these things are not of God. They are just pursuits of vanity to crowd our minds and cloud our spirits and cause us to forget that we were created for the man to whom we are married. We need to lay aside activities outside the home that push us and the kids to the edge of exhaustion and confusion. Homeschooling is not the problem. It is the ambitious goals you set. God's will for all married couples is that they walk life's path hand in hand. Many husbands and wives are running circles around each other, seldom meeting in the middle. We are so busy driving the kids to this class or that event that we lose sight of being heirs together. Even church activities rob us from God's plans for us as a couple.

Get off the phone, lay down romance novels, turn off the TV, stay off the web, reduce outside visits or women's classes, and focus on putting your time into what your

Learn to be his soul~mate

husband is doing and what your children need. That is how you can better meet his needs, and **it is the beginning of learning to be an heir together with him of the grace of life.**

Pastor Ben's soul hungered for a real *soul-mate*. He did not want his wife to be a performer for the church, the homeschool committee leader, or to win the best housekeeping award; he wanted a woman to tell him he was wonderful. He needed a woman to meet him at the door with a smile. He longed to be the most important activity in her life. He needed her with him. **"… And the wife see that <u>she reverence her husband</u>"** (Ephesians 5:33). He needed to be HER king.

Many couples live their whole lives together and never really bond. They are just two people sharing the same house and dividing up responsibilities. They live together, never fuss or fight, raise their children, yet never function as a team. He does his thing, and she does hers. She doesn't really know his business or care. He is bored with her "many" daily activities. There is little in their lives that couldn't be done just as well apart. When he drives to the store, it never occurs to him to have her ride along. When she goes out for a few minutes, it feels as though it would be a nuisance to have to tell him where she is going and when she will be back. They are married, sleeping together, raising children, sharing duties and chores, but they are two separate people going about life. The wife gets busy with her children and church and bonds with her best friend at church. She shares more emotionally with another woman than she does with her own husband. Women bonding with other women? Instead of the perfect picture of Christ and the Church, today we have a perverted expression of woman satisfying woman. What a disgusting mess!

The husband works and finds fulfillment in his success, yet in his heart he is just like Adam was before Eve was created—incomplete—and, **like Adam, he is alone, and it is "not good."** Life passes him by, leaving him unfulfilled. Children grow up, and somewhere around 40 or 50 years old, when the husband has built his personal empire, hubby's long-lost need for **a *real* soul-mate** is revived. Suddenly, his goals and accomplishments don't seem so important. That man, who has sexually resisted other women all his life, is suddenly vulnerable to women who show interest in him as a human being and as a man. He can now enjoy the "alien" company of some lady who shows him deference through her interest in his dreams, hopes, and joys.

Your husband needs you to be his help meet, his lover, his best friend. You need to lay down your own agenda and become his Queen.

Chapter 24 ~ Heirs Together of the Grace of Life

I Stand Amazed

Dear Debi,

I found your website! What a blessing. I have learned so much from the submissive-wife-type comments. I am learning about being a submissive wife, and it is amazing to see my husband absolutely bloom before my eyes. We have been married for 15 years, but this is the first year I have kept my tongue quiet. Any request that I have, I tell God about it and he provides through my husband. It is sooo coooool! Things have changed so very quickly. If you only knew what life was like before. I won't go into detail, but let's just say, I now have beauty for ashes. And it is absolutely God's doing. I know that I had nothing to do with it, and I am glad for that. **God is jealous for my husband,** and He will not allow me to change him. Sometimes I can almost hear God tell me, "See, daughter, you finally gave him to me, and now I am fixing him better than you would have even thought! He is my son, and I take pleasure in working with him. Keep having that faith that I will work in your husband's life, because I am not done with him yet; and I am not finished with you, either. Lift up your head, and praise me with joy as I complete this work. This is your job, daughter; praise him with joy always for the work that I am doing in him."

When things go hard, I praise God and give the circumstance to him. I've learned that our prayers will not be answered if we harbor bitterness. Deb, my house is changing from week to week. I can see the work going on before my eyes, and I stand amazed. The more I forgive in my heart, the more wonderful changes there are. Please let your people know that forgiveness really is a key, and yes, <u>continual forgiveness</u>, so that our prayers will be answered. I Peter 3:7 "Likewise, ye husbands, dwell with them according to knowledge, giving honour unto the wife, as unto the weaker vessel, and as being heirs together of the grace of life; <u>that your prayers be not hindered</u>." When I stopped dictating the answers to God, then some of the questions got answers, better than I had even hoped. If you only knew where I was a few years ago. God is so good. Be blessed.

Jill

Early Roots

The seeds of bonding are planted early in the marriage. When a young wife gets bored and lonely being at home by herself, she spends her days preparing for her husband's return each evening, and she looks forward to their weekends together. She spends the lonely hours planning for him, cooking for him, cleaning for him, and eagerly hungering for him. His spirit flourishes, and his love for her grows <u>when he sees</u> her need of him. It is this process that makes two people learn to depend on each other.

When a young wife gets on the phone with her friends or leans heavily on her mother, she never develops the need to depend on her husband emotionally. Her husband has spent his youth without her, and so he tends to keep on functioning as an independent man. He doesn't instinctively sense her needs, and she doesn't yet know that it is he that she needs. They too often end up as two people living in the same house, raising children, leaders in the church, and are what the world thinks of as the perfect family. Yet both know that something is missing.

> ♥ ——— ♥
> Bonding, and becoming heirs together, starts with the wife.
> ♥ ——— ♥

Bonding, and becoming heirs together, starts with the wife, because she is the weaker vessel and has the greatest need. It is her "visible" need of him that awakens him. **If she pours her life into pleasing her husband and serving him, he will develop a protective, nurturing instinct toward her**. As he gains confidence that his heart is safe with her and that she places his welfare first, he will begin to trust her with his innermost being. The Proverbs 31 woman was a major success in many areas of her life, but in laying a foundation for her success, the verses tell us that **"The heart of her husband doth safely trust in her, so that he shall have no need of spoil. She will do him good and not evil all the days of her life"** (Proverbs 31:11-12). Without this foundation, a man will never bond. Remember my queenly friend who was a crown to her husband? Even in his unsaved condition, he knew that when he brought those men home, his wife would not disgrace him by being moody or upset.

When a woman bonds with her man, she gains his strength and stability. As a couple, they can accomplish more than they would ever accomplish standing alone. He gives her emotional strength to deal with the issues of life. When he can trust her judgments, it will help him become wiser and more in tune with the needs of others.

A man does not have to be a nice, sweet guy who never once forgets a special occasion. He doesn't even have to be saved, but if he trusts his wife to do him good, he will bond with her. If she opens up to him, he will fill her need. The wife does not need to be cute, hardworking, or smart, but *if she honors and loves her man, she will have his strength helping her become more than what she would have ever been without him.* **He only needs his woman to pour her life into his, for him to pour his soul back into hers**. But if she stands apart and complains because he is angry, lazy, not a good daddy, or works too much, he will never pour his soul into that kind of woman. If she spends her days running from event to event or from person to person, and if she finds emotional solace in her daughters, mother, or friends, he will not pour his strength into her. Someday, her daughters will get married and no longer need a mother. In time, her mother will pass on, her friends will move, and she will find that he has found someone else to be his soul mate, his help meet, because he didn't find it in her.

Yet, when a plain, ordinary woman, with a dull personality, without many skills, pours herself, her time, joy, thanksgiving, and even her praise, fear, and uncertainty into a plain ordinary man, they both become stronger, more capable, and wiser human beings. People will come to them for help and encouragement.

It is so easy to spend your life lamenting, "Oh, if only my husband were saved or more spiritual or not so angry." No matter who or what your husband is, *your job is to be his help meet.* When you approach him with light in your eyes, that light will reflect back to you.

Becoming heirs together of the grace of life is God's highest plan for husband and wife. It is the great mystery, the pattern of Christ and the Church. The inheritance is great passion, stability, wisdom, joy, love, and balance. God's blessings are so much greater than any tongue or writer can ever tell.

God is the master at making heavenly marriages

From a Thankful Help Meet

(Here is a letter that was sent to me from a thankful lady.)

Dear Mr. and Mrs. Pearl,

I thought you might be interested to hear of my husband's passing, and what a blessing it is to have been married to a husband who lived what you teach. He went out to do yard work in the afternoon of September 24 and as he went out the door, he turned and said to me, "It has been a wonderful life with you." Those were the last words I ever heard him say. He came in a few minutes later, went into a back room, and dropped dead of a heart attack. He was always telling me how he loved me and would always thank me for meals and all the things I did for him. He was a wonderful, godly husband, and it is so lovely to have those words to remember.

We were married for 56 years.

Keep reminding people that marriage is the most precious relationship we have on this earth, and it is ONLY FOR THIS EARTH, so make the most of it, and don't waste the time. The Lord is sufficient for all things, and I am receiving from Him all I need, but oh, how I miss the half of me that is gone!

Love in our Savior,

Marian

Marriage is the most precious
relationship we have on earth.

REFLECTING ON
The Things we have Learned

➤ **Things that can break a man's spirit and cripple a marriage:**
- ◆ A wife who is spiritually critical.
- ◆ A discontented wife.
- ◆ A wife who is not fulfilling the eight priorities listed in Titus 2 for a wife.

➤ **Eight things that women must <u>do</u> or <u>be</u> to avoid <u>blaspheming the written Word of God.</u>**

Titus 2:3-5

[1] sober, [2] love their husbands, [3] love their children, [4] be discreet, [5] chaste, [6] keepers at home, [7] good, [8] obedient to their own husbands.

➤ **Tools of our Glorious Marriage Warfare are:**
- • Joy
- • Thankfulness
- • Contentment
- • Reverence
- • Submission
- • Prayer
- • Believing God's Word

"And the LORD God said, It is not good that the man should be alone; I will make him a help meet for him....the LORD God... brought her unto the man" (Genesis 2:18,22).

"Whoso findeth a wife findeth a good thing, and obtaineth favour of the Lord" (Proverbs 18:22).

I Am His Water

by Debi Pearl

I am his water;
He gazes at me as I ripple over the rocks,
The sun glistening in a thousand places over my surface.
I dance and play,
Delighting him day after day;
So beautiful! I hear him say;
I am his water, lovely and laughing.

He thirsts for me
Like a man in a burning desert,
Hot, dry sand burning his throat,
The scorching sun beating upon him.
He seeks me.
I am his deep well filled with fresh, clean,
abundant water;
Always there, waiting to quench his thirst;
I am his water, fresh, clean, abundant.

He looks for peace;
His soul grows troubled.
Rumors abound, he struggles;
He comes to me;
He lies in the soft green carpet of my banks;
I am the deep, still water.
Although he does not touch me, I give him rest.
Solace.
I am his water, deep, still; I bring him peace.

He has forgotten who he is;
He searches for reality, to reclaim his
personhood.

He stumbles and falls on his knees beside me;
He stares into my depths, searching for truth.
I lie still and reflect the man he is, good, strong, true;
He sees and is reassured.
I am his water, reflecting, reassuring,
Reminding him of who and what he is.

He has learned to trust me;
I have earned his trust.
I have danced and laughed for him.
In the bright sunshine he thought me beautiful.
I have been clean, fresh, and abundant water;
I have yearned always to quench his thirst;
Waters, abundant water.

I have been quiet and deep;
I have soothed his troubled soul;
He has found rest beside me.
When he peered into my depths, searching,
I reflected back to him strength and honor.
He had no fear with me;
He was safe being the man he was created to be.
Now he plunges into my cool, deep water;
I hear him laugh as he surfaces; I feel his
muscles relax;
I see him find glory and honor—
Other men marvel.
I am. . . his water.

God is awesome and terrible in his judgments. He is also full of mercy, and of grace.

His strong desire is to bless his people, but too often by our "carelessness," we force him to judge. I believe he wearies of judgment.

He is looking, searching, calling out to those who will hear him. He calls your name, just as long ago in the night hours he called the boy, Samuel. Just as he came to the handmaiden, Mary, he softly calls your name. Will you hear him?

God is looking for *help meets*, ladies who will honor what he said in his "letter of instructions," so he can use them as vessels of blessings. Blessings! He has so many blessings and so few willing vessels.

I can almost see him standing there, leaning over the portals of Heaven, watching, waiting, and listening for that lovely musical sound of joyful laughter wafting up through the heavens. "Yes, I hear one answering the call. Bring me the cup." An angel hands over the cup of chastisement and judgment, and God replies, "No, not THAT one; the large one full of blessings is what this little gal needs." And the angel smiles as he puts the large Blessings Cup into God's eager hands. Smiling, God begins to pour the blessings forth, spilling out blessings faster than they can be received. The angel leans over so he can see, and then he, too, hears the beautiful sound of thanksgiving floating ever upward as a sweet aroma to God. He is an Awesome God of blessings and delight. He is ever willing and ready to bless those who honor him.

Do you hear him? He is softly and tenderly calling your name: "Be the *help meet* I created you to be. Believe me, trust me, obey me, and then watch what I will do."

Showers of blessings!
Oh, that today they might fall.

Scripture List

This scripture list is included as a reference for those of you who wish to study the role of women and wives in the Word of God for yourselves. This list is not exhaustive but contains all major verses pertaining to the subjects addressed in this book.

REFERENCE	TEXT
Gen 1:27-28	...male and female created he them
Gen 2:15	...put him into the garden of Eden
Gen 2:18	I will make him an help meet for him
Gen 2:20	...for Adam there was not found
Gen 2:22-23	...made he a woman
Gen 3:1-24	Now the serpent was more subtil...
Gen 12:10-20	Abraham allows Sarah to be taken
Gen 18:12	...I am waxed old shall I have pleasure
Gen 18:19	For I know him, that he will command
Gen 19:26	Disobedient wife
Gen 20	Abraham allows Sarah to be taken
Gen 20:18	Closed womb
Gen 24	Finding a bride
Gen 29:31	Opened womb
Gen 41:33,34	...look out a man discreet and wise...
Ex 2:1-22	Mothers of Moses
Ex 34:14	...for the Lord, whose name is Jealous...
Lev 18	Sexual perversion
Deut 22:5	Men's clothing
Deut 24:1-4	Her former husband, which sent her...
Deut 28:28	The LORD shall smite thee with madness
Deut 28:47-48	Because thou servedst not the LORD...
Judges 13	Miraculous birth (Samson)
Ruth	Story of Ruth
I Sam 1	Miraculous birth (Samuel)
I Sam 25	Story of Abigail
II Sam 11-12	Read the story of David and Bathsheba
I & II Kings	Story of Jezebel and her rebellion
I Kings 17:9-24	Story of a widow
Neh 8:10	...the joy of the LORD is your strength
Esther	Story of Esther
Job 5:2	For wrath killeth the foolish one...
Ps 33:18	Behold, the eye of the LORD...
Ps 37:3-8	Commit thy way unto the LORD...

REFERENCE	TEXT
Ps 51	A Psalm of David, repenting of his sin
Ps 90:12	So teach us to number our days...
Ps 100	Make a joyful noise unto the LORD...
Ps 107:22	...sacrifice the sacrifices of thanksgiving...
Ps 111:10	The fear of the LORD is the beginning...
Ps 139:13-16	The unborn
Prov 1:3	To receive the instruction of wisdom...
Prov 1:7	The fear of the LORD is the beginning
Prov 2:2	So that thou incline thine ear unto wisdom...
Prov 2:10-11	When wisdom entereth into thine heart...
Prov 4:7	Wisdom is the principal thing...
Prov 5:15-19	Marital faithfulness
Prov 6:21	Bind them continually upon thine heart...
Prov 6:24-35	Adulterous women
Prov 7:1-27	Unfaithful woman
Prov 9:10	The fear of the LORD is the beginning
Prov 9:13	A foolish woman is clamorous...
Prov 11:16	A gracious woman retaineth honor...
Prov 11:22	...a fair woman which is without discretion
Prov 12:4	A virtuous woman is a crown...
Prov 13:24	He that spareth the rod hateth his son
Prov 14:1	Every wise woman buildeth her house...
Prov 14:18	but the prudent are crowned...
Prov 15:13,15	A merry heart maketh a cheerful...
Prov 16:3	...and thy thoughts shall be established
Prov 16:21	The wise in heart shall be called prudent...
Prov 17:22	A merry heart doeth good...
Prov 18:9	He also that is slothful in his work...
Prov 18:15	The heart of the prudent...
Prov 18:22	Whoso findeth a wife findeth a good thing...
Prov 19:13	...and the contentions of a wife...
Prov 19:14	...and a prudent wife is from the Lord
Prov 20:5	Counsel in the heart of a man...
Prov 21:9	...brawling woman in a wide house

Phil 2:5	Let this mind be in you, which was also...	Titus 3:14	...maintain good works for necessary uses...
Phil 3:14	I press toward the mark for the prize...	Heb 6:7	...and bringeth forth herbs meet for them...
Phil 4:6	Be careful for nothing...	Heb 11:11	...she judged him faithful who had promised
Phil 4:8	...whatsoever things are true...	Heb 13:4	Marriage is honourable in all...
Phil 4:11	...I have learned, in whatsoever state...	Heb 13:5	...be content with such things as ye have...
Col 1:12	...meet to be partakers of the inheritance...	Heb 13:8	Jesus Christ the same yesterday...
Col 3:15	...and be ye thankful	Jas 1:5	If any of you lack wisdom...
Col 3:18	Wives, submit yourselves...	Jas 2:25	Rahab, the harlot, is justified...
II Thess 1:3	We are bound to thank God always...	Jas 3:1	My brethren, be not many masters...
I Tim 2:9-10	In like manner also, that women adorn...	Jas 3:1-12	The tongue is a fire...
I Tim 2:11	Let the woman learn in silence...	Jas 3:17	But the wisdom that is from above...
I Tim 2:12-15	But I suffer not a woman to teach...	Jas 4:17	Therefore to him that knoweth...
I Tim 3:11	Even so must their wives be grave...	I Pet 1:8	...joy unspeakable and full of glory
I Tim 5:3-16	Widows—younger and older	I Pet 2:13-23	...be subject to your masters with all fear
I Tim 6:6-8	godliness with contentment is great gain	I Pet 3:1-17	Likewise, ye wives, be in subjection...
II Tim 1:5	Grandmother Lois	I Pet 4:8	...for charity shall cover...
II Tim 1:7	For God hath not given us a spirit of fear...	I Pet 4:9	Use hospitality one to another...
II Tim 2:21	...meet for the master's use...	II Pet 1:13	Yea, I think it meet, as long as I am...
II Tim 3:6	...and lead captive silly women laden with sins...	III John 1:4	I have no greater joy than to hear...
Titus 2:3-5	...that the word of God be not blasphemed	Rev 2:20	...thou sufferest that woman Jezebel...

If you enjoyed this book, consider these and other products by Michael and Debi Pearl that can purchased through www.nogreaterjoy.org

To Train Up a Child
- 500,000 In Print! -

From successful parents, learn how to train up your children rather than discipline them up. With humor and real-life examples, this book shows you how to train your children before the need to discipline arises. Be done with corrective discipline; make them allies rather than adversaries. The stress will be gone and your obedient children will praise you.

122pg Book

The Joy of Training Video

Michael and Debi Pearl tell how they successfully trained up their five children with love, humor, the rod, and a King James Bible. The 2 DVD set contains the same high quality, digitally filmed content as the video set and hundreds of snapshots and video clips of family and children, illustrating the things being taught.

Available on DVD or VHS

Marriage God's Way Video

A good marriage is 50/50. A perfect marriage is 100/100. It is a man and a woman giving 100% to the other. What if he or she won't give 100%? Then you can match his 10% with your 10% and continue in an unfulfilling relationship, or, by the grace of God and the power of the Holy Spirit, you can give 100% of your talents and abilities to your spouse for their sake and blessing and watch their 10% grow into 100%. Someone has to start the process. Holding out will never do. Only by giving do you receive. Love and honor make more love and honor.

Michael takes the viewer through the Word of God to uncover the Divine plan for husbands and wives. These two messages have been used by God to restore many failing marriages.

Available on 2 DVDs or 2 VHS

Holy Sex

God created his children as sexual opposites, and designed marriage to be the context of erotic pleasure. While the church as been mostly silent on the subject of sex, the world and the devil have attempted to make it their domain.

The church has rightly proclaimed biblical prohibitions on the misuse of sex, but it has failed to speak out on the godliness of erotic pleasure in the context of marriage.

Out of 66 books composing the Bible, one whole book is dedicated to promoting erotic pleasure—the Song of Solomon. Michael Pearl takes his readers through a refreshing journey of Biblical texts. This sanctifying look at the most powerful passion God ever created will free the reader from false guilt and inhibition. Michael Pearl says, "It is time for Christian couples to take back this sacred ground and enjoy the holy gift of sexual pleasure."

82pg Book

Only Men

Michael Pearl speaks directly and frankly to men about their responsibilities as husbands. Wives should not listen to this tape. We don't want you taking advantage of your man.

Sin No More

The big question is: "So how do I stop sinning?" You have confessed your sins, received the baptism of the Holy Ghost with evidence of everything but ceasing to sin, yet you are still a Romans 7 defeated Christian. I assure you, God not only saves his children from the penalty of sin but he saves them from its power as well. You **can** stop sinning.

Available in a 9 CD set or 7 Cassette set

Created to be His Help Meet

This book is also available at 40% discount when purchased in unbroken boxes of 24.

FREE Magazine Subscription

No Greater Joy Ministries Inc. publishes a bimonthly magazine with answers to questions received in the mail.

Send us your name and mailing address to the address below, and we will put you on our mailing list. Your information is confidential. We do not share your information with anyone.

If you are on our mailing list, you will also receive notification of when the Pearls are speaking in your area.

You can also read additional material on our website www.nogreaterjoy.org or you can sign up on our website to receive No Greater Joy.

NGJ is a 501(c)3 Non-profit organization dedicated to serving families with the good news of Jesus Christ.

Other books by *Michael Pearl*

To Train Up A Child
No Greater Joy Vol. 1
No Greater Joy Vol. 2
No Greater Joy Vol. 3
Romans - Commentary
By Divine Design
Repentance
To Betroth or Not to
    Betroth
Pornography–Road to
    Hell
In Defense of *Biblical*
    Chastisement
Holy Sex

Baptism in Jesus' Name
Justification and the book
    of James
1 John 1:9 the Protestant
    Confessional

No Greater Joy Ministries Inc.
1000 Pearl Road
Pleasantville TN 37033
United States of America
www.nogreaterjoy.org

"Therefore to him that knoweth to do good and doeth it not, to him it is sin"
(James 4:17)